Edward Thoma

Writing Wales in English

***CREW* series of Critical and Scholarly Studies**
General Editor: Professor M. Wynn Thomas (CREW, Swansea University)

This *CREW* series is dedicated to Emyr Humphreys, a major figure in the literary culture of modern Wales, a founding patron of the *Centre for Research into the English Literature and Language of Wales*, and, along with Gillian Clarke and Seamus Heaney, one of *CREW*'s Honorary Associates. Grateful thanks are due to the late Richard Dynevor for making this series possible.

Other titles in the series

Stephen Knight, *A Hundred Years of Fiction* (978-0-7083-1846-1)
Barbara Prys-Williams, *Twentieth-Century Autobiography* (978-0-7083-1891-1)
Kirsti Bohata, *Postcolonialism Revisited* (978-0-7083-1892-8)
Chris Wigginton, *Modernism from the Margins* (978-0-7083-1927-7)
Linden Peach, *Contemporary Irish and Welsh Women's Fiction* (978-0-7083-1998-7)
Sarah Prescott, *Eighteenth-Century Writing from Wales: Bards and Britons* (978-0-7083-2053-2)
Hywel Dix, *After Raymond Williams: Cultural Materialism and the Break-Up of Britain* (978-0-7083-2153-9)
Matthew Jarvis, *Welsh Environments in Contemporary Welsh Poetry* (978-0-7083-2152-2)
Diane Green, *Emyr Humphreys: A Postcolonial Novelist?* (978-0-7083-2217-8)
Harri Garrod Roberts, *Embodying Identity: Representations of the Body in Welsh Literature* (978-0-7083-2169-0)
M. Wynn Thomas, *In the Shadow of the Pulpit: Literature and Nonconformist Wales* (978-0-7083-2225-3)
Linden Peach, *The Fiction of Emyr Humphreys: Contemporary Critical Perspectives* (978-0-7083-2216-1)
Daniel Westover, *R. S. Thomas: A Stylistic Biography* (978-0-7083-2411-0)

Edward Thomas

The Origins of his Poetry

Writing Wales in English

JUDY KENDALL

UNIVERSITY OF WALES PRESS
CARDIFF
2012

British Library Cataloguing-in-Publication Data
A catalogue record for this book is available from the British Library.

ISBN 978-0-7083-2403-5
e-ISBN 978-0-7083-2452-3

Typeset by Mark Heslington Ltd, Scarborough, North Yorkshire
Printed in Wales by Dinefwr Press, Llandybïe

Diana Louise Kendall
1924–2008

Contents

General Editor's Preface

The aim of this series is to produce a body of scholarly and critical work that reflects the richness and variety of the English-language literature of modern Wales. Drawing upon the expertise both of established specialists and of younger scholars, it will seek to take advantage of the concepts, models and discourses current in the best contemporary studies to promote a better understanding of the literature's significance, viewed not only as an expression of Welsh culture but also as an instance of modern literatures in English worldwide. In addition, it will seek to make available the scholarly materials (such as bibliographies) necessary for this kind of advanced, informed study.

M. Wynn Thomas
CREW (*Centre for Research into the English Literature and Language of Wales*)
Swansea University

Acknowledgements

Thanks to Shelley Saguaro, Alan Brown and Simon Dentith for patient advice during the germination of the ideas in this book; Philip Gross for tactful, astute responses; University of Gloucestershire for practical support; University of Salford, and in particular Jocelyn Evans and Lucie Armitt, for practical support and publication funding; Lorna Scott and Caro McIntosh of University of Gloucestershire Archives; Colin Harris and the staff of Oxford University Bodleian Special Collections Reading Rooms; the Battersea Public Library Local History Department; the Hawthornden Fellowship for an extended secluded period of support; and the Kendall family for the loan of Barrow Road.

Thanks also to Martin Randall, Diana Kendall, Geoff Caplan, Edward Thomas Fellowship, Richard Emeny, Anne Harvey and Chris B. McCully for scholarly support.

I am grateful to the Edward Thomas Estate for generous permission to use unpublished and published material on Edward Thomas; the Bodleian Library, University of Oxford, owners of Letters to Walter de la Mare (Eng lett 376), for kind permission to use Edward Thomas's unpublished letters to de la Mare; and Alec Finlay for graciously allowing the use of an unpublished circle poem.

Note on the Text and Abbreviations

Thomas's editors seem at times to have viewed the provisional quality inherent in his poetry too literally. In *PN Review* 103, John Pikoulis detailed the liberties taken by R. G. Thomas in the classic *Collected Poems* (1978). Subsequent editors silently amended some of these, as in the 2004 Faber and Faber re-issue of R. G. Thomas's edition. In 2008, the record was set straight in more than one sense by Edna Longley's *Edward Thomas: the Annotated Collected Poems*, a substantial revision of her 1973 *Poems and Last Poems*. Her 'Note on texts' acknowledges the difficulty of alighting on final versions or titles of Edward Thomas poems, and states her editorial decision to stay with titles that have run the course of time. She generously gives context to apparently high-handed dealings with Thomas manuscripts in the past, revealing how R. G. Thomas's selection, and creation, of titles for poems in the definitive *Collected Poems* resulted from lack of access to the printer's typescript of Edward Thomas's choice of text in the 1917 *Poems*. Such scrupulousness asserts Longley's edition as a genuine contender for the new definitive Edward Thomas text and it remains therefore the main text referred to here, although note is taken of the different versions and successive drafts of poems recorded in R. G. Thomas's 1978 edition. For the sake of consistency, titles are taken from Longley's *Annotated Collected Poems*, but a list of major differences from R. G. Thomas's *Collected Poems* appears in the appendices. For frequently appearing sources, abbreviated references are given in the text. Less obvious abbreviations include:

ANCP	*Edward Thomas: the Annotated Collected Poems*, ed. Edna Longley (Newcastle: Bloodaxe Books, 2008)
Berridge	*The Letters of Edward Thomas to Jesse Berridge*, ed. Anthony Berridge (London: Enitharmon, 1983)
Between	Virginia Woolf, *Between the Acts* (London: Hogarth Press, 1941)
Blackbirds	Edward Thomas, *Four-and-Twenty Blackbirds* (London: Duckworth, 1915)
Bottomley	*Letters from Edward Thomas to Gordon Bottomley*, ed. R. G. Thomas (London: Oxford University Press, 1968)
Celtic	Edward Thomas, *Celtic Stories* (Oxford: Clarendon Press, 1911)
CP	*The Collected Poems of Edward Thomas*, ed. R. G. Thomas (Oxford: Oxford University Press, 1978)
DC	*Daily Chronicle* (London, August 1901 to February 1913)
ETF	*Edward Thomas Fellowship Newsletter*
Eng lett 376	Bodleian MS, Eng lett c 376, Letters to Walter de la Mare
FIP	*Feminine Influence on the Poets* (London: Martin Secker, 1910)
Georgians	*Edward Thomas on the Georgians*, ed. Richard Emeny (Cheltenham: Cyder Press, 2004)
Garnett	*A Selection of Letters to Edward Garnett*, ed. Edward Garnett (Edinburgh: Tragara Press, 1981)
LFY	Eleanor Farjeon, *Edward Thomas: The Last Four Years* (Oxford: Oxford University Press, 1958)
Light	*Light and Twilight* (London: Duckworth, 1911)
NLW	National Library of Wales
Norse	*Norse Tales* (Oxford: Clarendon Press, 1912)
Portrait	R. G. Thomas, *Edward Thomas: a Portrait* (Oxford: Clarendon Press, 1985)
PW	Edna Longley, *Poetry in the Wars* (Newcastle: Bloodaxe, 1986)
'Reading'	'Reading out of doors', *Atlantic Monthly*, 92 (1903), 275–7
SC	*The South Country* (London: Dent, 1909)
Selected Letters	*Edward Thomas: Selected Letters*, ed. R. G. Thomas (Oxford: Oxford University Press, 1995)

Sheaf	*The Last Sheaf* (London: Jonathan Cape, 1928)
Welsh Writing	Judy Kendall, '"A Poet at Last"; William H. Davies and Edward Thomas', in Katie Gramich (ed.), *Almanac: Yearbook of Welsh Writing in English* (Cardigan: Parthian, 2008), pp. 32–54

P. J. Croft notes, 'the continual fluctuations in shape and size and the flexible spacing of handwritten text cannot be accurately imitated in the relative fixity of print'.[1] Reproductions of Edward Thomas's handwritten orthography in the mechanical medium of print are therefore necessarily approximate. The appendices include an example of his handwriting and original manuscripts are accessible on the Oxford University First World War Poetry Digital Archive. The abbreviations and lack of punctuation in a number of Thomas's notes and letters are left strategically in place since these reflect their status as immediate comments on his composing processes.

Introduction: Studying the Composing Process

> There is nothing to it. You only have to hit the right notes at the right time and the instrument plays itself.
>
> Johann Sebastian Bach[1]

Edward Thomas: the Origins of his Poetry takes the reader into dark, unknown areas of poetic composition in order to excavate a tunnel to a more illumined place. The focus is on the poems and prose of Edward Thomas, a fearless, challenging, typically elusive writer on the composing process. To assist on this journey, reference is made to a range of his writings. These offer a wealth of information on the subject from varying angles: notes prior to writing poems, letters, reviews, prose essays and books, drafts and completed poems. Study of this material offers a rounded picture of Thomas's poetic processes, since it both documents them and indicates his understanding of them.

Examination of Thomas's linguistic, literary and historical context provides further insight. William James, Richard Jefferies and Oscar Wilde were major influences. Japanese aesthetics had an enormous effect on poets of Thomas's time and, coupled with the legacy of the Romantic poets, the Japanese concept of *ma* ('space' or 'interval') and the appreciation of absence and shape are evident in Thomas's work. The preoccupations of near contemporaries Virginia Woolf, Sigmund Freud and Gertrude Stein, herself initially a student of William James, also had important bearings on Thomas's writing.

Thomas wrote a great deal on the composing process. The most highly regarded critic of contemporary poetry of his day, he produced numerous reviews of other poets. These often refer in passing to aspects of composing, a subject that appears frequently in his prose books and poetry. He conducted several epistolary conversations on his writing with a select group of friends. These included frequent incidental references to his experiences of composition.[2] To some extent, therefore, *Edward Thomas: the Origins of his Poetry* provides an epistolary reading of his poetic processes.

Although Thomas often alluded to the composing process, he rarely made it his main subject, with the exception of *Feminine Influence on the Poets*. However, his writing often implies that darkness and inaccessibility are vital conditions for poetic composition which takes place 'out in the dark', a phrase that forms the title of one of his poems. He emphasized the mystery of this process and the importance of retaining lack of awareness of it, and expressed hesitancy in his explanations of it, observing, in an attempt to gloss one of his poems, that 'I am afraid I am meddling now'.[3]

Many twentieth-century and twenty-first-century poets share his tendency to shy away from examination of this subject. It is as if they wish to preserve a degree of inaccessibility, or 'unknowingness' in their composing processes. In C. B. McCully's *The Poet's Voice and Craft*, a collection of twentieth-century poets' responses to questions about poetic craft, Douglas Dunn observes:

> Accepted wisdom would have us believe that when a poet sets out to explain his methods of working, the risk that is run is nothing less than the possible killing of his gift. I feel inclined to agree. Having accepted the invitation to participate in this series, I now find myself in a state of funk.[4]

In the same book, Edwin Morgan reveals an overwhelming sense that lack of awareness is essential to the craft of poetry: 'to many of the questions my answer was "I don't know [. . .] And I don't want to know!"' Anne Stevenson declares: 'I do not believe anyone sitting down with a like set of questions could write a poem.'[5]

W. N. Herbert and Matthew Hollis's introduction to *Strong Words: Modern Poets on Modern Poetry* also emphasizes inaccessibility as crucial to poetic composition: 'We have attempted in each case to find the illuminating moment in a poet's prose, the point at which they reveal something of their own process.' Their choice of the verbs 'attempt', 'find' and 'reveal' suggests, as does *The Poet's Voice and Craft*, that details of composing processes are not directly accessible. Many of the poets' statements corroborate this. Elizabeth Bishop states: 'It can't be done, apparently, by will-power and study alone – or by being "with it" – but I really don't know *how* poetry gets to be written. There is a mystery & a surprise, and after that a great deal of hard work.' Brendan Kennelly describes poetry as 'an attacking force born of a state of conscious surrender', turning 'the whole self into a river of uncertainties', in 'an act of rebellion against the poet himself'.[6]

Thomas provided a detailed account of an attempt at writing a poem in 1913 in *The Last Sheaf*, its biographical accuracy confirmed by a letter to Walter de la Mare. However, he did not approach the subject directly. The relevant passage is buried in a piece apparently focused on the subject of insomnia. This tangential approach to the subject occurs repeatedly in Thomas's writing, as if to preserve something of the hidden quality of what is revealed. As this book will show, a lateral approach is a quintessential part of the composition process.

Thomas's rapidity of composition, sometimes completing more than one poem a day, resulted in only brief records of the process involved. As a result, despite his evident interest in this subject, access to his composition processes is to some extent adventitious, limited to what he chose to, happened to or had the opportunity to write down. This is appropriate to the subject matter of this study, which is in part an examination of ways in which drafts and the process of their development into poems are affected strongly by the conditions in which they are written. In Thomas's case, adventitious circumstances played a crucial part in the emergence and completed content and form of many of his poems.

The influence of the external environment is evident not only in Thomas's work but in the research that has led up to the writing of this monograph. This research was carried out in tandem to the creation of my first poetry collection *The Drier the Brighter*. I documented my own processes of composition of this collection as an aid and testing ground for my explorations of Thomas's composition processes.[7] The simultaneous composition of both texts has resulted in a number of coincidences in subject matter, form and style, both deliberately and accidentally. Points relating to composition unearthed in this book are explored in *The Drier the Brighter*. Insights into Thomas's processes revealed in here have their origins in observations of the composition of *The Drier the Brighter*.

My seven-year residency in Japan prior to the start of this research also informs this exploration of Thomas's writing, applying aspects of Japanese aesthetics to his work. Equally, my assimilation of fragmentary postmodernist approaches to poetry and my experimentations in shaped poetry, visual text and collaborative digital poetry have bearings on the argument of *Edward Thomas: the Origins of his Poetry*.

Different aspects of Thomas's composing processes are woven together in his practice, as a perusal of this monograph soon makes clear. The book works chronologically through the process of poetic composition, each chapter examining in detail various aspects as they relate to Thomas's writing. These include elements present before and during the composition process, as well as in the completed pieces and eventual collection of those pieces as a body of work. Since each chapter builds on ground covered in previous chapters, this book makes most sense if read sequentially, although the explanation of references in previous chapters means that the chapters also stand alone.

The first chapter looks at the physical context of the composing process and the influence of external writing conditions on Thomas's poetry. It focuses on the point at which a poem emerges in the poet's awareness, the processes that precede that point and the influences of external writing conditions on the poem. It includes a study of Thomas's explorations of birdsong.

The second chapter examines links in Thomas's work between poetry composition and oral tradition. It shows how the beginnings of the composing process can be said to lie within experiences of the physical environment, and continues the discussion on birdsong, referring to Virginia Woolf's work and responses to Thomas's writing. This chapter also examines Thomas's attempts to re-invent the anonymous through land and landscape in his writing of poetry and prose. His experience of external conditions when composing is explored in the context of Wordsworth's and Coleridge's descriptions of composition in natural surroundings.

In the third chapter, emphasis is placed on ways in which absence is used to articulate experiences of the environment in Thomas's writing. Attention is paid to absence as it appears in his drafts and poems: in the form of ellipses, indicators of omission, and aporia, representing what is inaccessible. This chapter also looks at the active part blank space plays in drafts and in completed works, and the emotional import of such space. Absence as a measure of the point at which a work coheres into a completed text is also discussed, as is the play of fore- and backgrounds in Thomas's work and the influence on him of Keats's theory of negative capability and of Japanese aesthetics.

Chapters 4 and 5 continue the work on absence, examining, in Thomas's composing process and completed pieces, his use of absence as gaps or unfilled space, and as 'unfinishedness'. This is discussed also in the context of the Japanese aesthetics of absence; the research of William James; Freud's work on the role gaps play in thought processes; James's and Woolf's emphasis on the importance of vagueness in the writing process; Richard Jefferies's suspended endings; and Oscar Wilde's experimentations with the spoken voice. Discussion of the art of submission in composing leads to an analysis of the ways in which a writer learns to submit to the unfolding patterns revealed by a work in progress, and the ways in which that work continues to be in process even when completed.

The sixth chapter investigates the crucial role in Thomas's writing of dislocation resulting from physical and temporal disturbances caused by changes in external writing conditions or by the transforming effects of memory. This chapter also examines Thomas's use of temporal dislocation, drawing, once again, on the work of James and Freud. Reference is also made to the importance of physical dislocation when composing.

Chapter 7 continues examining the role of dislocation in composing, looking at distraction, associative non-logical or other indirect connections, and the resultant shifts in attention. It draws on the writings of James, Freud and Coleridge, and experiments conducted by Gertrude Stein. The distancing of the writer from works in progress that occurs as a result of readers' feedback on drafts and completed poems, and the effects on the poem of a focus that tracks the present moment and immediate physical sensations are also discussed.

The eighth and concluding chapter argues for the importance of a sustained, open and exact attention to immediate perceptions and thoughts when composing. Making reference to James, Freud and Woolf and to Japanese aesthetics, Thomas's development of the art of 'divagations', perfected by him in his poetic work, is examined, as is the way his poetry, controlled but flexible, resists conclusions, and so succeeds, even in its completed forms, to remain in process. This chapter also refers to Thomas's use of enveloping perspectives and concludes with a discussion of the lack of conclusiveness in his writing, confirming his special position and importance as a poet of the composing process.

Although the focus in this book remains on Thomas, much of what is said applies to other poets and artists. The epigraphs prefacing each section of the book encourage such readings. Some show Thomas approaching the subject from unexpected angles. Others shift the focus to poets from different times and contexts and artists in varying creative disciplines, suggesting, intentionally, that elements of Thomas's composition processes identified and isolated here apply also to musicians, artists, thinkers, dictionary-makers.

We are all creators.

Judy Kendall
Salford Quays

1

Starting Points – How Poems Emerge

> that other thing whats looking out thru your eye hoals. It aint you nor it don't even know your name. Its in us lorn and loan and sheltering how it can.
>
> Russell Hoban[1]

Much of Thomas's life was spent not writing poetry. From 1897 to 1913, he produced extensive criticism on poetry and poetic prose but practically no poems. His mature poems surfaced only in his last two years. Poised, for several years, at the brink of poetic composition, his writing career is like an analogy, writ large, of the process of composing a poem. Andrew Motion notes of the development of Thomas's prose writing style: 'With hindsight it is obvious that he was clearing the ground for his poems.'[2]

As a result, an obvious place to start observing Thomas's poetic process is the point at which a poem emerged in his awareness. The importance this initial phase in poetic composition held for him is suggested in his continued exploration, in his criticism, prose books and poetry, of the beginnings of articulation. However, it is possible that he took so long to embark on his later poetry, as opposed to his early juvenilia, because his poetic composing processes began prior to that point of awareness. Perhaps a protracted composing process, leaving little visible trace, was long underway before the poem appeared in his mind and on the page. Investigation of the external conditions in which his composing processes took place is necessary to establish whether such conditions were a contributing factor.

The unusually large proportion of critical biographies in Thomas's critical heritage demonstrate scholarly recognition of the importance external conditions held for Thomas. These works make several connections between his writing and life, including the outburst of poetry in his late thirties and the onset of the First World War, and, more proleptically, his impending death in that war. The implication is that foreknowledge of this fate spurred him on to write his lyrics, a suggestion a number of his poems appear to confirm.

Similarly, the context in which Thomas wrote seems, like his writing career, to act as an analogy for the emergence of a poem. Thomas published his writings from 1895 to 1917, a period of rapid urbanization leading up to the First World War, and on the cusp between the grand traditions of the Romantics and the Victorians, and modernist experimentation. This was a period also of revolution in fine arts; in linguistics and philology; in studies of the mind in psychology and in the new 'science' of psychoanalysis. Language itself was under severe scrutiny, evident in Oscar Wilde's earlier experiments with the spoken voice; the Georgian poets' attempts to revitalize poetic language; the multiple manifestos on poetic writing produced by the various movements of the Imagists, Vorticists and Futurists; and the keen interest shown by poets of this time in Japanese literary aesthetics. Japanese aesthetics were an important influence on the creative work of W. B. Yeats; Thomas's close friend and collaborator, Gordon Bottomley; and the Imagist poets. Thomas, the major critic of contemporary poetry of his day and reviewer of most of these writers, also wrote about Japanese writers and showed himself keenly aware of Japanese aesthetics.

Just as a poem before it emerges may hover on the cusp of articulated form and structure, so Thomas himself was on the peripheries of, but not fully allied to, the literary movements of his time. He was closely connected with writers in Edward Marsh's Georgian anthologies, particularly Bottomley and Walter de la Mare, exchanging criticism and ideas on writing with them. However, his work never appeared in these anthologies and he remained to some extent critical of them. Similarly, his opinion of early modernist work was muted, although features of his writing very much anticipated later modernist writings and, in particular, strong parallels exist between his work and Virginia Woolf's later writings. Julia Briggs observes how Woolf's later work is like Thomas's writing in its revelation of 'disruption quite as much as continuity'.[3] Thomas, therefore, mirrored the conflicts of his time, as Edna Longley recognizes, calling him a 'radical continuator' who stands '"on a strange bridge alone" ('The Bridge') between Romantics and Moderns'.[4]

This image of a man on a bridge is typical of Thomas. The speakers of his poems express and inhabit indecision and indeterminacy. D. J. Enright calls the slippery syntax of his poetry 'unamenable to high-level exegesis'.[5] Other Thomas scholars emphasize the lacunae, contradictions and ambiguities in his writing. John Lucas refers to the 'carefully weighed qualification of utterance – the brooding hesitancies that are unique to Thomas's mode of spoken verse'.[6] These qualities reflect crucial elements in the composition process, re-enacted by Thomas in his poetic work, which itself remains in some sense in process, cut short by his early death.

IN THE PHYSICAL CONTEXT: NOTES FROM THE ENVIRONMENT

> the water over green rock & purple weed in a cove near Zennor
> where I bathed & the little circle of upright stones at Boscawen Inn
>
> Edward Thomas[7]

Analysis of the context in which Thomas is writing or not writing his poetry is most easily quantifiable as the physical environment. This is most evident in the note-taking that preceded his prose writing. These notes recorded impressions of his immediate physical environment that were later worked into creative pieces.

He showed concern that this reliance on notes was affecting his writing processes detrimentally, writing to de la Mare on 9 October 1909:

> There may be excuses for inconclusiveness but not for negligence. I didn't realise, till I saw these in print, what a hurry I had been in. Probably at the back of it all is my notebook habit. Either I must overcome that or I must write much more laboriously – not mix the methods of more or less intuitive writing & of slaving adding bits of colour and so on. Bottomley sternly advises me to burn my notebooks & buy no more.[8]

In 'How I Began', Thomas recorded how this 'notebook habit' reached back to his childhood:

> At that age [eight or nine] I was given a small notebook in a cover as much like tortoiseshell as could be made for a penny. In this I wrote down a number of observations of my own accord.[9]

The habit continued throughout his writing life. His topographical or 'travel' books were regularly preceded by periods of walking the ground to be covered, accompanied by copious note-taking. As the eighty preserved notebooks that he used on his walks indicate, it became Thomas's constant practice to write his prose works from such notes, so much so that his early mature poetry was created out of prose versions of the same material as if these prose versions too were notes, sources of creative material. R. George Thomas's edition of Thomas's poems cites the first lines of one source of 'Old Man' as a prose piece, 'Old Man's Beard':

> Just as she is turning in to the house or leaving it, the baby plucks a feather of old man's beard. The bush grows just across the path from the door. Sometimes she stands by it squeezing off tip after tip from the branches and shrivelling them between her fingers on to the path in grey-green shreds.[10]

In her *Annotated Collected Poems*, Longley notes that '"Old Man's Beard" sounds like a prose poem or prose from which poetry is trying to get out.'[11] She instances 'Up in the Wind' and 'March' as poems worked up from previous prose sources, and 'November' and 'After Rain' as poems worked up from notebooks.

Thomas admitted to a heavy reliance on notes as a writer, 'I go about the world with a worried heart & a notebook', and instructed his wife to file or return his letters for use as notes, 'I hope you won't mind if I make this a notebook as well as a letter'.[12] When burning his correspondence prior to setting out for the front, he chose to retain these notebooks.

He received authoritative confirmation of the value of notes early in his writing career. At the suggestion of the publisher Blackwood, his first book *The Woodland Life* concluded with a selection of *in situ* field notes, 'A diary in English fields and woods'. Blackwood therefore set Thomas's notes on an equal footing with his more worked creative pieces.[13] Subsequently, in 1907, Thomas made use of 'open-air' diaries when editing *The Book of the Open Air*.

After his death, Thomas's editors continue to recognize the importance of notes in his creative *oeuvre*. In *Edward Thomas: Selected Poems and Prose*, David Wright separates Thomas's war diary from other prose items, placing it next to the poems. R. G. Thomas included the same diary as an appendix to his edition of Edward Thomas's *Collected Poems*, observing that it 'is carefully phrased and Thomas corrects words and phrases as in all his working drafts'.[14] R. G. Thomas also wrote that the diary

> seems to contain the germs of ideas, books, and poems that were never to be written but that were surely present in his mind. Even more clearly it reveals the consistency of the poet's entire writing life grounded as that was upon his powerful sensuous response to the world of living and natural things.[15]

In the preface to *The Icknield Way*, Edward Thomas makes clear that his notes, taken while travelling along the Icknield Way, are not merely preparatory but integral to the composition process. He observes how, in the course of writing the book, both the ancient road and his physical journey along it become images of the book's composition process. *The Icknield Way* is 'in some ways a fitting book for me to write. For it is about a road which begins many miles before I could come on its traces and ends miles beyond where I had to stop.'[16] His composing process starts, literally as well as metaphorically, 'many miles' before he actually begins to write the book, initiating with his travels along the road; the notes he takes during this journey; and the ways in which the subject matter and style of those notes are affected by the journey. The environment and the composing process are closely entwined. Thomas's awareness of this comes to fruition in *A Literary Pilgrim in England*, written in 1914 although not published until 1917. This book observes the close relation between the composing activity of a disparate number of poets and their environment. They include, among others, Matthew Arnold, Hilaire Belloc, William Blake, George Borrow, Emily Brontë, Robert Burns, William Cobbett, S. T. Coleridge, Thomas Hardy, William Hazlitt, Robert Herrick, W. H. Hudson, Richard Jefferies, William Morris, P. B. Shelley, A. C. Swinburne, Alfred Tennyson and William Wordsworth.

Thomas's poems also relate closely to the environment. They refer to journeys, roads and the dark, conditions in which many were drafted. He told Frost that 'I sometimes write in [*sic*] the train going home late', and described to Farjeon the 'long slow' train journeys from military camp.[17] The length of these journeys is mirrored in the winding, clause-ridden sentence constructions of poems such as 'The Owl', 'Good-night', 'It rains', 'It was upon' and 'I never saw that land before'. The rapidly changing perspectives in 'The Barn and the Down' also suggest a train journey:

> Then the great down in the west
> Grew into sight,
> A barn stored full to the ridge
> With black of night;
>
> And the barn fell to a barn
> Or even less
> Before critical eyes and its own
> Late mightiness. (pp. 68–9)

Similarly, Thomas wrote 'Roads', an exploration of roads, while travelling home.

R. G. Thomas recognized the connection in Edward Thomas's work between physical environment and poem when he observed that the 'train journey home [from military camp] was long and roundabout and two poems at least, "The Child in the Orchard" and "Lights Out", were worked on in semi-darkness'.[18] As Thomas told Farjeon, he began writing 'Lights Out' while 'coming down in the train on a long dark journey when people were talking and I wasn't'.[19] Lack of light is present not only in the poem's title, but in the sense of blurred vision and silent isolation in stanzas that describe entering a dark forest,

> the unknown
> I must enter and leave alone, (p. 136)

The almost mnemonic repeated lines and nursery-rhyme-like echoes of 'The Child in the Orchard' also reflect external writing conditions. The darkness of a train journey forces the composing poet to depend more on memory than on the written page.

Thomas's habit of composing poems on train journeys from military camp to his home resulted in work that refers constantly to the search for a home. The word 'home' forms the title of three poems, and references to buildings occur in at least eleven other titles. The poems allude frequently to lost, present, ideal or fleeting senses of home. The opening and ending lines of 'The Ash Grove' run:

> Half the grove stood dead, and those that yet lived made
> Little more than the dead ones made of shade.
> If they led to a house, long before had they seen its fall:
> But they welcomed me;

At the end of the poem, a snatch of song signals a brief rediscovery of a paradoxically fleeting sense of rootedness:

> The song of the Ash Grove soft as love uncrossed,
> And then in a crowd or in distance it were lost,
> But the moment unveiled something unwilling to die
> And I had what I most desired, without search or desert or cost. (p. 108)

Thomas's care in noting the conditions of composition of eleven of the poems in the fair handwritten copy of sixty-seven poems in the Bodleian manuscript of 1917 *Poems* indicates the important connection he saw between physical conditions experienced in the composition period, such as travel, direction of travel and a strong sense of home, and the completed poem. In each case he observed that the poem was composed in transit and, apart from once, when the note does not specify the destination, he recorded that he was 'going home' or 'coming home', mainly from military camp.

Early versions of 'Liberty' and 'Rain' are among the drafts including indications of composing conditions. Both poems focus on solitude, loneliness and homelessness, at night, the time when Thomas often travelled. Other poems refer to a longing for home. 'No one so much as you' suggests separation from home in its emphasis on the distance in an apparently close relationship. 'I never saw that land before' describes a search for, and loss of, an ideal home: 'some goal / I touched then', and 'Some eyes condemn', written eight or nine days later, echoes this in 'I had not found my goal' (pp. 120, 121). 'What will they do?' revolves around the sense of a lost home, while 'The Sheiling' celebrates the discovery of a spiritual home. In the case of 'The Sheiling', the composition process begins while 'travelling back from Gordon Bottomley's (Silverdale)', a spiritual home or place of sanctuary for Thomas, as the poem's content declares.

'Some eyes condemn' and 'What will they do?' reflect physical conditions particular to train journeys. The traveller, stationary in a moving vehicle, watches through the window people apparently moving away from him. In 'Some eyes condemn', composed in Hare Hall military camp, 'Hare Hall & train', the speaker appears passive, while the 'eyes' he observes move restlessly, the movement emphasized by a twisting enjambement:

> Others, too, I have seen rest, question, roll,
> Dance, shoot. And many I have loved watching. Some
> I could not take my eyes from till they turned
> And loving died. I had not found my goal. (p. 121)

A draft of 'What will they do?' includes the note 'going home to Steep'. The speaker's observations in this poem also suggest a position behind a glass window, echoing the conditions of composition on a long, slow train journey:

> I have but seen them in the loud street pass;
> And I was naught to them. I turned about
> To see them disappearing carelessly. (p. 133)

Physical conditions of composition have a strong effect on 'The Lofty Sky', composed while Thomas was confined inside at home with an injured ankle. On the same day that 'The Lofty Sky' was composed, Thomas wrote, 'I am downstairs but worse off because I know how helpless I still am. I can only hop.'[20] Confinement and the desire to escape it form the subject of 'The Lofty Sky', which focuses on the outdoor environment to which the poet and speaker are denied access.

Coleridge's 'This Lime Tree Bower My Prison' was composed under similar restraints. In his chapter on Coleridge in *A Literary Pilgrim in*

England, written the summer before the composition of 'The Lofty Sky', Thomas clearly linked Coleridge's completed poem to its conditions of composition, observing how Coleridge,

> disabled from walking, sat in 'this lime-tree bower my prison,' and followed in imagination the walk which his friends were taking, and wrote a poem on it, half 'gloomy-pampered' at his deprivation, half happy both with what he imagined and with the trees of his prison.[21]

The echo of 'This Lime Tree Bower My Prison' in 'The Lofty Sky' indicates another condition of composition: the strong influence of the Romantic legacy on Thomas as poet and critic. His admiration for Coleridge in particular was unequivocal. For Thomas, the *Biographia Literaria* contained 'the most profound literary criticism which has so far been written in English. His [Coleridge's] scattered pages on poetic diction, due to his disagreement with Wordsworth's theory, are all that can at present form the basis of any true criticism of Poetry.'[22]

'Words' is another poem directly affected by its physical conditions of composition. Thomas's letters reveal that it was composed on a bicycle, scribbled on various 'scraps' at intervals on a cycling trip up and down the steep hills of Gloucestershire.[23] This external environment is reflected in the content, form and rhythm of the poem. In '"The shape of the sentences": Edward Thomas's tracks in contemporary poetry', Lucy Newlyn points out that the shape of 'Words', formed from a series of very short lines, is recognizably that of a long, thin path, a visual form also used in Henry Thoreau's 'The Old Marlborough Road', a poem Thomas knew.[24] The typical short up-down rhythm created by cycling also has a partner in the accumulation of brief phrases that make up the short lines of 'Words'. More pragmatically, short lines are easier to hold in the head, which is helpful when composing while cycling.

Earlier in the same essay, Newlyn observes how the rhythm of Thomas's writing on walking reflects his tendency to navigate away from prescribed pathways. His sentences 'follow an easy, meandering pattern, accommodating obstacles and pauses, as well as distractions *en route*'. She refers to 'Thomas's development of a "pedestrian" prose style – one that explored the three-way connection between walking, talking, and sentence structure', and discusses in detail the way Thomas's skilful use of complicated sentence structure in 'Women he liked' forces readers to re-trace their steps in an effort to disentangle the sentence, the process enacted being 'remarkably like a walk that ends in a clearing – one of Thomas's favourite experiences'.[25]

Thomas showed acute awareness of how physical conditions impinge on composition in his introduction to George Borrow's *Zincali*. *Zincali* was 'written, as he [Borrow] tells us, chiefly at Spanish inns during his journeys', and Borrow's subsequently published letters from Spain,

> which formed the basis for a great part of *The Bible in Spain*, show us that he wrote his portly but vigorous prose fresh from the saddle and from the scenes depicted; and upon some of these letters or the journals, their sources, he drew for the earlier book.[26]

In his critical biography of Borrow, Thomas measured the success of *The Bible in Spain* by its ability to conjure up the environment and conditions in which it was written. He praised the book for being 'just as fresh as the letters'.[27]

Thomas did not always take notes with particular pieces of writing in mind. He often discovered composition subjects when re-reading his notes, writing in 1903 that 'I sit down with my abundant notebooks and find a subject or an apparently suggestive sentence.'[28] At the point of making those notes, he was unaware of the eventual creative form or forms that they would take. Similarly, some initial prose versions of his mature poems exist in texts written long before he conceived of himself as a poet and before he worked them into a poetic form.[29]

Other details of the conditions of composing indicate the unplanned onset of that process. Thomas wrote 'Words' on whatever scraps of paper he could find. This resulted in '2 lines that got left out owing to the scraps I wrote on as I travelled'.[30] His lack of appropriate writing material suggests the unexpected advent of the composing process. He did not choose the moment of composition but was instead compelled to write, despite unfavourable conditions. The poem hijacked the poet.

The content of 'Words' reflects the unplanned onset of its composing process. Words choose the poet, or to be more precise, the poet pleads with words to choose him, placing himself at their mercy:

> Choose me,
> You English words? (p. 92)

Similarly, the very short lines in 'Words' suggest uncertainty and a lack of preparedness, echoed in the way the lines break across syntactical pauses, fragmenting the text, and in the quick reversals of point of view:

> And as dear
> As the earth which you prove
> That we love.

Emphasis on uncertainty of cause and outcome is also present in Thomas's unorthodox use of rhyme and metre. As Ian Sansom suggests in a review of *Collected Poems* (2004), Thomas's completed poems tend to reflect the uncertainty accompanying their beginnings:

> [M]any of the poems read like echoes of themselves, like broken-up, vaguely blank-verseish prose (and indeed, in many instances, that's exactly what they are).
>
> If anything explains the continuing appeal of his poems, it's probably that Thomas seems to have no clear idea of what he's doing or where's [*sic*] he's going; the effort is all.[31]

Sansom implies that this uncertainty is unintentional and is linked to an essential lack of clarity in Thomas. However, Thomas's continued emphasis in poems on beginnings or endings, and on moments that precede or mark the close of a period of articulation, suggest deliberate decision. This is evident in 'Adlestrop', where the celebration and analysis of a moment of epiphany is heralded both by a pause in a train's unscheduled stop and by the regular accompanying litany of sounds. The effect is that of a considered and strong evocation of the moments just before or after an event, such as preparation for speech, cessation of mechanical action and arrival or departure of people:

> The steam hissed. Someone cleared his throat.
> No one left and no one came
> On the bare platform. (p. 51)

Thomas's dealings with contemporaries' criticism of his poetry similarly show deliberate, intended and knowing striving after uncertainty of effect. The response of Blackwood, one of the first publishers to whom he sent his poetry, was typical of Thomas's early readers:

> The poems are to me somewhat of a puzzle, and I do not think I could venture upon them. They are, however, exceedingly interesting, and I shall be very pleased indeed to consider anything else which Mr Eastaway may write at any time.[32]

Thomas's reaction, recorded in a letter to Farjeon, was perceptive and defiant: 'I suppose Blackwood just thought it looked very much like prose and was puzzled by the fact that it was got up like verse. I only hope the mistake was his and prefer to think it likely.'[33] A few weeks later, Thomas wrote,

> Did I tell you that I sent Monro a lot of verses in hopes he would make a book of them? Well, he won't. He doesn't like them at all. Nor does Ellis – he says their rhythm isn't obvious enough. I am busy consoling myself. I am not in the least influenced by such things: but one requires readjustment.[34]

These reactions to negative criticism of his poetry show Thomas resisting, despite his acute sensitivity to the reception of his poems, the pressure to make them and their rhythms more 'obvious' or certain. He rarely bowed to a plea for more clarity. The compromise he reached in 'Digging ("What matter makes my spade")' is unusual: 'I have a laugh at you for not detecting the rhyme of soldier and bear. However to please you I bring the rhyme nearer.'[35] Most often he seemed bent on widening the gap between his work and conventional expectations of rhythm and rhyme, as if celebrating the ambiguous inception of this work, which remained beyond his control, dependent on the physical environment in which he happened to be placed.

IN THE PHYSICAL CONTEXT: THOMAS ON HOW HIS POEMS EMERGE

> I need to be in a position to write when writing comes.
>
> Carol Ann Duffy[36]

Thomas's poems and their composing processes have an unplanned air, an air he courted and fostered, as suggested in his references to his habit of note-taking. He stressed the primacy of the environment and its role in dictating the form and style of notes made within it. The notes were written as responses, and he re-read them because of their ability to evoke the environment. This allowed him to write further and produce a completed creative piece. Their main purpose is revealed in his lament: 'One little note used to recall to me much of the glory or joy of former days out of doors. Now it is barren.'[37]

Thomas's words suggest that he saw the beginnings of the composing process as lying in the experience of the environment, not in notes on it. He was moving towards the extreme claim that human language has developed from man's relation with his environment and depends upon that relationship. In terms of poetic composition, this implies that the composing process commences with the poet's interaction with the environment. In 'Reading out of doors', he developed this idea, tentatively positing not man but the environment as the initiator of the creative process:

> I have ever found that my own thoughts, or those which the landscape and the air thought for me, were far beyond the range of such as they [Spenser, Wordsworth, Thoreau]. There is more wisdom in the amber maple leaf or the poise of a butterfly or the silence of a league of oaks than in all the poems of Wordsworth.[38]

This passage implies that the 'landscape and the air' are not merely conditions existing before language and from which language springs. They offer the first moments of the creation of that language. To some degree they write the creative work that follows, thinking the writer's thoughts for him with a 'wisdom' to be favoured over that in a Wordsworth poem, the writer's role in this process being that of amanuensis.

If, as Thomas suggested, the composition processes begin in the environment, then further examination of such processes necessarily entails focus upon experience of the environment. This is exactly what happens in his account of poetic composition in the essay 'Insomnia'.

Comparison with a letter Thomas wrote to Walter de la Mare in 1913 makes clear that the account of composing in 'Insomnia' is to a great degree autobiographical. It matches detail for detail the description of attempted poetry composition in the de la Mare letter.[39] In both, the speaker is a 'non-poet' who, suffering insomnia, finds himself trying to write a poem that reflects his mood. Failing to complete the first verse, he remains plagued by the rhyme of 'ember' and 'September'.[40]

The significance of 'Insomnia' to Thomas's composition processes and to a more accurate understanding of the chronology of those processes is so crucial that it will be examined from several angles in the course of this book. It is worth therefore spending some time detailing the conditions and date of composition of this essay.

Most critics and biographers of Thomas date the inception of his mature poetry to late 1914. However, an examination of the accounts of composing in 'Insomnia' and the related letter to de la Mare point to an earlier start date for his first mature attempt at poetry. This is an incomplete attempt since the poet gives up after three lines. Nevertheless, it comprises a highly significant record of his first moments of poetic composition.

The exact date of 'Insomnia' remains unknown. However, it can be assumed that it was written after the de la Mare letter, since the letter contains the germ of the essay. The letter, although undated, was almost certainly written in the later months of 1913. Penned on notepaper headed 'Selsfield House', it has been filed in the Bodleian manuscripts between letters dated end of October 1913 and 2 January 1914, a period when Thomas was staying at Selsfield House. However, a much more likely date lies between 5 and 13 September 1913, since both letter and essay refer to the month of September, and letters to Farjeon confirm that Thomas was also staying at Selsfield House at this time. Discussion in the de la Mare letter of Thomas's arrangements to meet de la Mare suggest it was written on Sunday, 7 September, the date mentioned at the end of 'Insomnia': 'And so I fell asleep again on the seventh of September'.

This proof that Thomas's first foray into mature poetry occurred in late 1913 affects the commonly accepted view that his attempts at mature poetry were largely instigated by Robert Frost in the summer of 1914. Instead, it acknowledges the contributory influence on Thomas of other poet friends, such as de la Mare.

In a letter to W. H. Hudson, Thomas named November 1914 as a start date for his mature poetic compositions. He appeared to have forgotten or to discount his earlier failed experience of poetic composition, writing of his first successfully completed poems that they had

> all been written since November [1914]. I had done no verses before and did not expect to and merely became nervous when I thought of beginning. But when it came to beginning I slipped into it naturally whatever the results.[41]

The unsuccessful attempt recorded in 'Insomnia' and the de la Mare letter has been relegated to an experience of feeling 'nervous when I thought of beginning'. This dismissive reference, however, was written in 1915 after Thomas had successfully completed many poems. The 1913 letter to de la Mare, written before Thomas's poetry had begun to flow, records in detail the earlier attempt at poetic composition, suggesting that at the time he saw it as highly significant.

A second indication of Thomas's awareness of the significance of this attempt lies in his decision to communicate it to de la Mare. He held de la Mare in very high regard, particularly esteeming his poetry collection *Peacock Pie*, which he was reading in the summer of 1913, and later rated him 'second [to Frost] among all living poets'.[42] Thomas had long been in the habit of sharing his writing ideas with de la Mare. They worked closely on creative compositions, de la Mare sending Thomas his own poetry for comments and advice. Theresa Whistler records how they agreed to write stories on the same topic of time, Thomas publishing his story in 1911 and de la Mare writing his in 1917.[43] They shared creative material, such as accounts of dreams, a frequent source of creativity for de la Mare, and also for Thomas, as his 1915 poem 'A Dream' bears witness. A 29 March 1911 letter to de la Mare, describing a dream, concludes with the words 'this is my copyright', showing a keen awareness in Thomas of the potential of dreams as creative material.[44]

Although in 1913 Thomas was in awe of de la Mare's poetic gift, in the following approximation of the spacing in the handwriting of the September 1913 letter, Thomas described his friend, in a rephrasing of Pope's words, as one of those

> mob of gentlemen that rhyme
> with ease .[45]

The word 'rhyme' is Thomas's choice, not Pope's, and the idiosyncratically spaced handwriting emphasizes this word, as does its position at the end of the line. The spacing frames, and therefore isolates, the word 'gentlemen', which, presented thus, suggests an apparently select group of poets, a group from which Thomas excluded himself.[46]

Previously, this sense of exclusion as a writer was very strong in Thomas. In 1909 he wrote to Bottomley: 'By comparison with others that I know – like de la Mare – I seem essentially like the other men in the train & I should like not to be.'[47] However, by 1913, Thomas's view of himself had changed subtly. He showed greater confidence in his writing abilities, as indicated by the fact that he replaced Pope's 'wrote' with 'rhyme', suggesting awareness of his own possible gift as poet. Also, these lines denigrate not Thomas but the 'mob of gentlemen'. Thomas's exclusion has become a position of choice, not regret. The 'ease' with which the 'mob of gentlemen', poets such as de la Mare, 'rhyme' is perhaps too easy and not altogether admirable. This emphasis on subtlety in rhyming manifested just over a year later in reference to Thomas's poetry, when he discussed the rhymes of 'inlaid' and 'played' in his poem 'After Rain' (p. 38) with Farjeon, allowing them to stay because 'neither is a rhyme word only'.[48]

Thomas's awareness of the significance of his early attempt at composing poetry is also indicated in the graphology and layout of the letter. He placed brackets around the words 'for the first time'. The positioning of 'trying' at the end of the page delays the crucial word 'rhyme' – which, significantly, rhymes with 'the first time' – to the following sheet of the letter. The result is an emphasis on the difficulty of this attempt at poetic composition. The dramatic delay of this first mention of 'rhyme' is also strengthened by the fact that when it finally appears, it is underlined:

I found
myself (for the first time) trying
[new page]
hard to rhyme my mood &
failing very badly indeed , in
fact comically so ,

As if to reiterate the importance of this attempt, both uses of the word 'rhyme' in the letter occur in emphatic positions, either at the end of a line or underlined near the start of a new page. This stress on the difficulty in rhyming 'with ease' also points the way to later daring experiments with the loosened, and therefore uneasy, rhyme schemes.

The account of the would-be poetic attempt in 'Insomnia' emphasizes links between the experience of composing and the conditions of composition. It begins with a description of the would-be poet's experience of the external environment, particularly of the song of a robin:

> I strove to escape out of that harmony of bird, wind, and man. But as fast as I made my mind a faintly heaving, shapeless, grey blank, some form or colour appeared; memory or anticipation was at work.
>
> Gradually I found myself trying to understand this dawn harmony. I vowed to remember it and ponder it in the light of day. To make sure of remembering I tried putting it into rhyme.

The narrator's attempts first to avoid and then to record the birdsong appear to trigger the composing process and also to provide a subject for it. The outcome is only three lines, consisting of

> The seventh of September

and

> The sere and the ember
> Of the year and of me.

Although these lines include references to the season, the date and the speaker of the poem, they omit to mention the birdsong that was their initial impetus. They are as a result completely distanced from the experience of the environment that prompted their inception. Their failure as a poem suggests therefore a possible relation between success in composing and specific reference to the external environment in which the composition occurred. This is borne out by the many successfully completed poems by Thomas, such as 'Good-night', 'It rains', 'Words' and 'Lights Out', which contain circumstances of their composition. Long, dark train journeys or hilly cycle rides are indirectly reflected in sentence structure and shape.

IN THE PHYSICAL CONTEXT: THE VERNACULAR OF BIRDSONG

> chack, chack –
> what a note – what a note!
> the sharp wet snap of a pebble on slate:
>
> Geoffrey Winthrop Young[49]

Birdsong frequently appears in Thomas's writing. In his growth as a poet, he showed awareness of its importance for poetry as a means of connecting with the environment in which both birdsong and poems are situated and composed or performed. Such awareness is already implicit in 'Insomnia', in which the attempt at composition is fired by the sound of birdsong.

However, the later poems indicate a gradual but significant shift in his attitude to birdsong. Coinciding with this change is an increased confidence: 'I think perhaps the Ash Grove is really better and I know the sonnet is (you didn't realise it was a sonnet I suspect).'[50] The fact that his new confidence in his poetry ran parallel to his changing approach to birdsong suggests a study of birdsong in 'Insomnia' and his drafted and completed mature poems may illuminate his development as a poet and track his progression from failed attempts at poetry to successfully completed works.

The thrushes in 'March' are 'unwilling' singers, just like the robin in 'Insomnia' (p. 35). The robin's song occurs in the moments between night and day, in the transitions in light, and the thrush's song is placed in intervals between different weather patterns. However, in 'March', the interaction between the birds and the weather and light patterns is made more explicit, as an examination of its sources indicates. In the *Annotated Collected Poems*, Longley points to the start of Thomas's *In Pursuit of Spring*, written in early 1913, as a source of 'March'. The opening of *In Pursuit of Spring* emphasizes close interaction with the weather, and suggests an ultimate potency of birdsong:

> The missel-thrush sat well up in a beech at the wood edge and hailed the rain with his rolling, brief song; so rapidly and oft was it repeated that it was almost one long, continuous song. But as the wind snatched away the notes again and again, or the bird changed his perch, or another answered him or took his place, the music was roving like a hunter's

and

> with the day came snow, hail, and rain, each impotent to silence the larks (p.148)

In 'March', this potency also infects silence. Although the song of the thrushes is set in direct combat with adverse weather conditions, 'Rain, snow, sleet, hail, / Had kept them quiet', and, in a moment of meteorological calm, the thrushes earnestly sing to 'keep off / Silence and night', silence itself is then depicted as 'Rich with all that riot of song'. The birdsong not only wards off the silence, but adds to it, inhabiting it, merging with it, surrounded by it. Reminiscent of the 'harmony of bird, wind, and man' in 'Insomnia', this poem includes an essential ingredient of silence, previously lacking. 'March' shows birdsong holding some undefined inexplicable knowledge that the listener, both while listening and for a short period afterwards, is enabled to share, if uncomprehendingly: 'Something they knew – I also, while they sang / And after' (p. 35) or, as an earlier draft of 'March' puts it, 'And for a little after'.[51]

'The Other', written about three to five days later than 'March', explores further the relation between birds and silence, depicting birds as struggling less triumphantly with silence:

> The latest waking blackbird's cries
> Perished upon the silence keen. (p. 42)

The importance of 'silence keen' and its primacy over bird or human song or speech is suggested in 'The Combe', written a few days later. The mouth of the combe is 'stopped with brambles', and it is 'ever dark, ancient and dark'. All singing birds, except for the missel thrush, 'are quite shut out' (p. 48).

Further lines in 'The Other' indicate another development in Thomas's treatment of birdsong. These lines describe birds as imitative: starlings 'wheeze and / Nibble like ducks' (p. 42). This characteristic is also implied in the disturbing exchanges in attributes between birds, men and fish in 'The Hollow Wood', composed a day later than 'The Combe', on 31 December 1914.

A comparison of 'Adlestrop', written on 8 January 1915, with a passage in its source notebook, dated 24 June 1914, shows another change in Thomas's treatment of birdsong. One of his field notebooks refers to a 'chain of blackbirds [*sic*] songs' (p. 176), reminiscent of his description of birdsong in 'Insomnia' as a song 'absolutely monotonous, absolutely expressionless, a chain of little thin notes linked mechanically in a rhythm identical at each repetition'. However, in 'Adlestrop', the birdsong coincides with a sense of epiphany. The focus is on not an 'identical' and 'monotonous' chain-like rhythm but on a specific moment, with the many blackbirds of the notebook becoming one: 'for that minute a blackbird sang' (p. 51).

References to birdsong in Thomas's poems frequently evoke not only the close relation of song and land, weather and silence, but also the emotional charge of that environment for the listener and the singing bird. 'The Hollow Wood' emphasizes the effect of sunlight and darkness on birdsong: 'Out in the sun the goldfinch flits' (p. 48). The goldfinch has a 'bright twit', while the birds in the dark forest are 'Fish that laugh and shriek'. The word 'drop' in 'the bright twit of the goldfinch drops' into the wood suggests both downward movement and a drop in mood as the bird enters the darkness.

Thomas's first mature poem, 'Up in the Wind', written on 3 December 1914, investigates connections between the song of the stone curlew and the land. The song speaks with, if not for, the land. The lines relate the song to wildness and a lack of man-made boundaries, and show the bird nesting in half-cultivated fields that hark back to the communality of land:

> the land is wild, and there's a spirit of wildness
> Much older, crying when the stone-curlew yodels
> His sea and mountain cry, high up in Spring.
> He nests in fields where still the gorse is free as
> When all was open and common. (p. 31)

This stress on the link between birdsong and the land is countered by an awareness of the distance between human song or poetry and land and birdsong. Such an awareness of, in particular, the inaccessibility of bird-song is already evident in Thomas's early writings. A letter to his future wife Helen in 1897 runs:

> I enjoy the songs of birds at times, but not often: I never could enjoy them much, though doubtless they have combined with other things to cause my delights; perhaps my surroundings are too imperfect for it; but more likely I am incapable of it.[52]

His later poetry, too, although it often refers to birdsong as a language, emphasizes its distance from human language. 'If I were to own', written in April 1916, employs the phrase 'proverbs untranslatable' (p. 115) to describe a thrush's song, encouraging a view of birdsong as a vernacular language, but also stressing its inaccessibility – it cannot be translated. This image recalls Thomas's implicit criticism of Keats in his critical biography of the poet, also published in 1916, which observes how '[t]he great odes, the poems to Autumn, and "The Eve of St Agnes", could never have been translated out of a thrush's song'.[53] An earlier poem of Thomas's, composed on 26 December 1914, 'An Old Song II', is less explicit about levels of comprehension and accessibility but combines the sounds of human singing and a gull's 'mewing' in the fading light of dusk that threatens oblivion:

> The sailors' song of merry loving
> With dusk and sea-gull's mewing
> Mixed sweet, the lewdness far outweighed
> By the wild charm the chorus played: (p. 47)

Longley has interpreted these lines as art that has become 'inseparable from Nature', art being represented by the sailors' song.[54] However, 'An

Old Song II' draws its rhythms from traditional song, and the example of human song is a generic sailors' song of a 'lewdness' that is 'far outweighed' by the 'wild charm' of the birds' chorus. Such detail undermines Longley's reading, reversing it to suggest, as Harry Coombes has phrased it in a comment on the robin's song in 'Insomnia', a 'sense of the alien' in nature.[55] Whichever reading is adopted, however, the emphasis remains on the extent to which human composition, particularly vernacular song, is connected with or divided from the environment, as articulated in birdsong.

In the 17 January 1915 poem, 'The Unknown Bird', the bird, as in 'Up in the Wind', acts as a buffer between man and what remains inarticulate. Birdsong is presented as superior to human attempts at articulation of what is 'bodiless' (p. 55). This pre-empts the later celebration in 'The Word', composed on 5 July 1915, of the 'pure thrush word' (p. 93). In 'The Unknown Bird', the speaker admires the bird's song, but is unable to replicate it satisfactorily: 'that La-la-la! was bodiless sweet'. The poet's efforts to reproduce the song are limited and second-hand: 'Nor could I ever make another hear' and 'All the proof is – I told men / What I had heard.' The song and the bird remain 'wandering beyond my shore'. In contrast, the bird's song is successful in articulating, or being, 'bodiless'. The poem therefore celebrates birdsong's unreproduceability, evoking the peripheral quality of the experience of listening to such song, just beyond the 'shore'. It explores and articulates not the song, but the distance between that song and human language, and the possibility of connection between the two. Such writing as this shows the importance for Thomas of an indirect approach. Instead of attempting to reiterate mechanically and monotonously the bird's notes, which in 'Insomnia' seem to describe not only the robin's song but the would-be poet's failed attempts to reproduce it, this passage in 'Insomnia' does not strain to complete the process but focuses on that process, the attempt itself. Interestingly, although the approach to composition recorded in 'Insomnia' is direct, the importance of an indirect approach to song and poetry is implicit in the tangential appearance of the account of poetic composition. The body of the essay is devoted to the narrator's struggles to sleep. The truncated process of attempting to compose lines and rhymes of a poem, linked with the experience of birdsong and other sounds from the external environment, is recorded only in the last few paragraphs, which finally revert once again to the topic of insomnia.

An emphasis on process also informs 'I never saw that land before', composed on 5 May 1916:

> if I could sing
> What would not even whisper my soul
> As I went on my journeying.
>
> I should use, as the trees and birds did,
> A language not to be betrayed;
> And what was hid should still be hid (p. 120)

The conditional 'if I could' not only reinforces the difficulty of attempts to reproduce the environment in language but the difficulty of reproducing the language that is written into the environment. The poem focuses on the attempt rather than its successful conclusion. The use of the conditional signals incompleteness, and the impossibility of completion. The emphasis necessarily remains on the process of articulating or describing the environment. This process is one that cannot be totally successful.

Thomas's explorations of birdsong and its connection with human language and poetry were strongly influenced by W. H. Hudson's work, and in particular Hudson's bird-girl in the novel *Green Mansions*.[56] Thomas admired Hudson highly: 'Except William Morris, there is no other man I would sometimes like to have been, no other writing man' and he described *Green Mansions* as 'one of the noblest pieces of self-expression'.[57]

Hudson's bird-girl can communicate with birds as well as people. Hudson named her Rima. The evocation in this name of 'rhyme' suggests the high value Hudson placed on the power of poetry as a means of connecting with the environment. In his *Green Mansions* review, Thomas emphasized the power of communication that Rima possesses: 'her singing was a mode of expression which Nature had taught her. It was attuned to the voices of animals and birds and waters and winds among the leaves; it was more a universal language than Latin or English.' In the novel, however, the close connection she enjoys with birdsong is contrasted with her uneasy relationship with humans and the human voice. Unlike the facility with which she communicates with her natural environment, Rima finds communication with human beings limited and unsatisfactory. Returning from a venture out of her forest habitat into the world of men, she is fatally silenced, implying a doubt, on Hudson's part, as to how far the environment, represented by birdsong, could be connected, or translated, into human speech or poetry.

Thomas explored the issues raised by *Green Mansions* in a description of a woman in his prose piece, 'A Group of Statuary', first published in *Light and Twilight* in 1910. As if echoing Hudson, Thomas referred to birdsong in this piece as a way of articulating the uneasy relationship between the human voice and, by implication, the woman who possesses that voice, and her environment. She is 'a lovely woman living among mountain lakes', whose eyes 'were like wild-voiced nightingales in their silence', a silence imposed upon them by their present 'imprisonment' in the urban 'cage' of London.[58] Like Rima, Thomas's woman also appears to have been silenced. Her impoverished existence in an urban setting is emphasized. Her overlooked status is highlighted with the image of a statue: 'no one notices the statuary of London'. Her fate as a forgotten or overlooked figure is re-enacted when an image of her eyes speaking like nightingales is continued with the words 'but in this cage . . .'.[59] The ellipses imply silence, although it remains uncertain whether the woman's divorce from her environment results in a loss of the power to articulate or to be heard. This suggests another important feature in Thomas's explorations of the composing process – the relation of the progressing poem not only to its human maker but to its potential listener or reader.

2

Poetry and Oral Literature

> [The Forest miners] singing their yearning hymns through the dark, wet woods on their way home.
>
> Dennis Potter[1]

In Thomas's writings he alluded to a language of the physical environment, an anonymous language residing in features of the land or in the birdsong that emanates from it. He repeatedly examined the distance between this language and contemporary human forms of articulation like human song, speech or poetry. However, he also used oral tradition to link the language inscribed in or expressed by the physical environment to the written text of poetry. Such language of oral tradition is a near cousin to the language of the land, sharing its quality of anonymity, distanced from it only relatively recently, and holding within it records of the land, as Thomas made clear in his preface to the retold legends in *Norse Tales* (1912):

> These stories are taken from poems in the Old Norse tongue. The stories, created in the ninth and tenth centuries, remain in touch with ancient pagan traditions. Their names have been lost, their poems confused and mutilated, in the course of a thousand years. Even the land where they wrote is unknown, and scholars have tried to discover it from the nature of the landscape and the conditions of life mentioned in the poems.[2]

This link with the land helps explain the power Thomas saw imbued in oral tradition, positing it as a key to the invigoration of imaginative writing in his time:

> I cannot help wondering whether the great work done in the last century and a half towards the recovery of old ballads in their integrity will have any effect

> . . . Can it possibly give a vigorous impulse to a new school of poetry that shall treat the life of our time and what in past times has most meaning for us as freshly as those ballads did the life of their time? It is possible; . . . their style is commonly so beautiful, their pathos so natural, their observations of life so fresh, so fond of particular detail – its very lists of names being at times real poetry.[3]

Thomas's early championing of the poet W. H. Davies was closely connected with his sense of the importance of oral tradition to poetry. His first review of Davies, in 1905, highly favourable, was given the title 'A Poet At Last!'[4] He supported Davies in other ways. Almost immediately after their first meeting, Thomas invited Davies to share his study cottage, which Davies did for over a year. After that period, Thomas continued working very closely with him, advising and encouraging him as a poet and frequently reviewing him. He presented Davies to the public as an exciting and unusual figure, emphasizing his unique success as a contemporary writer in remaining in connection with the neglected heritage of folksong, ballads and the oral tradition. He described Davies's work as part of 'an old literary mode charmingly and unconsciously revived, without any sense of artifice', and praised Davies's drinking songs in *New Poems* (1907) for 'their vigour, their truth, their splendid spirit [which] is inestimable'. It is clear that, for Thomas, Davies formed a model of the invigorating power of old songs. Davies's poems represented the 'vigorous impulse' referred to in *The South Country* in two ways. They were a source of stimulation for further 'vigorous' writing by Davies or other poets, and also embodied the results of such an impulse. Thomas attributed their vigour to Davies's refreshing and unusual lack of education and literary knowledge, writing that his poetry came from a 'strange, vivid, unlearned, experienced' condition and quoting G. B. Shaw's response to Davies's collection, *The Soul's Destroyer*, as a delight in its 'freedom from literary vulgarity . . . like a draught of clear water in a desert'.[5]

Thomas made use of the 'vigorous impulse' of old songs and ballads in his own mature poetry, composed several years after the discovery of Davies's work. A considerable number of Thomas's poems lean significantly on traditional oral sources: his two 'Old Songs'; his three 'Songs', as they were entitled in the 1978 edition of his poems; the reference to traditional music in 'The Penny Whistle'; the reinvigoration of a ballad in 'The Ash Grove'; and the reworking of proverbs and folk tales in 'Lob'. 'An Old Song II' refers directly to the practice of drawing on folk lyric. The speaker imitates the song of a robin, also represented as a shade, shadow or echo. The word 'repeat' refers to the refrain from the folksong around which the whole poem is built. Thus, four lines of the poem comprise a neat acknowledgement of the debt it owes to birdsong and folksong:

> A robin sang, a shade in shade:
> And all I did was to repeat:
> 'I'll go no more a-roving
> With you, fair maid.'[6]

These lines also evoke Thomas's comment to Farjeon on 2 August 1914: 'I may as well write poetry', beginning 'at 36 in the shade', thus reinforcing the reading of these lines of 'An Old Song II' as an allusion to his debt as a poet to ballad, song and forgotten verse 'in the shade'.[7]

BEGINNING AGAIN: RETURNING TO THE OLD LORE

> To make new boots from the remains of old
> *Oxford English Dictionary*[8]

The final years of the nineteenth century corresponded with the beginning of Thomas's writing career. Linda Dowling's *Language and Decadence in the Victorian Fin de Siècle* observes the growing doubts at this time about the imaginative life of English literary language. She connects this with nineteenth-century developments in comparative philology, referring to the 'fin de siècle linguistic self-consciousness as it floated between the artificial dialect of literature and the "barbaric yawp" of vernacular speech'. She writes:

> Spoken dialects, that is to say, not only more perfectly reflected language reality than did written languages; they also persisted in their linguistic purity, whereas written languages, already falsified by orthography, compounded their falsity by incorporating the vogue words and constructions of civilized fashion. Thus did nineteenth-century linguistic science end by fully ratifying Wordsworth's belief in rural speech as the real language of men, and by deeply undermining Coleridge's idea of literature and the literary dialect as a *lingua communis*.[9]

Dowling's reference to rural speech as 'real language' resonates with Thomas's preference for the spoken vernacular and oral tradition. This was clearly stated by him in September 1913, the same month he attempted his own 'ember' / 'September' poem, when he extolled the poems of one contemporary, Ralph Hodgson, for their pre-Victorian, pre-Keatsian flexibility: 'They recall what poetry was before Keats and Tennyson had so adorned it that it could run and sing too seldom, when words were, and more often than they now are, dissolved and hidden in the beauty which they created.'[10]

Thomas's reviews often show him rejecting the more embellished poetic diction of recent Victorian verse and harking back to a Wordsworthian or pre-Wordsworthian approach to language. He praised Davies for writing 'much as Wordsworth wrote, with the clearness, compactness, and felicity which makes a man think with shame how unworthily . . . he manages his native tongue'.[11] Frost was applauded for the way in *North of Boston* he cast off out-worn literary conventions and 'refused the "glory of words" which is the modern poet's embarrassing heritage'. *North of Boston* was also lauded for its 'natural delicacy like Wordsworth's, or at least Shelley's, rather than that of Keats'.[12]

Thomas's dissatisfaction with an 'embarrassing heritage' was shared by many writers of his time. In *The Oxford Book of Modern Verse* (1936) introduction, W. B. Yeats, in a retrospective frame of mind, particularly attacked Victorianism:

> The revolt against Victorianism meant to the young poet a revolt against irrelevant descriptions of nature, the scientific and moral discursiveness of *In Memoriam* – 'When he should have been broken-hearted', said Verlaine, 'he had many reminiscences' – the poetical eloquence of Swinburne, the psychological curiosity of Browning, and the poetic diction of everybody.

Yeats continued by describing how 'in 1900 everybody got down off his stilts' in a 'reaction from rhetoric, from all that was prepense and artificial' and from 'what ailed Victorian literature'.[13]

For Thomas, getting off these stilts did not simply amount to retrogression to pre-Victorian poetic modes. In his *North of Boston* reviews, he took the time to distinguish Frost's approach from Wordsworth's. Frost 'sympathizes where Wordsworth contemplates and the result is a unique type of eclogue, homely, racy', moving from 'a never vulgar colloquialism to brief moments of heightened and intense simplicity'.[14] Thomas focused on the present in his celebration of Frost's 'colloquialism' and leaner more contemporary diction.

Like Thomas, modernist writers in the 1913 'Futurism' issue of *Poetry and Drama* expressed a sense of the urgent need for revolution in the use of language in poetry and literature. The opening article lays out the editors' position: '[W]e claim ourselves, also, to be futurists' and states some of 'the first principles of *our* Futurism' to be '[t]o lift the eyes from a sentimental contemplation of the past' and to avoid 'walking backwards with eyes of regret fixed on the past'.[15] In the same issue, the Imagist poet

F. S. Flint declared 'Are we not really spellbound by the past, and is the *Georgian Anthology* really an expression of this age? I doubt it. I doubt whether English poets are really alive to what is around them.'[16] Three of Thomas's reviews, including the Hodgson review, appear in this issue of *Poetry and Drama*. They are grouped in a cluster that immediately follows Flint's article. These pieces, published alongside other essays celebrating Futurism and its focus on the dynamic energy of new technology, include implicit dissatisfaction with much contemporary poetry. Hodgson's verse is praised for its remarkable lack of 'all weight of mere words, of undigested thought, of mechanical rhythm'.[17] The saving grace of John Alford's *Poems* lies in their 'freshness [which] is that of a little before sunrise, cool and blithe and yet solemn', suggesting a lack of such qualities in most modern poetry, and explicitly evoking a 'kinship to Blake and some Elizabethans'.[18] As in his reviews of Davies and Frost, the *Poetry and Drama* reviews recall a more distant era of 'the ballads which were sold in the street and stuck about inn walls two hundred years ago', when poetry was more closely connected to song, to music and to its environmental context, in this case on an inn wall.[19]

Other evidence of Thomas's propensity for poetry closely related to oral tradition, and his belief in its absolute appropriateness to his time and poetic language, is located in his descriptions of Davies's poems as 'simple, instantaneous and new, recalling older poets chiefly by their perfection'; de la Mare's song-like *Peacock Pie*, which gave him 'perfect pleasure';[20] and his heralding of Frost's *North of Boston* as 'one of the most revolutionary books of modern times' because it went 'back, through the paraphernalia of poetry into poetry again'.[21]

Yeats expressed similar sentiments in his *Oxford Book of Modern Verse*, pointedly snubbing the Victorian tradition as he traced the ancestry of the successful modern lyric:

> During the first years of the century the best known [poets] were celebrators of the country-side or of the life of ships; I think of Davies and of Masefield; some few wrote in the manner of the traditional country ballad . . . [and] De la Mare short lyrics that carry us back through *Christabel* or *Kubla Khan*.[22]

Thomas internalized his own criticism of contemporary poetry. In May 1914, he wrote to Frost of wanting 'to begin over again with them [his ideas about speech and literature] & wring the necks of my rhetoric – the geese'.[23] Like Yeats in his *Oxford Book of Modern Verse*, Thomas evoked Verlaine, alluding to his expression 'Take eloquence and break its neck'.[24] In typical Thomas fashion, he inserted the image of a domiciled farmyard bird with a notoriously unmelodic call, a stark contrast to the wild song of the untamed bird. In order to 'begin over again', Thomas was turning to the unwritten vernacular of popular songs and proverbs, and the calls or song of wild birds in their natural environment: such songs as the dawn chorus recorded in 'Insomnia'. For him, the sounds and rhythms of this environment and the vernacular formed the crucial preconditions of the composing process.

However, if Thomas saw creative writing as emerging from the natural physical environment, he also recognized the difficulties he and his contemporaries had in connecting with such pre-conditions of composition in the domiciled or urbanized settings of early twentieth-century towns. He often described himself as alienated from both wild birdsong and the vernacular: born in the suburbs of London, cut off from the rural countryside and from the vernacular of his indigenous Welsh roots. He borrowed the term 'superfluous men' from Turgenev to express this.[25] He praised Turgenev's novels and stories for the high value placed on the vernacular: 'He sends us continually out into the fields and the streets to men and women, reminding us that not long ago the ordinary man was discovered, and that he is great', and a passage from *Memoirs of a Sportsman*, in which Turgenev explored man's desire to merge with the environment in images of woods as sea inhabited by fish, became a source of two Thomas poems:

> 'Tis a wonderfully agreeable occupation, to lie on one's back in the forest, and stare upward! It seems to you as though you were gazing into a bottomless sea, that it spreads broadly beneath you, that the trees do not rise out of the earth, but, like the roots of huge plants, descend, hang suspended, in those crystal-clear waves; the leaves on the trees now are of translucent emerald, again thicken into golden, almost black green. Somewhere, far away, terminating a slender branch, a separate leaf stands motionless against the blue patch of transparent sky, and by its side sways another, recalling by its movements the play of a fish's gills[26]

This image of a fish out of water in a wood reappears in Thomas's 'The Lofty Sky' and 'The Hollow Wood', albeit with the introduction of a darker side. 'The Lofty Sky' includes a sense of imprisonment, as the speaker becomes a fish looking up through the sea of trees, desiring to escape and reach the surface 'where the lilies are' (p. 53). 'The Hollow Wood', written a few days earlier, accompanies the image of birds swimming in a dark wood like fish with a sense of mismatch and unhappiness. Their voices are discordant. They do not fit harmoniously with their environment. They 'laugh and shriek' in contrast to the bright singing of goldfinch in the light on the 'thistle-tops' (p. 48).

Thomas wrote that for Turgenev 'no sentiment obtrudes . . . his observation is supreme. There is no greater praise to be given to an imaginative writer than that.'[27] This reference to 'supreme' observation suggests the way forward for Thomas. Keen attention to features of the environment offers up poetic material. With such an approach, the land becomes a way of connecting with vanishing oral tradition, providing inklings of what has been lost.

BEGINNING AGAIN: VOICING THE LORE

Alec Finlay[28]

As his brother, Julian Thomas, has reported, Thomas cherished a Wordsworthian ambition to produce 'prose, as he said to me shortly after he had finished his critical study of Walter Pater, "as near akin as possible to the talk of a Surrey peasant"'.[29] This concern stemmed from Thomas's acute awareness of the fragility of vernacular knowledge, hovering on the edge of extinction. It was present in his writing as early as 1895 in the essay, 'Dad', where he described an old countryman:

> He certainly had no intention of allowing the old lore concerning herbs to die out. Dried specimens of any sort were always kept by him and roots of many more. Such knowledge as he was full of is fast decaying.[30]

The *Norse Tales* preface highlights the precarious existence of one form of vernacular knowledge, orally transmitted stories. The names of the story-tellers 'have been lost'; the surviving creative works are 'confused and mutilated'. Their geographical sources too are 'unknown' and, by implication, also 'lost' or 'mutilated'. Such stories remain in touch with an ancient tradition, with creators who were 'for the most part Christians, living in the ninth and tenth centuries amidst a still keen aroma and tradition of Paganism'.[31] This hint of antiquity coupled with their existence on the border of extinction contributed to their value for Thomas. In his 'Note on sources' in *Celtic Stories*, written a year earlier than *Norse Tales*, he declared: 'it is one of the charms under the surface of these stories that we can feel, even if we can never trace, a pedigree of dimmest antiquity behind them'.[32]

The *Norse Tales* preface describes how such stories are handed down: 'gradually collected and paraphrased . . . [t]he different poets tell them in their own ways, one often inventing or presenting scenes and characters incompatible with those in another's poem'.[33] These words, which could apply to Thomas's activity compiling *Celtic Stories* and *Norse Tales*, suggest that he saw the task of compilers, editors and rewriters of old tales, preserving and reclaiming oral traditions, to be also part of oral tradition.

In his later series of reviews of reprints and anthologies, published in *Poetry and Drama* in 1914, he suggested that anthologies share that role. He defined 'a genuine anthology, [as being] culled from obscure corners, from magazines, even from manuscripts' and argued that 'room should be found for songs, epitaphs, nursery rhymes, popular verse'.[34] He took great pains to include the unknown, neglected or hidden in his anthologies. He talked of the need to avoid '*Golden Treasury* obviousness' in *The Pocket Book of Poems and Songs for the Open Air* and celebrated the discovery of hitherto unprinted unknown material:

> 3 jolly unpublished sailors' songs for the Anthology: also 2 little known songs from *The Compleat Angler* . . . But in my endeavour to keep clear of what Lucas & other open air anthologists have used I daresay my poetry is not all good & not all popular enough[35]

Similarly, the *Pocket Book* 'Note by the compiler' emphasizes the oral sources of the songs: 'These Westmorland songs have, I think, never been published before.'[36]

However, he also acknowledged the very different effects created when putting oral literature in print. The 'Note on sources' alludes to the process of change that is part of oral literature. Stories are repeatedly modified so as 'to accord with changing taste and custom and belief'.[37] Reference is also made to the need to unravel 'these changes in order to trace the origin of the stories, or at least as early as possible a form of them', an activity best suited to print. This is made clear in Thomas's declaration of his own approach: 'Many of these tales have been re-written by poets and others in our own time. I have kept them as nearly as possible in their mediaeval form.' This is tempered by the need for accessibility, as indicated in the introductory note to the volume: 'The spelling of some of the chief names in these stories has been changed so that English children may at once be able to pronounce them.'[38]

Thomas's anthologizing work also sharpened his awareness of the looseness of the connections between music and lyrics. A letter to Bottomley shows Thomas continuing this tradition in his own recombinations of text and melody: 'I will add Masefield's version, but must retain that in the minor. Cecil Sharp (who knows) says no *old* sailor would sing the major tune that Masefield gives, & it was he who gave me the version I am using. It is not obvious but I have learned to like it well.'[39]

Thomas's efforts at reclamation of the vernacular are not only manifested in his activities as compiler, editor, rewriter and recorder of oral traditions, myth, legend and song. They are also evident in his scrupulous use of indigenous plant names in preference to Latin terms for flora and fauna and his record and celebration of the neglected and under-farmed countryside of the rapidly urbanizing Edwardian England in which he lived. This land, despite the neglect it had suffered, represented for him a long history of close human contact, correspondingly reflected in rural speech. The walls of the ruined cottage covered in periwinkle in 'A Tale', and his celebration of the 'corner of the farmyard I like most' with its 'rusty harrow' and 'long worn out' plough in 'Tall Nettles', are just two of many appearances of abandoned countryside in his poetry. Thomas's writing on this, as Stan Smith notes, is particularly focused on the impending loss of that world. The only remaining records that 'tell the tale' of the ruined cottage are scattered 'fragments of blue plates', and the farmyard nettles have grown so tall that they cover all but the 'elm butt' (pp. 73, 119). It is a world poised on the brink of extinction, just like the vernacular spoken within it. As Smith puts it,

> the rundown of the land, the demoralization of the farmers, and the poverty of the agricultural labourers, now the lowest paid of any large category of workers, created that landscape of picturesque abandon which is recognizably Thomas's own.[40]

Thomas's position, as a poet in search of origins and the words that issue from them, results in a focus on the possibilities of rediscovering a human understanding of the natural environment. His poem 'Home ("Often I had gone")' suggests that such an understanding is related to sustained contact with the land. The narrator, as the first words declare, is 'often' travelling, but momentarily achieves absorption in the natural world:

> one nationality
> We had, I and the birds that sang,
> One memory. (p. 81)

The narrator cannot articulate this experience, remaining caught in it, unable, like the birds themselves, to distinguish the end of the song:

> as he ended, on the elm
> Another had but just begun
> His last; they knew no more than I
> The day was done. (p. 81)

The narrator's experience is contrasted with the skilled and aware activity of a labourer. The last line of the poem refers to the sound of the labourer's sawing, which translates and completes not only the narrator's experience of the birdsong but the whole poem: 'The sound of sawing rounded all.' The labourer lives and works locally, inhabiting the land in the way the narrator, a passing traveller, does not. His sawing can be seen as an approximation of a local vernacular, having the power to 'speak' with and complete the birdsong that overwhelms the narrator. As Jonathan Bate declares in his analysis of this poem, the labourer presents a 'relationship with earthly things that is turned into language by the poetry of dwelling'.[41] Birdsong and its beginnings in the environment are linked to a completed poem by the everyday activities of a local, rural inhabitant in sustained contact with a particular area of land.

In early 1913, Thomas started work on a collection of retold proverbs, *Four-and-Twenty Blackbirds*. He rewrote vernacular proverbs to form a series of stories based on a literal reading of the images that they contain. *Blackbirds* has many connections with the voices of children. The writing of it coincided with a developing close friendship with Eleanor Farjeon, a writer for children, and a growing interest in the voices of children, recorded in a number of letters to Farjeon and his poet friend John Freeman who also had a young daughter. These letters repeatedly refer to Thomas's youngest child Myfanwy's experiments with incipient speech. Some of the *Blackbirds* stories began as oral literature told by Thomas and his wife to their children. Farjeon encouraged him in his work on these, and he later dedicated the published work to her. De la Mare also lent his support to *Blackbirds*, another writer friend whose work appealed to children, and whose work, *Peacock Pie*, Thomas was avidly reading at this time to his children and himself.[42]

The significance of *Blackbirds* in Thomas's development as a poet has been noted by a number of critics. In *Studies in Children's Literature*, Deborah Thacker argues that, by interpreting the *Blackbirds* proverbs literally rather than metaphorically, he 'undermines the authority of a moralising adult voice and, through entering into a playful relationship with the child-as-reader', challenges language as 'a socialising and controlling force', and that such 'childlike uses of language and the child-like studied misapprehension or "play"' with language reflected in these children's stories feed into and influence his poetry.[43] Similarly, R. G. Thomas suggested that Edward Thomas's intense 'desire to be "non-literary"' that manifests itself in his focus on the vernacular and the voices of children helps to release his poetry.[44] Thomas himself traced a similar connection between *Blackbirds* and 'Lob', which is, as Longley describes it, 'unequalled as a poem based upon English mythological material'.[45] He wrote: 'I wish I had gone on where the Proverbs [*Blackbirds*] left off. Probably I never shall, unless "Lob" is the beginning.'[46]

Just as the experience of listening to the robin's song in 'Insomnia' leads to the composition of a rhyme, the rewriting of vernacular proverbs for children, which is what *Blackbirds* entails, led Thomas to poetry. A number of times in his poems children are shown as conduits for an understanding of what is lacking in the adult world. They inhabit, in a way an adult cannot, the nameless natural world with its 'proverbs untranslatable', a kind of Eden that adults have left behind (p. 115). 'The Brook' evokes a Blakean innocence in the description of a child living and directly participating in her environment. Her superior powers of articulation are emphasized. Unlike the adult in the poem, she can 'translate' her experience and put it into words. This celebration of the special penetrative abilities of children chimes with Thomas's earlier delight in the childlike quality of Davies's poems, as when he quoted, in a review in April 1908 of *The Soul's Destroyer*, G. B. Shaw on how Davies's poetry shows 'no sign of his ever having read anything otherwise than as a child reads.'[47]

'Lob' continues to stress connections between birds, the vernacular, proverbs and rhymes for children, and poetry. The vernacular is translated into poetry, and the act of translating birdsong into human language is recorded:

> Our blackbirds sang no English till his [Lob's] ear
> Told him they called his Jan Toy 'Pretty dear'. (p. 77)

Longley observes how these lines connect 'blackbirds, an old proverb, Lob's sweetheart and a dialect poem by Thomas Hardy'.[48] As with the sailors' song, which is 'far outweighed' by the seagull's 'mewing', in 'An Old Song II' (p. 47), so, in 'Lob', the belatedness of Lob's act of naming the birdsong is highlighted by the reference to that song's pre-linguistic history.

In its connection of song, poetry, the vernacular and the environment Lob crosses both temporal and spatial boundaries. Lob is presented as a timeless figure appearing across generations, turning up in various locations in the rural countryside, often as a traveller. Steeped in the vernacular, and quotations and adaptations from earlier literature, the figure of Lob represents oral literature. He possesses the ability to name, but his words are subject to the transforming effect of oral tradition, as is evident in the reference to Lob's weather rhymes, which also, in the allusion to sleeplessness, evoke the failed poetic attempt recorded in 'Insomnia':

> On sleepless nights he made up weather rhymes
> Which others spoilt. (p. 78)

Lob's success in naming birdsong contrasts with Thomas's early failure to appreciate songs of birds, 'I never could enjoy them much . . . I am so miserably conscious of myself' and the attempt of the narrator in 'Insomnia', who, also suffering from excessive consciousness, fails to put the robin's song into rhyme.[49] The key to the power of 'Lob' lies in the conjunction of the environment, birdsong and plants, named and renamed by the fluid voice of anonymous indigenous tradition. Even the moniker for Lob constantly changes, from 'tall Tom' to 'Herne the Hunter' to 'Hob', reaching an apotheosis at the end of the poem in a litany of names that encompass time and space. Such a process also incorporates the reinvention of oral tradition in the context of printed texts by weaving in reworked proverbial sayings and text from Chaucer, Shakespeare, Hardy and de la Mare. This celebration of folk heroes, characters in proverbs and printed texts, indigenous plants, waste or common land includes what Longley calls a 'roll-call of battles' in which the common soldier has died.[50] The oral tradition and the vernacular are thus linked to a sense of place:

> The man you saw, – Lob-lie-by-the-fire, Jack Cade,
> Jack Smith, Jack Moon, poor Jack of every trade,
> Young Jack, or old Jack, or Jack What-d'ye-call,
> Jack-in-the-hedge, or Robin-run-by-the-wall,
> Robin Hood, Ragged Robin, lazy Bob,
> One of the lords of No Man's Land, good Lob, –
> Although he was seen dying at Waterloo,
> Hastings, Agincourt, and Sedgemoor, too, –
> Lives yet. (p. 79)

These lines draw together the richness and fluidity of oral tradition, represented by the many different names and guises under which Lob appears, and through the concluding recitation of names and places, root that oral tradition in specific geographical locations related to the experiences of common man. By recreating the process that is so essential to this tradition in a poem, Thomas has not only recorded that tradition as in earlier editorial work, but also participated in it, reliving it in process, linking past memories and legends to the present time and place.

BEGINNING AGAIN: WITH RE-INVENTING THE ANONYMOUS

> In my new robe
> This morning –
> Someone else.
> Matsuo Bashō[51]

Celtic Stories, *Norse Tales* and *Blackbirds* mirror the processes by which oral tradition is perpetuated in their reuse of proverbs and sayings. This also occurs in Thomas's intricate use of the vernacular in his poems, where sayings are woven in unannounced, as if, as Longley puts it, 'he had invented them'.[52] Many of what initially appear to be original turns of phrase hark back to previous texts or sayings. Myfanwy Thomas wrote:

> Not many people realize the implication of the line 'But if she finds a blossom on furze' [in 'If I should ever by chance'] and also the line in the poem 'October', 'And gorse that has no time not to be gay'. They have their origins in the country saying, 'When gorse is out of flower then kissing's out of fashion'.[53]

In such instances, Thomas ran counter to the trend of anonymity in oral literature, bestowing his own name or pseudonym on previously anonymous material. However, at other times, in line, incidentally, with the tradition of mythologizing Welsh history and literature recorded by Prys Morgan in *The Invention of Tradition*, Thomas reinvented himself and his writing as anonymous.[54] In *Beautiful Wales*, he presented his own lyric as an anonymous translation of a Welsh song:

> Here is one of his [Llewelyn the Bard's] imitative songs, reduced to its lowest terms by a translator:
>
> She is dead, Eluned,
> Whom the young men and the old men
> And the old women and even the young women
> Came to the gates in the village
> To see, because she walked as beautifully as a heifer.[55]

The uncovering of this deception left Thomas unabashed. He reported to Bottomley that '[t]o the Cymric enthusiast I only said that there was no Welsh original for "Eluned" & that therefore he wd be disappointed because anyone can make a pseudo translation that suggests a noble original.'[56]

He indicated this preference for anonymity and communality of literature over one individual's claim on a text in exchanges with Bottomley in 1904–5. They were discussing rearrangements in verse of prose versions of Welsh songs for *Beautiful Wales*. Initially, he informed Bottomley that 'your name would be mentioned if you were pleased with the verses'. Later, he changed his mind:

> I have already planned to use 'The Maid of Llandebie', I mean your translation. Of course it is not you, & it is not the Welsh lyric, but it can be sung & it has already reminded me of the original. Therefore, without your name, but with your apologies, I have inserted it in my 3rd. chapter.

Finally, a compromise was reached, with Bottomley being represented as an anonymous poet, credited but not named: 'Here follows the air and a translation by an English poet.' A subsequent apology to Bottomley employed the telling excuse that the lines 'were quoted in such intimate relations with the context that it would be difficult for me to mention your name'. In other words, the act of naming Bottomley would have run the risk of alienating the lines from their context.[57]

Thomas's preference for anonymity in the context of Welsh oral traditions is not surprising, given his special esteem for Welsh culture, seeing himself as 'mainly Welsh'.[58] However, he behaved in a similar fashion in other contexts, omitting to credit borrowed passages of contemporary texts. His *Swinburne* quotes unattributed passages from Edmund Gosse, causing Gosse to observe, a little bitterly, that Thomas 'is one of those people who grudge acknowledgement and he quotes metres of passages from me without mentioning my name. (He does mention it elsewhere.)'[59]

The difficult conditions in which Thomas produced his books, working to tight deadlines with limited funds for copyright, may have encouraged such behaviour, but a similar practice occurred in other circumstances. He reworked unacknowledged material from his own earlier texts in new uncommissioned pieces that were therefore unrestricted by publishers' demands. In 'Birds in March', possibly his earliest published piece, a description of 'a woodland mere' includes a chilling image: 'a moor-hen's nest approaching completion. It is made of the long bayonet-like reeds and other water plants.'[60] This image resurfaced over twenty years later in 1916 in 'Bright Clouds', also in reference to a moorhen:

Tall reeds
Like criss-cross bayonets
Where a bird once called, (p. 125)

Thomas not only employed anonymity within his texts. He extended it to completed works. His writing was often published anonymously or under a pseudonym. Such anonymity was sometimes imposed on him as a reviewer, but he actively pursued it in connection with the writing he most valued, his poetry. He posed as 'Edward Eastaway' in journals, anthologies and a booklet of six poems, and planned to use this pseudonym for his 1917 collection. He wanted to see how the poems would fare uninfluenced by his previous reputation as prose writer and critic: 'I prefer to remain Eastaway for the time being. People are too likely to be prejudiced for or against E.T.'[61] He was keenly aware of the detrimental effect of the declaration of individual ownership of a creative piece. Adding a name to a text risks distracting the reader from the creative piece, blurring responses to that piece with preconceived judgements about the author's capabilities. In this context, his vigorous activities in the realm of anonymity, editorializing, anthologizing and rewriting vernacular records of the environment and making unattributed use of other writers' material can be seen as exercises in restraint, of his own and other named voices, in order to foster complete focus on the current creative piece.

The introduction to Taylor's *Words and Places in Illustration of History, Ethnology and Geography* (1911) discusses the anonymous creation of place names, doubly significant as anonymous acts of creative composition and of naming the environment. They often precede written attempts to describe an environment and so remain closer to it. In addition, the environment, oral tradition and written and spoken language all coincide in place names. Thomas praised those who give inaccurate etymological histories for traditional place names for making 'England great, fearing neither man nor God nor philology'. Attempts to give such names finite histories and definitions are likely to have a reductive effect, so it is '[b] etter [to use] pure imagination than rash science in handling place names'.[62] Elsewhere, the inaccuracy of 'a thousand errors so long as they are human' is favoured.[63] Such apparent inaccuracy is more accurate since it closely reflects the fluid history of the names themselves.

He explored this topic further in relation to the names of plants in 'Old Man':

Old Man, or Lad's-love, – in the name there's nothing
To one that knows not Lad's-love, or Old Man,
The hoar-green feathery herb, almost a tree,

Various plant names 'half decorate, half perplex, the thing it is' (p. 36). Their proliferation emphasizes the ambiguities inherent in the naming process, and the importance of remaining aware of that ambiguity, challenging the ambition of taxonomy to classify definitively, a challenge that is reflected in the omission in this list of names of the plant's definitive Latin classification, *Artemesia abrotanum*.

BEGINNING AGAIN: WITH THE DANGERS OF APPROPRIATION

> I love a ballad in print, a-life, for then we are sure they are true.
>
> *The Winter's Tale*, Shakespeare[64]

Many writers in Thomas's time considered deeply the connections between the environment, oral literature and imaginative writing. As F. R. Leavis observed of Thomas's near contemporary Virginia Woolf: 'Edward Thomas's concern with the outer scene is akin to Mrs Woolf's.'[65] Her explorations in this area throw light on Thomas's views.

Woolf's regard for Thomas's writing on the land was apparent in her review of *A Literary Pilgrim in England*:

> We have seldom read a book indeed which gives a better feeling of England than this one. Never perfunctory or conventional, but always saying what strikes him as the true or interesting or characteristic thing, Mr. Thomas brings the very look of the fields and roads before us; he brings the poets too; and no one will finish the book without a sense that he [*sic*] knows and respects the author.[66]

In the initial draft of her last novel, *Between the Acts*, Woolf directly mentioned 'Old Man' and its exploration of words, naming and the environment. An allusion remains in the completed novel when Isa 'stripped the bitter leaf that grew, as it happened, outside the nursery window, Old Man's Beard. Shrivelling the shreds in lieu of words, for no words grow there, nor roses either.'[67] The importance of this poem to Woolf is indicated in her reference to its last lines when musing on the difficulty of memoir writing in her unpublished 'A Sketch of the Past', composed at the same time as *Between the Acts*: 'I see it – the past – as an avenue lying behind; a long ribbon of scenes, emotions. There at the end of the avenue still, are the garden and the nursery.'[68]

As her use of 'Old Man' suggests, Woolf shared Thomas's interest in the relationship between names and things, and the origins of naming. These relationships are examined in detail in 'Anon', on which she was working concurrently with *Between the Acts* in 1940–1. 'Anon' presents birdsong as the precursor to the human voice, echoing Thomas's placing of the robin's song before the poet's attempt at composition in 'Insomnia'. Longley has observed how birds 'often stand in for the poet' or 'provide aesthetic models' for him: '[He] assumes (rightly) that birdsong, the most complex utterance by any other species, and the lyric poem have a common evolutionary origin. Here [in 'Sedge-Warblers'] the sedge-warblers' song re-attaches the speaker-as-poet to the earth' (p. 241).

'Insomnia' shows a single instance of birdsong acting as stimulant for a poem. 'Sedge-Warblers' links the poet with one species of bird. Woolf, however, looked at the wider historical context, tracing the movement from birdsong to the anonymous vernacular of folk song:

> Innumerable birds sang; but their song was only heard by a few skin clad hunters in the clearings. Did the desire to sing come to one of those huntsmen because he heard the birds sing, and so rested his axe against the tree for a moment?[69]

In 'Anon' and other writings, Woolf was adamant about the importance of the anonymous voice. *A Room of One's Own* refers to Chaucer's dependence on 'forgotten poets who paved the ways and tamed the natural savagery of the tongue'.[70] Thomas's emphasis on the importance of anonymity was often accompanied by implicit references to the dangers inherent in naming. 'March the Third' celebrates anonymity of the 'day unpromised' which is 'more dear / Than all the named days of the year', and links that unnamed day to birdsong:

> 'Tis Sunday, and the church-bells end
> When the birds do. I think they blend
> Now better than they will when passed
> Is this unnamed, unmarked godsend.[71]

'October' includes a telling reference to the effect of naming:

> Some day I shall think this a happy day,
> And this mood by the name of melancholy
> Shall no more blackened and obscured be. (p. 101)

Woolf was even more explicit, particularly in her later work, written in the context of a period of increased upheaval in the late 1930s and early 1940s at the onset of a second world war. 'Anon' refers to *Morte d'Arthur*, the first printed text, as a symbol of printed literature, the fixing effect of print and its fatal effect on the anonymous voice:

> It was the printing press that finally was to kill Anon. But it was the press also that preserved him. When in 1477 Caxton printed the twenty one books of the Morte DArthur he fixed the voice of Anon for ever. There we tap the reservoir of common belief that lay deep sunk in the minds of peasants and nobles. There in Malorys [*sic*] pages we hear the voice of Anon murmuring still.[72]

The act of printing a text is connected with a sense of loss, and the acts of writing and remembering are associated with death, dependent upon the passing of what they record. Printed writing actively kills, or murders, 'Anon'.

In his prose piece 'Reading out of doors' (1903), Thomas also used Malory's *Morte d'Arthur* as a representative printed text. Writing about twenty years earlier than Woolf, he was distinctly positive in his approach, emphasizing the process of renewal and re-invigoration. He used *Morte d'Arthur* to show how, rather than the writer attempting to subsume the environment in words, words are subsumed in the environment. Read outdoors, the sounds of nature complement and redress the flaws of *Morte d'Arthur*:

> Immediately it is on the grass, the wood sorcery catches it. The birds fill with their softest notes the pauses of his halting stories. The flowers and the trees are glad to find the place in these stories, which Malory rarely gave to them.[73]

This exploration of print in a natural environment remains distinct from the very similar investigations of another contemporary writer, Hudson. In *Green Mansions*, Hudson described how, in the wildness of the forest, Rima shimmers in 'iridescent glory' but, when seen in human habitats, she appears 'like some common dull-plumaged little bird sitting in a cage'.[74] Seduced from her forest, she is eventually burnt to death. All that remains of her is an urn made by the narrator, who carves on it a textual inscription. Thomas noted how this acts as 'an imperishable and sacred memory', but also as a reminder of what has perished.[75] The inscription reads '*Sin vos y siu dios y mi*', translated in the novel as 'I, no longer I, in a universe where *she* was not, and God was not'. The urn and the epitaph serve as remembrances of the girl but also stress the irrevocability of death. The 'I' who carves the inscription is 'no longer I'.[76]

Woolf, Hudson and Thomas shared common ground. For all three, the act of writing words down, and, in Hudson's case, the act of speaking as an individual human voice, coincided with, involved and even caused creative loss. While emphasizing the limitations of the fixing quality of print, they also celebrated the printed book or word. For Thomas, it allowed space for the environment to have a voice. For Woolf, it preserved space in which anonymous voices could speak. For Hudson, the visceral physical experience of carving words on an urn offered comfort and consolation.

A foreshadowing of Woolf's explicit rendering of the tensions between anonymous and named printed text occurs in Thomas's comparisons of adult human voices with voices of unnamed and unself-conscious children. These children are closely connected with their environment, inhabiting it in a way that is evocative of Hudson's Rima. Their points of view are set against those of adults. Commonly, the adults remain distant, pronouncing on what they see, and attempting to contain or own a scene through their words. Commonly, too, they fail, and this failure alienates them further from the scenes that they observe. The children, on the other hand, remain part of the scenes. They inhabit them. Their voices come out of them, and are integral to them. In 'Old Man', the child is merely, effortlessly, 'perhaps / Thinking, perhaps of nothing' in the environment, while the more detached adult narrator is intent on trying 'to think what it is I am remembering' (p. 36). The children engage with their environment emotionally and imaginatively. The adult's observation of a child responding to a gloomy day of falling snow in 'Snow' is heightened and brightened by the child's direct speech, which provides the poem with its image of a bird, an image that the adult observer adopts in the last line:

> A child was sighing
> And bitterly saying: 'Oh,
> They have killed a white bird up there on her nest,
> The down is fluttering from her breast.'
> And still it fell through that dusky brightness
> On the child crying for the bird of the snow. (p. 51)

The child in 'The Child on the Cliffs' imaginatively inhabits the world he physically perceives, instilling it with drama and adventure: 'the grasshopper works at his sewing machine' is 'like a green knight in a dazzling market-place', while the 'foam there curls / And stretches a white arm out like a girl's' (p. 65). The child in 'The Child in the Orchard' similarly explores imaginative truth in nursery rhymes.

This combination of human language and the natural sounds and movements of the environment holds an echo of Wordsworth's 'The Thorn', in which a woman takes the part of Thomas's unself-conscious children. In 'The Thorn', Martha shudders and cries 'when the little breezes make / The waters of the pond to shake.'[77] It is as if she is a part of the land and her language synonymous with the sounds of nature. Wordsworth's note to 'The Thorn' reiterated this point, attributing the poem's use of repetition to the inadequacies inherent in human language, a point Thomas also drew on in his repetition of vernacular plant names in 'Old Man'. Wordsworth wrote:

> every man must know that an attempt is rarely made to communicate impassioned feelings without something of an accompanying consciousness of the inadequateness of our own powers, or the deficiencies of language. During such efforts there will be a craving in the mind, and as long as it is unsatisfied the speaker will cling to the same words, or words of the same character.[78]

Thomas spelt out the powerful effects of a deep unself-conscious engagement with the environment in 'The Mill-Pond' and 'The Brook'. While the adult narrators observe and muse on the natural scene, the younger voices unexpectedly translate that scene into speech. These poems echo and reflect on Wordsworth's illustration in 'The Prelude' of the nourishing effect of 'spots of time' in his description of a girl carrying a pitcher.[79] However, Thomas's poems demonstrate a sharper effect in which the voices of young girls shatter adult perceptions. In 'The Mill-Pond', when the girl speaks, interrupting the narrator's three stanzas of physical description, she startles him. In 'The Brook', the adult voice muses on the brook, the child's play in it and the 'fir-tree-covered barrow on the heath', but eventually acknowledges the superior success of the child as articulator of the natural scene and of the emotions of those inhabiting it:

> And then the child's voice raised the dead.
> 'No one's been here before' was what she said
> And what I felt, yet never should have found
> A word for, while I gathered sight and sound. (p. 97)

Woolf, like Thomas, also dealt with sounds and voices integral to the environment rather than distanced from it. In her case the catalysts were the calls of animals and the sounds of the natural environment. *Between the Acts* describes an interruption of the performance of an outdoor play: 'Then the wind rose, and in the rustle of the leaves even the great words became inaudible; and the audience sat staring at the villagers, whose mouths opened, but no sound came.'[80] The interrupted human speech is then followed by the bellowing of cows, as if in continuation.

Thomas's 'The Mountain Chapel' compares the human voice to the natural sound of the wind. The wind is unequivocally more powerful, more overwhelming and ultimately more lasting:

> The eternal noise
> Of wind whistling in grass more shrill
> Than aught as human as a sword,

And saying still:
''Tis but a moment since man's birth
And in another moment more
Man lies in earth
For ever; but I am the same
Now, and shall be, even as I was
Before he came;
Till there is nothing I shall be.' (pp. 43–4)

In 'The Word', a poem meditating on the elusiveness of words and names, 'There are so many things I have forgot', the speaker's thoughts are interrupted by 'a pure thrush word'. This interruption is unexpected and sudden, 'cried out to me' from the bushes. Intellectual and articulated thought is contrasted with physical and sensuous experience. The bird call, too, is sudden but also confirming, occurring, significantly, when the speaker is focusing not on intellectual thought but on how the physical experience of scents evokes 'food' and 'memory'. In contrast to the speaker's convoluted lists of lost or forgotten names, the bird call or 'word' is 'empty', 'thingless' and 'pure'. Not only is this particular name remembered even as the speaker cannot articulate it, but it completes and rounds off the poem:

the name, only the name I hear.
While perhaps I am thinking of the elder scent
That is like food, or while I am content
With the wild rose scent that is like memory,
This name suddenly is cried out to me
From somewhere in the bushes by a bird
Over and over again, a pure thrush word. (p. 93)

These voices from the natural world or from children raise rather than destroy the dead. They are 'empty' as Thomas described it in 'The Word'. They speak without risking the dangers of appropriation that Woolf identified in 'Anon' in her reference to Caxton fixing 'the voice of Anon for ever'.[81]

Between the Acts presents a gentler relationship between the sound of the wind and the cows and human efforts at articulation in an outdoor pageant. Although the play is interrupted by these sounds from nature, it picks up again after their cessation. Once the cows have bellowed, they 'lowered their heads, and began browsing' and the play moves on.[82] The temporary interruption of the performance by sounds from nature augments that performance, as the play interacts with and becomes more integrally connected with its physical setting. Cows, actors, director and audience all form part of the play experience, although the cows remain unaware of their contribution while the actors and director expend deliberate human effort, and the audience strains to interpret what is seen and heard.

Similar contrast is evident in 'The Mill-Pond' and 'The Brook' (pp. 56, 97). Both poems open with the narrator very deliberately watching and describing the scene, collecting rather than participating in what 'The Brook' terms the 'sight and sound' surrounding him. In contrast, the child and girl, like Woolf's wind and cows, are much more part of the land. In 'The Brook', the child paddles in the water. In 'The Mill-Pond', the narrator puts his feet near the water, but does not enter: 'my feet dangling teased the foam / That slid below'. At this point of not entering the water, isolating himself from his physical environment, a girl, dressed in white, perhaps implying a relation between her communion with the land and innocence, is introduced with the words 'came out'. It is as if she issues directly out of the landscape, like the 'thrush word' in 'The Word' out of 'somewhere in the bushes' (p. 93), or Wordsworth's woman in 'The Thorn', initially seen as a 'jutting crag' and only then as '[a] Woman seated on the ground'.[83]

However, unlike Wordsworth's characters, Thomas's children and Woolf's sounds of nature more evidently invade or interrupt the worlds of their detached narrators, actively engaging with or confronting them, often violently and unexpectedly. The rising wind and bellowing cows in Woolf's novel drown out the actors' words. In 'The Brook', the child's sudden speech 'raised the dead' (p. 97). The speaker's surprise in 'The Mill-Pond' at the girl's voice soon turns to anger and, as if in response to this building tension, a storm bursts forth in the natural world (p. 56).

The girl's ambiguous warning 'Take care!' in 'The Mill-Pond' demonstrates the power of this voice of the land. Her words herald the storm while advising the narrator of the need for caution and shelter. They also highlight the narrator's situation, poised on the brink, risking either alienation as a detached spectator, or loss of individuality if he should absorb himself in the landscape by dipping his feet in the dangerous mill-water. For the narrator, the land remains both a landscape viewed from a distance and a world that can harm and hurt. For the girl, the landscape is land, a place she inhabits and of which she is part, the power of her words residing in her unself-conscious position within this world.

BEGINNING AGAIN: WITH THE LANGUAGE OF THE LAND

> Nature, that universal and publick Manuscript that lies
> expanded unto the Eyes of all.
>
> Thomas Browne[84]

In 'The Brook' and 'The Mill-Pond', the narrator's self-conscious attempts at articulation divide him from the pre-linguistic experience he wishes to articulate. Thomas's writings suggest that poetry and the vernacular emerge without design from that pre-linguistic experience, emphasizing the importance of habitation or deep occupation of the land. He teased these ideas out in more depth in a review of an Australian poetry collection, arguing that the environment, in as much as it represents the past, is a crucial source of poetry:

> A race hardly develops a genuine poetry more rapidly than an oak achieves full maturity. Poetry is a natural growth, having more than a superficial relation to roses and trees and hills. However airy and graceful it may be in foliage and flower, it has roots deep in a substantial past. It springs apparently from an occupation of the land, from long, busy, and quiet tracts of time, wherein a man or a nation may find its own soul. To have a future, it must have had a past.[85]

The Australian poet, Thomas continued, 'is akin to the old ballad singers. He cannot tear the heart out of the mystery of the new lands, but he leads us up to the mystery, and we experience it.' The poet is an interpreter of the land, described as 'new' in this review, in a reflection of the colonial attitude to early twentieth-century Australia.

A few years later, in *The South Country*, Thomas talked more literally of the land as possessing language: 'If we but knew or cared, every swelling of the grass, every wavering line of hedge or path or road were an inscription, brief as an epitaph'.[86] Hans Ulrich Seeber observes how in 'Haymaking', 'February Afternoon', 'In Memoriam (Easter, 1915)' and 'Swedes', Thomas 'sees and reads the surface of English landscape and country life as a storehouse of memories; he transforms it into a text'.[87] Although features of landscape do not form words, they speak a language to those who can read it. The first lines of 'November' represent such an attempt, evoking the land's condition at a particular time of year by reading the marks left on it by living beings:

> the paths
> With morning and evening hobnails dinted,
> With foot and wing-tip overprinted
> Or separately charactered,

> Of little beast and little bird.
> The fields are mashed by sheep, (p. 34)

Thomas's interest in ways in which the land speaks results in repeated employment of geographically and historically rooted metaphors of place: buildings, landmarks, place names and indigenous, and therefore location-specific, flora and fauna. Examples occur in the loving descriptions of buildings in *Oxford*; the *Rest and Unrest* essay 'Snow and Sand'; his three poems entitled 'Home'; his ubiquitous use of place names, often in long topographical lists; and the indigenous plant names of 'Old Man'. Place names act as representatives of the poetry lying within the environment. Naming the land directly, land and words are clearly linked. Their power can subsume that of the writer's, and at times long lists of place names take over from Thomas's voice in his books, replicating the role played by the sounds of 'wood sorcery' and birds in 'Reading out of doors', or wind and cows in Woolf's *Between the Acts*.

Thomas's topographical lists come most evidently to the fore in *Richard Jefferies, his Life and Work*. The research for this book began with travel, interviews and note-taking *in situ*: 'I was nearly always out of doors & when indoors I was writing out my notes or writing to crowds of people who were supposed to be likely to help me to know Jefferies.'[88] The first chapter is a prime example of how the act of writing can relate to the physical environment in which it is initiated. The chapter returns repeatedly to the place names of Jefferies's childhood home, an important source of Jefferies's imaginative writing. They are strung together to trace ancient, '[u]ntrodden but indelible old roads'.[89] Significant landmarks are filled in on the way:

> Broad Hinton, the next village on this road, fills a considerable space in Jefferies' earliest descriptions; he mentions the small white horse on the downside near, the church, the mansion which its owner burnt to save from the parliament in the Civil War, and the legendary treasure in the well close by.

and 'At Clyffe there is a church, a manor-house, a pond, and a chestnut-tree; a hanging beech-wood above, ash-trees below' .[90] The result is a place name map of Jefferies's imaginative territory, highlighting the geographical and historical rootedness of place names as a vernacular and the importance of such rootedness to Jefferies. In the first edition of the book, a physical ordnance survey map of the area, inserted in the back of the book, accompanies the virtual map of place names. This inclusion of a physical map gives a close approximation in book form to the concept of language written on the land, providing further evidence of the link between creative writing and its external physical surroundings.

In the second chapter of *Richard Jefferies, his Life and Work*, a comparable feat is attempted with the personal names of the Jefferies family. However, these names, too similar to each other, have a weaker impact. They also lack any strong physical geographical base of place. To root them more securely in the land, Thomas has scattered among them more place names:

> Jefferies is, and has long been, a common Wiltshire name, spelt also Jeffreis, Jeffreys, Jefferis, Jefferie, Jeffereye, Jeffery, Jefferyes, Jeffereyes, Jeafries, Jefferes. They were farmers, coopers, and the like at Wootton Bassett, Clevancy, Chippenham, Marlborough, in the seventeenth century. In the parishes of Chiseldon and Draycot Foliatt they rank with the Webbs, Garlicks, Crippses, Lookers, Nashes, Woolfords, Chowleses, Pontings, and Jeroms for abundance and persistency. (p. 23)

BEGINNING AGAIN: WITH A PHYSICAL INTERDEPENDENCY

> the relics of every age, skull and weapon and shroudpin and coin and carven stone, are spread out upon the clean, untrodden sand
>
> Edward Thomas[91]

In 1903, Thomas presented 'landscape and the air' as prime movers in terms of human creative acts.[92] A more interdependent relationship was suggested in 1913: 'the literature of Nature represents rather the unsocial and unspoken thought of men'.[93] In 1909, *The South Country* showed how, although human beings may physically form marks on the land, these marks are dictated by the land's physical characteristics: 'The peculiar combination of soil and woodland and water determines the direction and position and importance of the ancient trackways'.[94] The role of creator is shared. Geographical locations rooted in particular temporal periods speak as a record of the physical movements and activities of human beings, but they also hold marks pre-dating those people's existence.

'Roads' emphasizes this interdependency of human beings and the language of the land. Human beings are presented as the main readers of the language contained in the manmade landscape feature of a road. However, the continuity of roads contrasts with their makers' fragile claim on continuing existence:

> Roads go on
> While we forget, and are
> Forgotten like a star
> That shoots and is gone.

On the other hand, despite the relative permanence of roads, they, too, depend on men they outlive:

> The hill road wet with rain
> In the sun would not gleam
> Like a winding stream
> If we trod it not again. (p. 106)

Just as language requires a speaker or a reader, so roads will not 'gleam' without the physical, and perceptive, contact of their human travellers.

The South Country involves 'history' rather than human beings in the act of creating landscape features, and the imagery employed in an investigation of history's impact on the land emphasizes the active physical movement and contact involved in the making of landmarks: 'In some places history has wrought like an earthquake, in others like an ant or mole; everywhere, permanently.'[95] The attribution of 'wrought', a verb of craft evoking strong physical activity, to 'history' rather than to man is a reminder that landscape features are both effects of the combined activities of man and nature and records of them. They act as a language that can be read.

In *The South Country*, history is physically and violently carved deep into the land. The land 'is an old battlefield, and the earth shows the scars of its old wounds'.[96] Woolf, too, observed how, from an aeroplane, 'you could still see, plainly marked, the scars made by the Britons; by the Romans; by the plough, when they ploughed the hill to grow wheat in the Napoleonic wars'.[97] She used a strong, startling and almost invasive physical image in her review of *A Literary Pilgrim* to express the impact a landscape can have on a book, writing of Thomas Hardy's and Emily Brontë's work that

> great tracts of Wessex and of the Yorkshire Moors [are] inhabited by a race of people who seem to have the rough large outline of the land itself. It is not with either of these writers a case of the word-painter's gift; for though they may have their detachable descriptions, the element we mean is rubbed deep into the texture and moulds every part.[98]

Despite this stress on the physical aspects of the language of the land, Woolf also highlighted uncertainty and lack of detail or location in her phrase 'rough large outline'. This phrase recalls Thomas's focus on places that do not possess names. He celebrated overgrown combes or stretches of undergrowth in poems such as 'The Chalk Pit' and 'The Hollow Wood', seeking connections between the environment, writing and places that are at risk, in their nameless state, of disappearing beyond the reach of history.

In particular, Woolf's phrase seems to echo Thomas's imaginary records of the first annals of human history in *The South Country*. These records start with nameless rather than named areas, 'begin[ning] with a geological picture, something large, clear, architectural, not a mass of insignificant names'.[99] Woolf's identification with what is nameless and uncertain in Thomas's work is further indicated in her later work on *Between the Acts*. Briggs observes how, in the initial draft of this novel, Isa, and possibly Woolf herself, misquotes Thomas, thus highlighting 'the gaps and uncertainties in Thomas's poetry'.[100]

A nameless starting point necessarily demands vagueness, as evinced in Thomas's reference in *The South Country* to an indeterminate, though demonstrative, 'something'. A similar indeterminacy is emphasized in 'The Word'. The 'pure thrush word' issues from a vague 'somewhere' in the bushes (p. 93). However, the lack of detail in 'something large' or 'somewhere' does not rule out specificity in the physical features that endure, as the accompanying qualifiers, 'geological', 'clear' and 'architectural' and 'in the bushes' declare.

The exploration of early history in Thomas's essay 'England' also highlights the importance of specific, physical, 'little things': 'two little things in early English history suggest England more vividly to me than bigger things. One is the very stunted hawthorn round which the battle of Ashdown mainly clashed.' The passage continues:

> Above all it tells me of the making of landmarks and the beginning of historic places. Of such things has England gradually been made, not lifted at one stroke by Heaven's command out of the azure main. The other little thing is the hoar apple tree where Harold's host met the Conqueror near Hastings.[101]

In *Flora Britannica*, Richard Mabey explains how enduring 'conspicuous landscape features' like indigenous crab-apple trees and hawthorn became important historical markers, respectively comprising the third and first most frequently mentioned species as boundary features in Anglo-Saxon boundary charters.[102] The 'little' hawthorn around which the battle clashes in 'England' also symbolizes the cause of that battle. Though 'little', it contains a large story. Thomas said that it 'tells' of that battle, suggesting that, as in the process of storytelling, it is necessary to listen, or pay attention, in order to uncover the historical information recorded on the land. The writer is as much discoverer as creator of a process, hence Thomas's praise of Wordsworth and Frost as visitors of and recreators of a past poetry, uncovering poetry and returning through its paraphernalia 'into poetry again', and hence, too, his preference for Frost's greater involvement in the process, sympathizing where Wordsworth contemplated, thus engaging emotionally.[103] The hawthorn in 'England' has a further function. It not only 'tells' the battle story but acts as a specific pointer to what Woolf and Thomas referred to as the larger, rougher 'outline' or 'something large, clear, architectural'.[104]

Thomas's awareness of the delicate balancing relationship between rough outlines and little individual points of attention informs his focus on the landscape features of inscriptions and epitaphs. He saw them as both enduring and beyond reach: physically and relatively permanently cut into the land 'in many languages and characters. But most of us know only a few of these unspoken languages of the past, and only a few words in each.'[105] He emphasized the peculiarly contemporary distance between human beings and the language of the land, and the contemporary loss of understanding of the indigenous knowledge, birdsong and language held within landscape features. It is as if, with the limitations of contemporary understanding of the land, the land itself has to interpret its history, a history that is often also human history, and the task of a contemporary writer becomes less interpreter and more transcriber or amanuensis.

BEGINNING AGAIN: WITH EMPHASIS ON PROCESS

> going on without end, touching here and there a farmhouse, crossing a road, passing in at the door of an inn and out through the garden, as if some friendly man had made the path by following his heart's desire.
>
> Edward Thomas[106]

Epitaphs involve very physical acts of writing. They are tangible, carved into stone, physically part of the objects on which they are written. Wordsworth's *Essays upon Epitaphs* emphasizes the particular relations epitaphs command between form, physicality, environment and language, relations that concerned Thomas deeply. Wordsworth called them the 'language of senseless stone'.[107] They 'personate the deceased, and represent him as speaking from his own tomb-stone', giving a distinctive image of the interrelation between language, land and human beings.[108] The human entity shifts from the eyes that read the stone-carved words, to a presence in the words, to the stone itself as the writer becomes part of the words written and even inhabits the object written upon, the tombstone.

Wordsworth's *Essays* also emphasizes the effect of the environment on epitaphs. The churchyard stone epitaph is weathered: 'the sun looks down upon the stone, and the rains of heaven beat against it'. It is 'half-overgrown with Hemlock and Nettles'. Coleridge, too, provided delicate descriptions of copying down epitaphs, acts that closely informed Wordsworth's *Essays upon Epitaphs*, and recorded his interaction with the plants growing around and over the grave:

> While I took the copy, the Groundsel showered its white Beard on me/ Groundsel & Fern on the grave, & the Thorns growing that had been bound over it – On a square Tomb as high as half up my Thigh, where the Tom Tits with their black velvet Caps showered down the lovely yewberries on me.[109]

Thus epitaphs and the nature surrounding them make up a complex and rich conversation with the people who come across them.

While appreciating the blurring effect of time on epitaphs, Wordsworth was clearly appreciative of the epitaph as fixed and located in the land, marking a particular temporal period. This value for specificity is reflected in the titles of his poems. Thomas observed this tendency of Wordsworth's in *A Literary Pilgrim* and Alain de Botton relates it to Wordsworth's belief in 'spots of time' in *The Art of Travel*:

> This belief in small, critical moments in nature explains Wordsworth's unusually specific way of subtitling many of his poems. For example, the subtitle of *Tintern Abbey, On revisiting the banks of the Wye during a Tour. July 13, 1798*, cites the exact day, month and year to suggest that a few moments in the countryside overlooking a valley could number among the most significant and useful of one's life, and be as worthy of precise remembrance as a birthday or a wedding.[110]

Thomas, too, saw epitaphs as both fixed and changing. His essay title, 'Epitaphs as a Form of English Literature' (1902) proclaimed a literary value for them, as did his inclusion of three epitaphs transcribed from cemeteries in *Pocket Book* (1907). He also wrote several poems that form epitaphs of reclamation and remembrance. 'In Memoriam' mourns those killed in the war. 'A Tale' commemorates an old cottage. 'Tall Nettles' remembers a neglected farmyard. 'The Cherry Trees' also remembers the dead.

Thomas's respect for epitaphs centres on a recognition of their role as a bridge between land and human language. Awareness of process is evident in his exploration of them. Although building on the Romantic understanding of the identity of things and persona as fundamentally insecure, he highlighted further the continual act of becoming. His epitaph poems lay stress on impermanence. The dust in 'Tall Nettles' is soon to be 'lost' in a shower and the petals in 'The Cherry Trees' are shed on 'the old road where all that passed are dead' (pp. 119, 120). These petals, acting as memorials to the dead who have already gone, are linked to them by the half-rhyme of 'dead' and 'shedding'. Such transformation of petals, a well-worn Japanese trope for what is transitory, into epitaphs becomes yet another reminder. It suggests not only impermanence, since petals soon deteriorate, but also the close relation between epitaphs and the natural environment.

Thomas's preference for what is marginal, transient and in transit is also indicated by his habit of titling and making notes on drafts and fair copies of poems. These notes and titles, although drawing on specificity of personal experience, lean towards movement and the ensuing blurring of vision, or vagueness, it can create. They show a propensity in Thomas for anonymity and removal of a sense of self from the poems. He decided also not to incorporate notes of composing conditions in the printed versions, unlike Wordsworth's detailed titles, and more akin to Keats's records of writing on the go, as emphasized by Thomas in his critical biography, *Keats*: 'we know that he wrote sonnets in Burns's cottage, on Ben Nevis, and in sight of Ailsa Craig, straight from his first shock of emotion'.[111]

Traditionally, the epitaph relates to the life and death of specific individuals, so it is illuminating to note that, in Thomas's writing, a more potent image is the pathway, road or river, continually in process. Once again, this shows a preference for anonymity. Thomas chose to title poems that relate to pathways not with reference to particular tracks, but with less specific monikers, 'The Path' and 'The Bridge', often making use of plurality, as in 'Roads' and 'The Green Roads'.

In 'Roads', the road 'winds on for ever'. It is a 'winding' stream. The dead are travellers coming back from France, dancing down the road. They accompany the living as they travel along the road and speak in a 'pattering' language that also represents their physical movement along the road:

> the dead
> Returning lightly dance:
>
> Whatever the road bring
> To me or take from me,
> They keep me company
> With their pattering, (pp. 107–8)

Such conversation between the road, bygone dead human travellers along it and the speaker of the poem evokes Thomas's use of place names in *Richard Jefferies, his Life and Work* as a token not only of past human interactions with the land, but of recreations of that past.

So, Thomas often expressed his repeated emphasis on process in his poems and composing in the flowing language of the land, fields, roads, houses, trees. He saw language as fashioned and refashioned 'like an earthquake' by history, 'everywhere, permanently',[112] 'fixed and free' (p. 93), fluid and continuous. Like Coleridge, he recorded how initial moments of composing could be affected strongly by their environment and literary context, and, to some extent, produced by that environment. He saw these initial moments as part of a much longer process, forming a continuum that includes features carved in the land by geological forces, the sounds of the natural environment, manmade landscape features and the body of oral and printed literature.

Thomas also suggested, like Woolf, that the fixing effect of printed literature and the resultant emphasis on individual writers put the rich flexibility and fluidity of language at risk. In completed printed texts it is difficult to articulate what is pre-linguistic and to make provision for the continuation of the process of creativity.

The epitaph provides one way of encapsulating that sense of continuing process. Stone-carved epitaphs situated in outdoor cemeteries preserve a close and changing relationship with the environment. Environmental weathering affects epitaphs long after the process of composition is apparently at an end. Thomas acknowledged this in a number of his epitaph-like poems. He also observed, in his exploration of the writing process in *The Icknield Way* dedication, a similar close changing and yet unending relationship between man, roads and the environment.

Thomas's explorations of the implications of this emphasis on process come together in one particular poem, 'Digging ("What matter makes my spade")', where excavation of the past is combined with burial of the present in the act of 'letting down two clay pipes into the earth'. One pipe belongs to Thomas and one, which his digging presumably uncovered, to 'a soldier of Blenheim, Ramilies, and Malplaquet / Perhaps' (p. 99). On a first reading, the owners of the clay pipes seem caught in separate moments of time, divided from each other. The 'perhaps', with which the list of possible locations in the past for the second pipe ends, reiterates this division. The division is so complete that Thomas, as owner of one pipe, is unsure of the exact whereabouts of the owner of the other. They are stuck in their separate layers of time. Their situation evokes that of the would-be poet in 'Insomnia', unable to progress in his poem from the temporally and seasonally fixed 'sere and the ember / Of the year and of me' to a more enduring 'empty thingless name' of birdsong, as evoked in 'The Word' (p. 93). Unlike the pipe-owners' apparent situation in 'Digging ("What matter makes my spade")', the 'thingless name' remains unmarked temporally or linguistically, harking back to a pre-linguistic era when, as 'Lob' puts it, 'our blackbirds sang no English' (p. 77).

However, a closer look at 'Digging ("What matter makes my spade")' reveals an emphasis on process, digging, uncovering and covering up. These activities and the physical juxtaposition of the uncovered pipes link two apparently divided layers of history. Despite the ages that separate them, the pipes are buried together: 'the dead man's immortality / Lies represented lightly with my own' (p. 99). The poem shows process, represented by the act of digging, both highlighting and eluding divisions caused by time. In its exploration of the act of digging, it also almost physically connects the poetry of the moment to the stories and memories of oral tradition. The spade uncovers two pipes that are buried just

> A yard or two nearer the living air
> Than bones of ancients, who, amazed to see
> Almighty God erect the mastadon,
> Once laughed, or wept, in this same light of day. (p. 99)

3

Ellipses and Aporia

> The very best poems are left unwritten or sung in silence. It is my opinion that the real test for poets is how far they resist their impulse to utterance
>
> Yone Noguchi[1]

In order to ensure that the printed poem retains some of the qualities of oral literature and of language held within the land, 'written' on it by man or geological forces in form of roads, furrows, hill, Thomas sustained emphasis on process both in the act of composition and the completed work. To achieve this, he employed certain techniques. These can be grouped under the broad headings of 'absence', 'dislocation' and 'divagations'. Examination of these techniques forms the basis of the ensuing chapters.

In Thomas's critical writing, absence features highly as a criterion of praise. The poetry of Frost, the contemporary poet he admired most, is valued precisely for its absences, for what it is not, 'extraordinary things have not been sought for', and for what the poems 'lack', 'appear to lack' or are 'free from'.[2] D. H. Lawrence is partly 'remarkable for what he does not do'.[3] The limited success Thomas allowed to Imagist poetry is attributed to the hint of an absent model, described in the case of Pound as 'the restraint imposed by Chinese originals or models'. When Imagist poems are criticized, it is for lack of absence, for the way they stick 'out of the crowd like a tall marble monument' and are 'conspicuous'.[4]

Thomas's use of absence as a yardstick for appraising literary work calls to mind the emphasis on absence, blanks and gaps in Japanese literary aesthetics. It indicates the great influence Japanese aesthetics had on many early twentieth-century Western poets, reaching far beyond the acknowledged debt of the Imagists. Thomas's value for absence in his criticism and in his poetry, as in the use of falling cherry blossom petals in 'The Cherry Trees' to evoke loss and death, resonates with the words of the fourteenth-century Buddhist priest Kenkō. Kenkō, one of the most highly respected writers on aesthetics in Japan, admired, not blossom in full bloom, but 'twigs which bear no blossoms as yet and a garden strewn with withered petals'.[5]

Appreciation of absence is so strong in Japanese literature that W. G. Aston in his *A history of Japanese literature* (1899) couched a mainly unsympathetic assessment of Japanese poetry in terms of lack, 'chiefly remarkable for its limitations – for what it is not, rather than what it has'.[6] Similarly, in the early twentieth century, Japanese writer and poet Yone Noguchi called this Japanese emphasis on absence 'the art of suggestion', the ability 'to read the space between the lines'.[7]

Thomas expressed his interest in Japanese aesthetics directly in his critical work. He reviewed a number of translations and paraphrases of Japanese writings and produced a critical study of Lafcadio Hearn in Constable's popular Modern Biographies series. Hearn was a key figure in Western understanding of Japanese aesthetics at this time. In 1896, his American publishers described him as 'the great interpreter of things Japanese to the West', and 'almost as Japanese as haiku'. As the Japanese critic, Yoshinobu Hakutani, put it in 1992, 'Lafcadio Hearn was best known for interpreting Western literature for the Japanese audience and, in turn, introducing the exotic [*sic*] culture and tradition to the West'.[8] Thomas appreciated Hearn's deep understanding of Japan, writing in 1907 that 'we had some right to believe that he was thinking like a Japanese', concluding in *Lafcadio Hearn* that 'I sometimes feel that with Japanese writers he should be compared', and quoting leading British Japanologist Basil Hall Chamberlain's *Things Japanese*: 'Hearn understands contemporary Japan better, and makes *us* understand it better, than any other writer.'[9]

Thomas also reviewed Yone Noguchi at least three times. As Hakutani records, Noguchi was 'perhaps the most influential professor of English in Japanese history', 'the only native [Japanese] scholar writing in English' and the first Japanese poet to write directly in English, so assuming 'a crucial role as an interpreter of Japanese culture for the West'.[10] Noguchi exchanged letters with many of Thomas's literary contemporaries, and was recognized as an important mediator and interpreter of Japan. Pound wrote to Noguchi that 'you are giving us the spirit of Japan is it not?' and compared Noguchi's work to his own efforts to reclaim Romance literature. Bottomley, in a dedicatory poem, referred to Noguchi's 'murmurs of hushed poetry that wait / On stillness to express what sound must lose', contrasting Noguchi's 'far land rare and desirable' with 'this greyer place of shadow and veil'.[11]

However, the emphasis on absence encouraged by Japanese aesthetics posed a dilemma: how is it possible to articulate absence, when absence necessarily precludes linguistic formulation? Thomas responded by focusing on process rather than completed work, a focus also found in Japanese art and poetry. In *The Icknield Way* preface he wrote of that ancient road: 'Today I know there is nothing beyond the farthest of far ridges except a signpost to unknown places. The end is in the means.'[12] He also wrote that the road is 'a symbol of mortal things with their beginnings and ends always in immortal darkness'.[13] The apparent rewording in this image of a road of what he described in *Keats*, composed contemporaneously with *The Icknield Way*, as the 'calm and penetrating' principle of negative capability evokes the Japanese emphasis on absence.[14] To focus on a particular end is to focus on an unknown remote location, on absence. To perceive that end, the attention must be turned to the process, which Thomas also expressed in terms of absence, focusing on the 'beautiful long straight line of the Downs in which a curve is latent – in the houses we shall never enter, with their dark secret windows [. . .] in the people passing whom we shall never know'.[15] A similar principle is evident elsewhere in the repeated use of interrelated aspects of absence: ellipses, aporia, gaps and unfinishedness in Thomas's writing.

ELLIPSES . . .

> *Vervain . . . basil . . . orison –*
> Whisper their syllablings till all meaning is gone,
> And sound all vestige loses of mere word . . .
>
> Walter de la Mare[16]

Thomas's letters and critical writings show that the presence of ellipses, whether typographical or metaphorical, in translations and original work, acted for him as a measure of a work's effectiveness. His creative writing reveals that ellipses were also central to his creative composing processes. This attraction to ellipses is unsurprising. They provide a convenient way in which to work with absence in a text or drafting process, serving as signposts to half-invisible, half-inarticulate absence. A particular characteristic of ellipses is that, while they signal an omission, they do not represent it.

Instead, they act as indicators of omission, pointing to the inaccessibility, albeit temporary, of an omitted part of a work. They represent, as the Cambridge handbook on copy-editing states, 'a pause, rather than an interruption'.[17] Instead of cutting a text short, they form a bridge between known areas of text. As a corollary to this, they invite the reader, and sometimes the writer, to supply, or imagine, the missing parts. Commonly, ellipses are marked in text with typographical dots or dashes. However, ellipses can also be signalled metaphorically. Frequently, in Thomas's work, words, phrases and even whole poems act elliptically, indicating other textually inaccessible parts of the piece in which they reside.

ELLIPSES . . . IN DRAFTS

> Finding themselves in a plot, they might suppose it appropriate to behave as though it were that sort of plot.
>
> A. S. Byatt[18]

R. G. Thomas identified one of Edward Thomas's drafts as the origin of no less than three poems, 'April', 'July' and 'The Glory'. The changes Thomas made when working on this draft give the impression of a redrafting process that largely consists of filling in missing words. The progression from the draft to the completed poems is not unlike the activity involved in finishing a partially completed jigsaw puzzle. The parts already selected form crucial aids in the search for what is still missing. They provide, together with the positioning and length of the spaces they surround, information on characteristics of the missing bits. These bits are missing in the sense that the person doing the puzzle has not yet found them. However, just as the picture on the lid of a puzzle box implies, these bits do already exist, simply waiting to be found.

Thomas's substantial use of typographical and metaphorical ellipses drives the drafting process of 'April', 'July' and 'Glory'. He marked the typographical ellipses with a continuous extended dash:

> As we met – the nightingale sang
> As we loved ________________
> As we parted __________the same.[19]

The extended dashes connect separate known areas of text. They also give information about the probable position, length and context of words not yet arrived at in the draft. In the above quotation, the dash linking 'As we parted' with 'the same' suggests both groups of words belong to one sentence. The omission of a word or words not yet arrived at is also signalled and the physical space to be taken up by them is approximated by the length of the dash.

The dashes in the 'April/July/Glory' draft also give information about the syntax of the missing words. The positioning of the long dash in line two of the draft indicates that the omitted words, when found, will syntactically complete the phrase 'As we loved'. Similarly, in line three, the long dash after 'As we parted' suggests that the omitted words, when found, will form the line's middle section.

The positioning of ellipses in the drafts, and the sections of known text that surround them, also indicate specific detail about the sound, rhyme, quantity and rhythm of the missing words. Thomas formed the concluding lines of two of the completed poems, 'The Glory' and 'July', by splitting up the last lines of the draft. The lines in the draft read:

> How swift time passes when nothing is
>
> _______
>
> In Time ________still hour after hour[20]

Their successors in 'The Glory', which R. G. Thomas dated as being completed one to two weeks later, run:

> How dreary-swift, with naught to travel to,
> Is Time? I cannot bite the day to the core.[21]

The positioning and stressing of 'How' and 'swift' in the draft are echoed in 'The Glory'. Both remain stressed, even though 'swift' is now preceded by 'dreary-'. In both cases, too, the words coincide with the beginning of the line and the beginning of a sentence. Similarly, the capitalized 'Time' is the first stressed word in a line in both 'The Glory' and the draft.

A similar pattern is evident when comparing the draft with the completed piece, 'July'. Edward Thomas made detailed changes to lines in the draft, but still retained the general position, rhythm and length of these lines in the completed poem. In the 'April/July/Glory' draft, the relevant lines read:

> Filled to content with what ring doves say.
> ~~I thought the above worth thinking of saying~~[22]

The concluding lines of 'July' are:

> Nothing there was worth thinking of so long;
> All that the ring-doves say, far leaves among,
> Brims my mind with content thus still to lie. (p. 88)

The ellipses in the draft mark characteristics of rhythm and stress that are retained in the completed poem. This suggests that Thomas was already aware of the specifics of rhythm and stress in the poem prior to his knowledge of the final form of words to be used. This is even the case when the length of a line appears changed from draft to completed piece. In the completed 'July', the 'ring dove' line has become 'all that the ring-doves say', acquiring an extra unstressed syllable, a hyphen and a shift in position from the second to the first half of the line. However, despite these alterations, as with the redrafted lines in 'The Glory', much of the phrasing and initial shape or length of the line is unaltered. Similarly, although the positioning of the lines in the completed poem 'July' has changed from the draft, the distance between these lines and their quality of sound has remained constant.

Thomas used the information held within the typographical ellipses in the 'April/July/Glory' draft to deduce details of the future completed poems. This suggests that the basic pattern of the completed poem was held in the first draft. It existed concurrently with that draft, perhaps even prior to it, taking shape before Thomas had begun to write anything down at all.

Metaphorical ellipses also play a significant part in Thomas's drafting processes. In the 'April/July/Glory' draft, the deleted line, '~~I thought the above worth thinking of saying~~', acts as a metaphorical ellipsis, standing in for words, or an order of words, not yet decided upon. In the completed 'July', this line has been reinstated, little altered, as the third last line: 'Nothing there was worth thinking of so long'. Although, in 'July', 'worth thinking of' now precedes the 'ring dove' line and is separated from it by a semi-colon instead of a deletion and indentation, the lines are linked by their similar-sounding final words, 'long' and 'among', and the retention in both draft and completed poem of a close juxtaposition between the phrase 'worth thinking of' and the 'ring dove' line. The order may have been reversed but the relations remain constant.

As with the development of 'The Glory', the reinstatement in 'July' of a line that was deleted in the draft indicates that, when Thomas continued to work on the poem, he discovered or uncovered pre-existing patterns. His deleted lines rarely remain legible, but in this draft the line can still be read under its scoring-out. It acts as a palimpsest, a subtle record of a previous pattern of words, and indicates Thomas's awareness that he might need it in a later version, as indeed he did. It signals a very specific gap, in which the alternative but rejected words remain discernible, both missing and present.

Examination of 'April/July/Glory' reveals how length, shape, sound, rhythm and patterning are leading factors in Thomas's composition processes. The sense of a work-in-progress might alter but qualities often resurface in successive drafts. This is particularly the case with sound, as can be seen in the line '~~I thought the above worth thinking of saying~~' which shifts from this affirmative if deleted statement in the draft to the negative 'Nothing there was worth thinking of so long' in 'July'. As it does so, it picks up the word 'nothing' from an earlier line in the draft: 'How swift time passes when nothing is'.[23] Although much changes in the transformation from draft to completed poem, the sound of most of the line remains constant.

Thomas's drafting decisions often stemmed from responses to words and patterns already held within a burgeoning draft. A comment to Frost indicated that sound rather than sense tended to lead the way: 'the rhymes have dictated themselves decidedly'.[24] Peter McDonald succinctly discusses this phenomenon, observing the dominant role each word, phrase or line selected in the composing process plays in subsequent drafting decisions:

> the requirements of poetic form have to do centrally with choice, with the exercise of an authorial free will in composition; but this is at every stage a choice compromised by the words available, and the relations with other words which they contain or uncover.

As McDonald phrases it, this situation necessitates 'mastery in the art of submission' involving a compromise between 'authorial free will' and 'submission'.[25]

McDonald's interpretation of the composing process echoes Thomas's view of the writer as amanuensis of what has already been 'written' in the environment. This is an interdependent process, as reflected in his poem 'The Sheiling', which uses the repeated end word 'kind' to express the exchange of benefits between a manmade house and the natural stone of the land:

> the house is kind
> To the land that gave it peace,
> And the stone has taken the house
> To its cold heart and is kind. (p. 137)

Thomas's practice of the 'art of submission' to patterns already buried or hidden in previous drafts means he acted at times like an external reader of his works-in-progress, looking for patterns that he was not already aware of. Just as earlier in the composing process the external environment provides stimuli that feed into the poem, so, at this later stage, an external eye is crucial. As Wolfgang Iser suggested, in his discussion of readers' responses to texts, the success of a text can be measured by anticipation of a possible or 'implied' reader's response to it:

> Texts must already contain certain conditions of actualisation that will allow their meaning to be assembled in the responsive mind of the recipient. The concept of the implied reader is therefore a textual structure anticipating the presence of a recipient without necessarily defining him: this concept prestructures the role to be assumed by each recipient, and this holds true even when texts appear to ignore their possible recipient or actively exclude him. Thus the concept of the implied reader designates a network of response-inviting structures, which impel the reader to grasp the text.[26]

In Thomas's case, the typographical and metaphorical ellipses in his drafts provide the 'textual structure'. At times successively and at times simultaneously, he acted as both composing poet and reader of his unfolding drafts, facilitating an 'art of submission' to 'the words available, and the relations with other words which they contain or uncover'.

This process can also involve an external reader's feedback on the work-in-progress. Thomas occasionally resorted to this, often to confirm his own ideas. After complaining to Frost of Bottomley's criticisms of his poems, Thomas continued:

> I am a little consoled too because what he liked most (& thought best) was a passage where I had allowed 'rain & wind' to come in 3 or 4 times or more usually at the end of a line, in about twice the number of blank verse lines.[27]

The anticipation of his own or other readers' responses influenced, and even drove, Thomas's drafting processes. His light deletion of a line in 'April/July/Glory' indicates his expectation that the line's value might become apparent on a rereading; the same applies to his use of extended dashes to mark the physical length of a missing piece of text. Such anticipation of future responses to a draft poem turns it into what Iser called a 'network of response-inviting structures'. In Thomas's case, actual external readers' responses to this structure helped him to identify further the work required in order to pick out the pattern of the completed poem. Similarly, readers' responses helped confirm to him the point at which the drafting process was completed, the point at which individual elements in the poem fitted the pattern held within it.

ELLIPSES . . . IN COMPLETED WORK

The longing to make the glimpsed good place permanent
R. S. Thomas[28]

Ellipses in drafts are often replaced with text in completed pieces. This is not the case, however, when typographical ellipses act as conventional markers of missing parts of quotations. Thomas also used typographical ellipses in completed pieces to indicate lack of connected thinking. The dying soldier in the prose piece 'Home' thinks of 'the inn dogs lying in the sun . . . the sun . . . the mist . . . his country . . . not the country he had fought for . . . the country he was going to'.[29] In the completed 'As the team's head-brass', ellipses represent the silences of taboo such as possible death in battle: 'If I should lose my head, why, so, / I should want nothing more . . .' (p. 124). Because ellipses always act as a pointer to what is not printed in the text, when, as in these instances, they form part of a work's final pattern, they help to convey the impression of the work still potentially in process.

In Thomas's completed poems, metaphorical ellipses share the impenetrability of typographical ellipses. They take the form of words with obscure semantic meanings that most readers do not know, often as unusual proper nouns: personal names or 'poems which are place-names' carrying impenetrable meanings.[30] He indicated his delight at such impenetrability and the elliptical effects of something half-eluded in his plea to de la Mare on 16 May 1911, written while composing *The Icknield Way*: 'please write a poem on "Puck Shipton" the name of an old farm close to the road I was following. The poem will enliven my dreary page'.[31]

'Adlestrop' draws on both metaphorical and typographical ellipses in its use of a place name and an em dash. Most readers are unfamiliar with the etymology of 'Adlestrop', and so are obliged to acknowledge possible levels of meaning inaccessible to them. The first stanza of the poem stresses the function of 'Adlestrop' as place name: 'I remember Adlestrop – / The name' (p. 51). This emphasis is repeated in the second stanza by the addition of 'only', and 'bare platform'. 'Adlestrop', with its initial capital letter, appears alienated and unattached, an impression reinforced by its juxtaposition with a stream of uncapitalized and more familiar plant names:

No one left and no one came
On the bare platform. What I saw
Was Adlestrop – only the name

And willows, willow-herb, and grass,
And meadowsweet, and haycocks dry, (p. 51)

'Adlestrop', as an ellipsis, both initiates and marks a pause in the flow of the text. In the first stanza, this pause is then extended by the means of the em dash, poised at the brink of an enjambement. In the second stanza, the addition of 'only' in the middle of a line similarly dislocates the flow of the text.

Thomas created similar effects with long lists of place names and personal names. The sheer weight of these names, tumbling one after another, renders redundant the use of typographical ellipses, since the impression of meaning eluded is already evident. Such lists occur most strikingly in the first two chapters of *Richard Jefferies, his Life and Work* and in *The South Country*, as in this passage on signboards:

> There is a wealth of poetry in them, as in that which points – by a ford, too – first, to Poulner and Ringwood; second, to Gorley and Fordingbridge; third, to Linwood and Broomy; and another pointing to Fordingbridge, to Ringwood, and to Cuckoo Hill and Furze Hill: and another in the parish of Pentlow, pointing to Foxearth and Sudbury, to Cavendish and Clare, and to Belchamps and Yeldham.[32]

He also praised W. H. Davies's 'Days That Have Been' for the 'exquisite music of some old Monmouthshire names that were sweet, but never so sweet'.[33] The list, by setting the sound of the names against their meaning, amplifies their sweet sound:

> Can I forget the sweet days that have been,
> The villages so green I have been in;
> Llantarnam, Magor, Malpas, and Llanwern,
> Liswery, old Caerleon, and Alteryn?

In a letter to J. W. Haines, Thomas, on 15 September 1916, stated that his 1916 'Household Poems' were 'I hope are among the best'.[34] The first of these, 'If I should ever by chance', begins with a place name list:

> If I should ever by chance grow rich
> I'll buy Codham, Cockridden, and Childerditch,
> Roses, Pyrgo, and Lapwater, (p. 115)

The second, 'If I were to own', composed almost in tandem with the first, employs a similar device:

> If I were to own this countryside
> As far as a man in a day could ride,
> And the Tyes were mine for giving or letting, –
> Wingle Tye and Margaretting
> Tye, – and Skreens, Gooshays, and Cockerells,
> Shellow, Rochetts, Bandish, and Pickerells,

> Martins, Lambkins, and Lillyputs,
> Their copses, ponds, roads, and ruts,
> Fields where plough-horses steam and plovers
> Fling and whimper, hedges that lovers
> Love, and orchards, shrubberies, walls
> Where the sun untroubled by north wind falls,
> And single trees where the thrush sings well
> His proverbs untranslatable,
> I would give them all to my son
> If he would let me any one
> For a song, a blackbird's song, at dawn. (p. 115)

The list of place names in this poem gradually transforms. First it is a list of unnamed places marked by human and animal action and seasonal changes. Then it itemizes specific 'single trees'. Finally, it resolves, with another form of metaphorical ellipses, into indecipherable birdsong, pointing the way to an elusive and 'untranslatable' absence.

In other Thomas poems, the whole of the written text forms an ellipsis. 'But these things also' enumerates emblems of spring, detailing a series of items found on marginal 'banks by the roadside': a little bleached snail shell, 'chip of flint, and mite / of chalk; and the small birds' dung'. Its title, and the repetition of the title in the first line, suggests the poem actually opens in the middle of a list that began, before the poem's first lines, with traditional emblems of spring, and now, in the poem, continues with less traditional emblems which form examples of mistaken identity:

> All the white things a man mistakes
> For earliest violets (p. 67)

The reading of 'white things' as traditional emblems of spring is re-enacted in 'But these things also' by reversing the usual positions of conventional and overlooked signs of spring. The overlooked items are placed in the centre of the poem. The conventional emblems, on the other hand, are pushed to the margins, visible in the poem only in the illusory misidentified 'earliest violets' and the background 'chattering' of 'starling flocks'. Otherwise, they are relegated to an unwritten list that precedes the poem and is only indicated in it by the 'But' of the poem's first line and title.

A similar process occurs in 'November'. In its celebration of November, this poem chooses to focus on overlooked characteristics, features that are literally trodden underfoot: the marks or imprints on land, mud and leaves, of birds, animals and human beings. The mud and the marks made on it are valued for what they are not, and for the way they highlight the brightness that is found elsewhere:

> without them, he sees clearly,
> The sky would be nothing more to his eye
> Than he, in any case, is to the sky;
> He loves even the mud whose dyes
> Renounce all brightness to the skies. (p. 34)

A comparison of mud and sky ends the poem, mud being valued for its function as foil to the sky. However, 'But these things also' goes further. It appears to present an ellipsis, containing overlooked emblems of spring, which is encased within a longer unwritten list of spring emblems. Such a presentation focuses attention on the peripheral. This slight poem manages to work not only as a sign of omission but also as the omitted thing itself, without ever losing sight of the peripheral quality of that omitted thing.

Conventional readers of Thomas's time found it difficult to view text as ellipses, as in Blackwood's misreading of Thomas's poetry as prose 'got up like verse'.[35] Iser interpreted such difficulties as arising out of too great a difference between the pattern of expectations held within the poem, its 'network of response-inviting structures', and the expectations of the readers.[36] If such sets of expectations are too remote from each other, it becomes impossible to accommodate both in a textual reading. Unless readers are prepared to let go of their expectations, they will find it hard to grasp the different pattern that the text actually contains. The poet's challenge is to find ways of persuading such readers to loosen their grip.

De la Mare commented on this in his foreword to the 1920 edition of Thomas's *Collected Poems*, warning readers that their expectations were likely to be at odds with the patterns held within the poems, and advising them to pay close attention to the 'network of response-inviting structures' that existed in the poems: 'loose-woven, monotonous, unrelieved, the verse, as verse, may appear to a careless reader accustomed to the customary'.[37] De la Mare's decision to employ syntax in this passage that itself demands close reading to disentangle, acts as further incitement to read in a different way.

Thomas's process of composing poetry involves gradual elimination of the obvious and increase of the elliptical, as in the inversion of the syntax of the deleted line in the 'April/July/Glory' draft, from '~~I thought the above worth thinking of saying~~' to the more convoluted 'Nothing there was worth thinking of so long' in 'July'.[38] A similar change can be discerned in a comparison of the 1895 prose piece 'Birds in March' and the 1916 poem 'Bright Clouds'. 'Birds in March' describes 'a woodland mere, and amidst the reeds and rushes growing along the shore, or in the shallow water at the edge, we spy a moor-hen's nest approaching completion. It is made of the long bayonet-like reeds and other water plants.'[39] 'Bright Clouds' contains a similar description, but it is sparser. Much of the subject matter is inferred from what is missing. There is no explicit mention of woodland, and while the poem goes on to refer to the bird, its half-made nest is not described. The gaps between the lines and phrases are important parts of the completed poem, resonating with the Japanese emphasis on absence and what is not said. A Keatsian state of negative capability when composing, 'of being in uncertainties, mysteries, doubts, without any irritable reaching after fact and reason' and 'taking hints from every noble mind that pays us a visit', is embedded in the completed poem, informing its effect. As Thomas put it in his critique of Keats's 'Endymion', 'In what obscures it lies the charm of the poem.'[40]

Japanese influence is also evident in the discretion of the references to war, death and loss in 'Bright Clouds'. The simile, 'bayonet-like reeds', lessens the effect of the tight metaphorical reference to weapons of destruction in the 'reeds / Like criss-cross bayonets' in 'Birds of March' (p. 125). Such discretion, common to Japanese soldiers writing death poems, is evident in a number of Thomas's poems and it has affected their reception. Although many were written during war time when he was making successive decisions to enlist and then volunteer for active service at the front, they deal so indirectly with the subject of war that some mid-twentieth-century critics have missed the references to it. Although some of his poems were included in war poem anthologies as early as the 1920s, John H. Johnston was able to write in 1964 that Thomas 'refused to let the conflict interfere with [his] nostalgic rural visions'.[41]

ELLIPSES . . . AS A MEASURE

> He talked too much; but now he has occasional flashes of silence, that make his conversation perfectly delightful.
>
> Sydney Smith[42]

Thomas's keen interest in ellipses is evident in his critical writings. He spoke approvingly of Noguchi's English poems as having 'seldom a quite definite significance. They suggest richly but mistily.'[43] He also extended this appreciation of ellipses to oral and traditional literature, praising Hearn's retold Japanese stories for containing 'that slight something absent which suggests the translation from a remote language'.[44]

In part, these approving allusions to Noguchi's elliptical English poems and Hearn's renderings of Japanese tales reflect a keen awareness of the emphasis on ellipses in Japanese literature, described by Noguchi as the ability 'to read the space between the lines'.[45] However, Thomas also praised the use of ellipses in non-Japanese contexts too. He commended the 'admirable' translations in Pound's 1910 survey of Romance literature for their ability to suggest 'the superiority of the original'.[46] Pound corroborated Thomas's comment when he explained to Noguchi that he was 'trying to deliver from obscurity certain forgotten odours of Provence and Tuscany'.[47] Similarly, Thomas's words, '[i]t is not you, & it is not the Welsh lyric', referring to his anonymization of Bottomley's rewritings of prose translations of a Welsh lyric, are revealing.[48] They suggest Thomas viewed translation as possessing a necessarily elliptical quality, anonymous and almost aporetic, belonging neither to the original writer nor to the translator.

Thomas's praise of Hearn's Japanese tales indicates that he saw the elliptical as an important measure of the success of written renderings of oral literature. In the 'Note on Sources' in his paraphrased *Celtic Stories*, written in tandem to *Lafcadio Hearn*, he wrote that 'it is one of the charms under the surface of these stories that we can feel, even if we can never trace, a pedigree of dimmest antiquity behind them'.[49]

Thomas extended his esteem for what was elliptical to his appreciation of original English work. He distinguished poetry from 'the amplification of prose' by means of its 'sensuous and elliptical forms'.[50] He saw the completed poem as only part of an unseen work. The ellipses of a written poem indicate unseen and unwritten but integral parts of the text, just as ellipses in a draft point to words not yet arrived at.

Thomas's book, *Feminine Influence on the Poets* (1910), presents ellipses as a common element in poetry and translation. A writer's personal experience is likened to the source text from which the target text, the poem, results:

> A man would give much to have a complete intimate account of the private life of a sonneteer during the period of conception and composition. This account might be printed on one side of the page and the sonnets on the other, like original and translation.[51]

In this passage, Thomas was echoing Wordsworth, who saw the poet as 'in the situation of a translator'.[52] In the case of Noguchi, this was almost literally true, since he was writing poetry in his second language, and Thomas was clearly attracted to the foreignness in Noguchi's work, writing of how '[h]is intimate foreign English rises up into mysterious intelligibility at intervals', and wondering 'how he could learn English and yet be so little tinged by our use of the language'.[53] He made similar remarks about Frost's American English, singling out for praise the elliptical quality of his 'good natural English with just that shade of foreignness'.[54] He also emphasized the strange abruptness of Pound's language, another American writer, likening him to 'a swift beetle that suddenly strikes your cheek' and confessing that it was Pound's '[c]arelessness of sweet sound and of all the old tricks' and his 'prickliness that incited us to read his book'.[55]

The close relation between the elliptical effect encouraged by Japanese aesthetics, the influence of those aesthetics on early twentieth-century poetry written in English and the elliptical quality that Thomas identified in both Noguchi's and Frost's writings in English coalesced in a performance, in Japanese, of one of Frost's poems nearly a hundred years later. 'The death of the hired man' appeared in Frost's collection, *North of Boston* (1914), which, Thomas wrote, 'put Mr Frost above all other writers of verse in America'. It was rewritten by John McAteer of *The No East West Company* in the early twenty-first century as an English Noh play entitled *Silas . . . the Hired Man*. McAteer inserted the ellipsis in the title as a reminder of the aesthetic of absence. They were intended to indicate a measure of respect of the original, of what was left out.[56]

Metaphorical ellipses can suggest absence in completed works. The half-inarticulate 'God bless it' in 'April' is a response to an onomatopoeic evocation of wild birdsong that focuses on sound rather than semantic meaning, embedded in lines that lean as much on domestic and traditional associations as literary explication. The poem draws on the traditional round, 'Sumer is icumen in', making use of the phrase 'loudly rings "cuckoo"'. This follows smoothly on from a sensuous domestic exploration of the image of an oven:

> When earth's breath, warm and humid, far surpasses
> The richest oven's, and loudly rings 'cuckoo'
> And sharply the nightingale's 'tsoo, troo, troo, troo';
> To say 'God bless it' was all that I could do. (p. 86)

As if to reiterate Thomas's conviction of the power of ellipses, the next verse employs the same elliptical technique, amending the phrase, however, from 'God bless it' to 'God bless you':

> But now I know one sweeter
> By far since the day Emily
> Turned weeping back
> To me, still happy me,
> To ask forgiveness, –

> Yet smiled with half a certainty
> To be forgiven, – for what
> She had never done; I knew not what it might be,
> Nor could she tell me, having now forgot,
> By rapture carried with me past all care
> As to an isle in April lovelier
> Than April's self. 'God bless you' I said to her. (pp. 86–7)

Emily's failure to articulate what she might have done wrong is accompanied and, it is implied, caused by 'rapture'. The repetition of 'God bless' suggests the poet is similarly inarticulate, and yet the poem ends with a sense of deep communication, partly achieved by replacing 'it' with the more personal 'you' to form 'God bless you', but also because the communicative effect of this phrase depends on its value as a metaphorical ellipsis signalling omission. 'God bless you' both indicates and stands in for a more direct expression of feeling.

Thomas's awareness of this elliptical effect is evident in his focus on the inarticulate 'it' of 'God bless it' in a letter to Frost written the day after the composition of 'April'. He wrote:

> By the way, there was a beautiful return of sun yesterday after a misty moisty morning, & everything smelt wet & warm & cuckoos called, & I found myself with nothing to say but 'God bless it'. I laughed a little as I came over the field, thinking about the 'it' in 'God bless it'.[57]

Metaphorical ellipses also appear at the end of 'Up in the Wind'. A girl's lament about her life in a remote rural inn is interrupted by a glimpse of the world outside. The quietening elliptical answer to her troubles created by this interruption evokes Wordsworth's privileged 'spots of time'.[58] The lines run:

> ['] I do wish
> The road was nearer and the wind farther off,
> Or once now and then quite still, though when I die
> I'd have it blowing that I might go with it
> Somewhere far off, where there are trees no more
> And I could wake and not know where I was
> Nor even wonder if they would roar again.
> Look at those calves.'
>
> Between the open door
> And the trees two calves were wading in the pond,
> Grazing the water here and there and thinking,
> Sipping and thinking, both happily, neither long.

> The water wrinkled, but they sipped and thought,
> As careless of the wind as it of us.
> 'Look at those calves. Hark at the trees again.' (p. 33)

The thinning that occurs between Thomas's prose piece 'Birds in March' and his poem 'Bright Clouds' is replicated in the elliptical progression from the prose version of 'Up in the Wind' to the poem. The prose version contains more detail:

> all she could see there was nothing but the beeches and the tiny pond beneath them and the calves standing in it drinking, alternately grazing the water here and there and thinking, and at last going out and standing still on the bank thinking.[59]

The 'nothing' that is reported in the prose piece is acted out in the poem, which removes the beeches, the pond size and the calves' exit from the pond. In the poem, the scene is presented more elliptically, pushing 'nothing' into the centre of the reader's awareness.

Thomas also created metaphorical ellipses in his prose, especially in his use of asides encased within further asides like a nest of Russian *matryoshka* dolls. The frequent incidence of a clause-embedded syntax that refers to topics outside the main focus of the piece alerts the reader to potential unwritten text, and to the existence of alternative forms of articulation. Thomas sometimes used such *matryoshka*-like asides to highlight the obligations and resultant ellipses that tended to accompany his commissioned prose, and so was able subtly to indicate his dissatisfaction with this situation: 'I mention these trivial things because they may be important to those who read what I am paid for writing.'[60]

An example of the spiralling connections made by such asides can be found in Thomas's exploitation of a forty-word place name list in *The South Country*. This list acts as an aside within the main text. It also contains a further *matryoksha*-like aside, which refers to creative belatedness, expressed as the failure to create an original place name. Immediately prior to, and confirming, the expression of failure in this second aside is the inclusion of the very place name that the writer mistakenly viewed as an original creation. This is also, dizzyingly, the same place name that initiates the second aside by stimulating the writer's memory of the previous attempt at originality:

> Lydiard Millicent, Clevancy, Amesbury, Amberley (I once tried to make a beautiful name and in the end it was Amberley, in which Time had forestalled me); what sweet names Penshurst, Frensham, Firle, Nutley, Appleshaw, Hambledon, Cranbrook, Fordingbridge, Melksham, Lambourne, Draycot,

> Buscot, Kelmscot, Yatton, Yalding, Downe, Cowden, Iping, Cowfold, Ashe, Liss . . . Then there are the histories of roads.[61]

Thomas recorded how the commissioning publisher of *The South Country*, Dent, had instructed him to 'scatter *real place names* plentifully' in the text.[62] By including this forty-word place name list, and the reference within it to his belatedness as a creator, Thomas skilfully met his publisher's demands while also asserting his identity as a creative composing writer. In addition, he was able to use this device to acknowledge the body of oral literature that lay behind his creative work, since the list highlights place names both as names and as ellipses for what is not written down. Thus, the list of '*real place names*' and the descriptions encased in those names form an elliptical aside that presents to the reader alternative ways of describing the countryside. In addition, the length of the list ensures that the names have a considerable impact on the flow of the main text. Momentarily, the apparent authority within the text is destabilized as the names edge, briefly, from an elliptical to a central position.

The typographical ellipses into which the forty-word place name list eventually drops indicate the provisionality of any text as a definitive description of the countryside: 'Cowfold, Ashe, Liss . . .' The reader is left with an impression of virtual endlessness. The list could go on and on. The individual writer is belated and insignificant, only sharing in what has already been created. The list is part of a larger unwritten whole. It does not simply belong to the written work in which it is inserted, but is, like 'But these things also', also part of a longer unwritten piece. In the same way that an examination of the drafting process of the 'April', 'July' and 'The Glory' poems indicates unwritten but nevertheless still present text, so Thomas's completed works provide a glimpse of a larger unwritten whole.

APORIA: OF?

> The forest foxglove is purple, the marguerite
> Outside is gold and white,
> Nor can those that pluck either blossom greet
> The others, day or night.
>
> Edward Thomas (p. 130)

Thomas's subscription to a state of negative capability and to the Japanese emphasis on the unwritten and unsaid in his composing processes and completed poems frequently resulted in what can be termed aporia, poised at the borders of articulation. In this context, Alan Bass's gloss of the Derridan use of aporia provides a useful definition: 'an excess which cannot be constructed within the rules of logic, for the excess can only be conceived as *neither* this *nor* that, or both at the same time – a departure from all rules of logic'.[63]

For the purposes of this book, the term 'aporia' refers to absences, interruptions, contradictions or doubtful areas that present impassable barriers to further expression. These are distinct from absences illuminated by the term 'ellipses', since ellipses not only indicate the absence of text from the work in which they are contained but invite the reader to fill them in. They do not cover what cannot be said, but signal, unlike aporia, the existence of an unwritten but potentially available text, suggesting that a creative piece is greater than its written parts. When the paradoxes and ambiguous resonances of ellipses, 'trailing off or fading away', form irresolvable logical difficulties and expressions of doubt, they are better termed aporia.

In keeping with their identity as markers of omission and doubt, the dividing line between aporia and ellipses is often blurred. A text may exhibit aporetic and elliptical qualities at the same time. Nevertheless, since the use of ellipses and aporia reveal different aspects of the composing process, it is helpful to examine them separately.

APORIA: OF PRESENT ABSENCE

> Well, you know, you have only to look. Claude is the artist who knows there is no painting the sun itself, and so he chooses the moment after the sun has set, or has hid behind a cloud, and its light fills the sky, and that light he suggests as no other painter ever could.
>
> James McNeill Whistler[64]

Thomas was appreciating aporia when he praised the tralatitious uncertainty of the linguistic relations between individual words in Noguchi's poetry, and the touch of synaesthesia:

> His world is his own. It is a nebulous, changeful one where few things retain their customary values and frequently lose their individuality altogether. In *My Heart* he is uncertain whether a sound be that of his heart or of the sea, of his tears or of 'the rain carrying tragedy from heaven'. A footstep heard is 'grey and soft'. He does not ask if the voice of his mother is heard in the wind, but 'Is the wind my mother lost?'[65]

The features Thomas admired in Noguchi's work suggest the effects of the Japanese literary device, *kakekotoba*, a fundamentally aporetic device that epitomizes the ambiguities lying at the core of Japanese grammatical constructions, literature and aesthetics. Critics of Thomas's time highlighted these ambiguities. As Chamberlain observed of Japanese poetry, 'the impression produced by these linked verses is delightful in the extreme, passing as they do before the reader like a series of dissolving views, vague, graceful, and suggestive.'[66]

A similar delight in ambiguity can be found in Thomas's determination to focus in his writing on the border between language and the pre-linguistic, the moment prior to a poem's emergence into words. Such an approach necessarily involves focus on what is not said and cannot be said. It is therefore unsurprising that, as Longley observes, Thomas showed a predilection for a construction that 'combines absence and presence', denoting absence while also alluding to what is missing: 'houseless', 'nameless', 'flowerless', 'beeless', 'lightless', footless', 'sunless', 'branchless' (p. 146).

'The Castle of Lostormellyn' exemplifies well Thomas's aporetic tendency to focus on both presence and absence. This story aptly illustrates the aporetic quality of the moment before articulation. A prince, in search of 'that which is most worthy of desire', is directed from castle to castle in an ever-extending quest, his destination always shifting to the castle beyond, on the horizon, that he has yet to reach.[67] This is a quest that he can never fulfil. The story is an analogy of Thomas's composing experiences. By determining to articulate, or perceive, the pre-linguistic moment and areas on the margins of the attention, he had to grapple with the fact that, once a marginal area had, like the nearest castle, moved towards the centre of his attention, it was no longer marginal, the quality that initially made it his desired point of focus. In order to retain his interest in articulating what was peripheral to the attention, he had continually to abandon the areas he was focusing on and approach the new areas hovering in the margins. Like the prince's search for the castle, this was a never-ending and essentially inconclusive quest.

A similar aporia was created when, in the title and first line of 'Home ("Often I had gone")', Thomas linked together a fixed idea of place and a sense of transitoriness, a search for place: 'Often I had gone this way before' (p. 81). His use of the first person in this and other poems allowed him to tackle the question of aporia more directly than in 'The Castle of Lostormellyn' and to work on how to articulate oblivion and what lies beyond words. His first person voice, however, retains marginality, frequently only appearing in one line, or at the end of a poem.

Aporia also make up much of the content of Thomas's poems. The forest is one common aporetic trope, as Coombes has observed,

> 'forest' in Thomas's poetry is the dark region of human experience which cannot be illuminated by thought or reason, a pathless region; it is the gulf of nothingness or eternity that waits behind the temporal and the tangible; or it is simply sleep, or death.[68]

This motif of forests looms largest in Thomas's later poems, reflecting both his more mature sense of poetic composition and his personal situation facing the possibility of death at the front. 'Out in the dark', 'Lights' Out', 'The Dark Forest' and 'The Green Roads' are all set on the edge of forests, revolving around the moment of entry and the impossibility of return. The characters are neither in nor out of the forest, and often the way forward or back is rendered impassable. 'The Green Roads' records

> marks left behind by some one gone into the forest
> To show his track. But he has never come back. (p. 128)

In the same poem, Thomas resolved the contradiction implicit in attempts to articulate aporia by setting the speaker apart, like the 'superfluous' man in *The South Country*, looking on from the outside, observing what happens:

> all things forget the forest
> Excepting perhaps me, when now I see
>
> The old man, the child, the goose feathers at the edge of the forest. (p. 129)

This sense of the speaker in the poem as outsider reflects Thomas's keen awareness of his 'superfluous' position as neither rural dweller nor city man, neither Welsh nor English, in pursuit of what could not be put into words or 'of one whom to pursue is never to capture'.[69] His attempts to articulate served to distance him further from the experience that he observed.

In later poems the uncertainty as to what can be articulated grows until, often in the last lines of a poem, it includes the poet's self in an act of aposiopesis. This development, chillingly reflecting the uncertainties facing Thomas as a soldier bound for the front, creates an aporia that takes over the whole poem, retrospectively affecting all the previous lines.

'Lights Out' presents five stanzas of meditation on

> the borders of sleep,
> The unfathomable deep
> Forest, where all must lose
> Their way, however straight,
> Or winding, soon or late;
> They cannot choose. (p. 135)

In the first four stanzas, the speaker stands, almost detached from the process. He hovers at the 'borders', observing the effects and implications of crossing that line. However, at the end of the poem, he records his entry into the forest and into oblivion:

That I may lose my way
And myself. (p. 136)

This aposiopesis both echoes and develops the Romantic mingling of self and object, where, as Lawrence Kramer writes of Shelley's 'Ode to the West Wind', 'the poet's self is mingled figuratively with the forest and the falling leaves just at the moment when both he and they begin to be transfigured: "Make me thy lyre, even as the forest is!"'[70]

A similar aposiopesis is implied in 'And you, Helen'. Thomas's offer of gifts to his wife Helen appears to build up to an ultimately precious present of 'myself', which is then almost immediately qualified by 'too, if I could find / Where it lay hidden' (p. 117). This qualification, suggesting aposiopesis, impinges on, and encourages, less favourable readings of the earlier gifts proffered, which, in their offer of 'youth', 'loveliness and truth', 'A clear eye' and so on, now suggest the present lack of such qualities in Helen.

'Out in the dark', too, holds the threat of a loss of self. The speaker describes the menace of the haunting dark forest in which 'all else is drowned' (p. 138). In the first stanza, the emphasis on the menace of the forest taints what is otherwise a beautiful scene of fawns in snow, demonstrating how focus on the process of articulation and resultant emphasis on its uncertainty as represented by the overwhelming engulfing forest affect attempts to articulate a particular experience or scene.

APORIA: OF LANGUAGE BREAKDOWN

His greatest hope, to become a poet without words
Yone Noguchi[71]

A number of Thomas's poems show how attempts at articulation undermine their objectives, obstructing further articulation. This occurs most often with duplication or repetition of words. Christopher Ricks refers to the 'achieved irresolvability' in 'Old Man'.[71] The sufficiency of each single plant name in this poem is challenged by its juxtaposition with several synonyms. As the names multiply, the confusion intensifies. The first two lines set the stage when they reverse and repeat the phrase 'Old

Man, or Lad's-love' as 'Lad's-love, or Old Man'. This develops into a list of alternative names that moves from the detailed 'the hoar-green feathery herb, almost a tree' to 'the thing it is', 'the herb', 'the bush', 'a low thick bush', and, finally, prefixed with a negative, 'no hoar-green bush' (pp. 36–7). While appearing to celebrate these names, the list exposes their fundamental emptiness. Their physical juxtaposition with other monikers for 'Old Man' highlights each name's individual inadequacy. The effect is similar to that achieved by *The South Country*'s list of forty place names, where the list is both part of the whole work and also, helped by the insertion of a pertinent aside, calls attention to the work as a constructed piece of writing. However, in 'Old Man', there is no need of an authorial aside to highlight the poem's status as a composed piece of work. The poem itself refers repeatedly to this status in its musings on the subject of naming.

A similar effect is achieved in 'Lob':

> There were three Manningfords, – Abbots, Bohun, and Bruce:
> And whether Alton, not Manningford, it was,
> My memory could not decide, because
> There was both Alton Barnes and Alton Priors.
> All had their churches, graveyards, farms, and byres,
> Lurking to one side up the paths and lanes,
> Seldom well seen except by aeroplanes;
> And when the bells rang, or pigs squealed, or cocks crowed,
> Then only heard. (p. 76)

The same name carries such different meanings, each obscuring each, that the speaker, or as Thomas specifically phrased it, the speaker's memory, cannot decide between them.

In 'Lob', 'Hog's Back' is used to refer both to a place currently holding that name and to the same place before it was named: ''Twas he first called the Hog's Back the Hog's Back' (p. 77). The effect is curious. The sentence blocks itself. There is a sense of obstructed progression, of language jamming or breaking down. 'Hog's Back' is obliged to do double duty. It refers both to the present named place and to its past existence as a nameless place. The repetition of the name reinforces the sense of the inaccessible remoteness of a pre-linguistic world. Necessarily, in his attempts to articulate a pre-linguistic state, Thomas has made use of the very names that supersede such a state. By so doing, he has sabotaged his own attempt at articulation. The name obstructs as much as, or more than, it elucidates.

In 'Up in the Wind', Thomas suggested that the act of naming is itself divided from subsequent human use of names produced. The extraordinary lines relating to the stone-curlew's song and to a much older 'spirit of wildness', imply that the land's name, 'Common', is created by the land. The object named chooses its own name. Such a name, therefore, both pre-exists and survives human use and exploitation:

> He nests in fields where still the gorse is free as
> When all was open and common. Common 'tis named
> And calls itself, because the bracken and gorse
> Still hold the hedge where plough and scythe have chased them. (p. 31)

The juxtaposition of 'common' in lower case with 'Common' as a capitalized name also exemplifies the ease with which the meanings of these words can shift and the effect that a geographical and ever-changing neighbourhood can have on a name.

In *Maurice Maeterlinck*, Thomas declared that 'no word, outside works of information, has any value beyond its surface value except what it receives from its neighbours and its position among them'.[73] He later exemplified this in poems like 'Old Man' and 'Lob'. They show how repetition, which might be expected to dispel aporia, helps create it, depriving a word of neighbours and of a 'position among them'. Repetition exposes the 'surface value' of words, revealing the emptiness behind them. As Stuart Sillars puts it, with reference to the repetition in 'Old Man', the effect is 'the tearing away of language from object' and 'the beginning of a process of aporia'.[74]

As Sillars's reference to a 'process of aporia' suggests, even in completed poems aporia remains, turning the poem into a procedure in the making. It is not surprising, therefore, to discover similar features in the composing process. In 1902, Thomas told Bottomley his play, *The Crier by Night*, was 'brilliant', hovering 'continually on the verge of what is probably inexpressible'.[75] Several years later, he was less enthusiastic about Bottomley's work, attributing what he saw as a critical lack of aporetic uncertainty in Bottomley's later play, *King Lear's Wife*, to a composing process too driven by its writer's need to fill the emptiness that Thomas himself chose to expose in 'Old Man' and 'Lob'. Thomas wrote that Bottomley's *King Lear's Wife* 'was all the result of thinking out an explanation' and 'it is made up. B. had thought out the motives.'[76]

In contrast, Thomas, in his own development as a writer, retained the qualities that he admired in Bottomley's early work, qualities he himself had experienced in his composition processes, as suggested in a letter to Bottomley in 1904:

> while I write, it is a dull blindfold faring through a strange lovely land: I seem to take what I write from the dictation of someone else. Correction is pleasanter then for I have glimpses of what I was passing through as I wrote.[77]

This awareness of the presence in composition of a context that expands beyond what is articulated or written down is later reflected in Thomas's use of naming both to expose and accept the superficiality inherent in printed texts, and also to allow room for potential, but invisible, alternative texts. Such awareness informs a crucial passage in *Beautiful Wales*, which Thomas began writing a few months after the Bottomley letter. In *Beautiful Wales*, the natural environment is described in a way that parallels Thomas's accounts of glimpsing a work that is larger than the marks on the page: 'And outside, the noises of a west wind and a flooded stream, the whimper of an otter, and the long, slow laugh of an owl; and always silent, but never forgotten, the restless, towering outline of a mountain.'[78] The emphasis on the barely perceptible background mountain brings the exact detail of the foreground 'whimper' or 'laugh' into focus, giving a concrete illustration of the crucial effect the awareness of what is not written, or in full view, can have on the visible work.

APORIA: OF UNCERTAINTY

> L'objet et le sujet sont donc irrémédiablement mouvants, insaisissables et insaisissants.
>
> Jules Laforgue[79]

Aporetic contradictions are rife in Thomas's writing. His convoluted sentence constructions and *matryoshka*-like asides appear to offer interpretations, cancel them, and then subsequently throw doubt upon the validity of those cancellations. Few of his statements about his work can be taken as definitive. An interpretation of 'Out in the dark' ends with the apparently throwaway phrase 'or so I fancy', indicating a possible reversal of everything Thomas had just expressed:

> It is really Baba [his younger daughter] who speaks, not I. Something she felt put me onto it. But I am afraid I am meddling now. A real poem would include and imply all these things I am writing, or so I fancy.[80]

Aporetic use of syntax often occurs at the end of his poems. The last stanza of 'Out in the dark' presents contradictory readings, depending on the reader's interpretation of the caveat 'if you love it not'. It could equally refer to 'all the universe of sight' or to 'the might' of 'night':

> How weak and little is the light,
> All the universe of sight,
> Love and delight,

> Before the might,
> If you love it not, of night. (p. 139)

In Thomas's work, uncertainty, when related to knotted and difficult syntax, often occurs in relation to difficult emotional truths. This is the case with the convoluted syntax of the last three lines of 'Aspens'. Thomas confirmed to Farjeon that these lines allude to emotional difficulties:

> About 'Aspens' you missed just the turn that I thought essential. *I* was the aspen. 'We' meant the trees and I with my dejected shyness. Does that clear it up, or do you think in rereading it that I have not emphasised it enough?[81]

Farjeon 'missed just the turn' because by the last line the closing sentence of 'Aspens' has undergone an unexpected change in direction, confounding previous expectation of that sentence's trajectory. However, the twisting aporetic syntax ensures that what is eventually conveyed semantically is still touched with a hint of what was earlier implied:

> We cannot other than an aspen be
> That ceaselessly, unreasonably grieves,
> Or so men think who like a different tree. (p. 97)

The syntax obscures the fact that the speaker might not think that the aspen's grieving is played out 'unreasonably'. The grief appears to be unreasonable until the last line is reached, and, even then, this impression remains while the reader attempts to disentangle the syntactical knots.

The understanding that the aspen represents Thomas, '*I* was the aspen', is also elliptical. The identification of the aspen with him is suggested, but not spelt out, by the first person plural in the last stanza, leaving an alternative possible reading, as Thomas discovered from Farjeon's response to the piece. Previous to this line, 'Aspens' records minutiae of an exterior world, locating in it aspens, a crossroads, an inn, smithy and shop. The interior emotional turmoil detailed in Thomas's letter to Farjeon resides only vestigially in the poem, and it is easy, or was for Farjeon, to miss the connection between him and the trees. Something, the poem perhaps, lies outside the reach of words. It is only indirectly present in the shift in perspective that occurs in the third last line of the last stanza when 'we' introduces what could be the poet's voice. What is seen and read combines with what is not read or half-read to form aporia.

Thomas's tendency to end poems by hijacking an expected trajectory with a surprising twist or an intricate semantic knot is also evident in the unexpected qualifications in the last lines of 'And you, Helen', which render the apparent offer of love not only unlikely but, confusingly, suggest that the offer was not of love in the first place:

And myself, too, if I could find
Where it lay hidden and it proved kind. (p. 117)

The aporetic twists of syntax ensure that the reader has to work to get at the unpalatable meaning of these lines. In fact, they encourage such a response, as is reflected in critical writing on 'And you, Helen', which tends to focus on the interpretation of these two last lines. Such an emphasis shows how Thomas's apparent avoidance of explicit expression of emotion in his poetry, replacing it with absence and aporetic syntactical twists, can have the perverse effect of placing emphasis upon that emotion.

It does not take long, when reading Thomas, to learn that the trajectory of his verse is not predictable. Careful attention is required in the reading of many of his poems. This results in a focus more on the phrases immediately before the reader's eyes and less on predictions of sentence or phrase continuation. In this context, Thomas's words in a letter to his wife from the front are pertinent. He discussed with her his need to avoid explicit emotion and to keep the bitter truth aporetic, half-elliptical, half-hidden, as if not consciously seen:

> I, you see, must not feel anything. I am just as it were tunnelling underground and something sensible in my subconsciousness directs me not to think of the sun. At the end of the tunnel there is the sun. Honestly this is not the result of thinking; it is just an explanation of my state of mind which is really so entirely preoccupied with getting on through the tunnel that you might say I had forgotten there was a sun at either end[82]

The syntax in his poems, his subsequent interpretation of them and the completed poems in their entirety all remain so much in uncertainty that several of his titles, such as 'It was upon' and 'How at once', are cut short of specific meaning. They appear to be still in the process of being formed. Others carry the same title. In R. G. Thomas's *The Collected Poems of Edward Thomas* (1978), two poems are entitled 'Digging'; two are called 'An Old Song'; three are called 'Song'; two are named 'Home'; and a third '"Home"' is only distinguished from its siblings by an additional pair of quotation marks. Yet other poems carry similar titles, make use of the first phrase or line as their title, or simply remain untitled. Edward Thomas's reluctance to title is articulated to Farjeon: 'On the whole I do like the trumpet verses. If they have to be named, "The Trumpet" will do.'[83] It results in some confusion in subsequent editions of his work. Poem titles vary considerably.[84] The three poems called 'Song' in R. G. Thomas's edition are reduced to two in Faber's reprint in 2004, while Longley's

Annotated Collected Poems (2008) refers to them by their first lines or phrases only.

To some degree this repetition in titling has the same effect as the repetition of 'Hog's Back' in 'Lob' and the duplication of plant names in 'Old Man'. It stresses the slipperiness of attempts at articulation and distrust of any act of definitive naming. This is also reflected in Edward Thomas's choice of *Poems* as the preferred title for the collection. However, the fact that he included no more than one of each of the groups of identically titled poems in his *Poems* of 1917 also suggests that he gave works identical titles either because he considered them provisional rather than completed, or closely connected versions of a similar subject or theme.

Other poem titles seem to act as attempts, on his behalf, to counter the tendency for titles to shift emphasis away from a work. Some of these consist of half a phrase, such as 'How at once', or a tangential phrase, such as 'Women he liked' which introduces a poem that almost immediately turns sharply away from the subject indicated in its title.

Thomas's wariness of definitive titles prefigured Derrida's concerns in 'The Double Session', originally presented by Derrida in two sessions in February and March 1969 and left title-less in homage to Stéphane Mallarmé, who also saw titles as tending to dominate or usurp text, and had written a similar piece intended to take place over two sessions. In 'The Double Session', Derrida declared that 'the title carries its head high, speaks in too high a voice, both because it raises its voice and drowns out the ensuing text, and because it is found high up on the page, the top of the page becoming the eminent center'.[85] Aware that even title-less pieces are likely to acquire a title eventually, as became the case with his own paper, Derrida suggested provisional titles for Mallarmé's work. These emphasize falling between, and echo Thomas's emphasis on 'betweenness' in titles such as *Light and Twilight* and *Rest and Unrest*:

THE 'INTO' OF MALLARMÉ
THE 'INTER' OF MALLARMÉ
THE ANTRE OF MALLARMÉ
THE IN-TWO OF MALLARMÉ[86]

A sense of betweenness is also pronounced in Thomas's later works, as demonstrated by his use of the same title in successive poems and a gradual increase in uncertainty and ambiguity. This is clear in the shift in subject matter between the two 'Digging' poems. The first evokes autumn through imagery of scents released by digging. The metaphor of digging is also used in the second poem, but it digs deeper than the first, uncovering further layers as it questions concepts of time, presenting, as Longley describes it, an act of 'imaginative archaeology [that] uncovers the common humanity, and inhumanity, that links the ages'.[87]

Neither of the 'Digging' poems is included in the 1917 edition of *Poems* but perusal of the contents of other poems that share titles shows that Thomas tended to select later over earlier pieces. Longley notes how the structure of the second 'Old Song', the poem selected for the collection, 'contrasts with the homogenousness of the first "Old Song"'.[88] A similar incremental shift in uncertainty can be found in the three 'Home' poems. The last poem is the most uncertain, as reflected in the qualifying quotation marks that suggest a provisionality which extends even to its title, '"Home"'. This is the poem Thomas selected for the 1917 collection. His apparently casual reuse of poetry titles, as in the cases of frequent repetition of the first few words of a poem instead of a separate title, or omissions of titles altogether, are indicative therefore of a desire to continue the sense of process even in apparently finished work. His habits of selection for *Poems* also suggest that he saw looseness in titles and uncertainty in poems as crucial components of completed pieces.

APORIA: OF FORE- AND BACKGROUND

> To leave the page covered, and the silence intact,
>
> Don Paterson[89]

Poems such as 'Lights Out', 'And you, Helen', 'But these things also' and 'Old Man' highlight the essential marginality of the printed words. In 'Lights Out' and 'And you, Helen', the aposiopesis of the cancellation, or suggested cancellation, of self in the last lines affects and impinges on the rest of the poem to the point where the aporia produced by this aposiopesis takes over the whole poem. The elliptical evidence of spring in the body of 'But these things also' pushes conventional emblems out of the printed text of the poem. Each successive name in 'Old Man' both dislodges its predecessor and, by virtue of following on from that predecessor, renders itself aporetic. These poems turn their visible words into frames for other invisible parts.

The issues raised in these pieces act as precursors for Derrida's questions in the 1970s on framing and context, topics that will be discussed further in the ensuing chapters on dislocation and divagation. As Derrida put it:

> Every sign, linguistic or nonlinguistic, spoken or written (in the usual sense of this opposition), as a small or large unity, can be *cited*, put between quotation marks; thereby it can break with every given context, and engender infinitely new contexts in an absolutely nonsaturable fashion. This does not suppose that the mark is valid outside its context, but on the contrary that there are only contexts without any center of absolute anchoring.[90]

Thomas's description of trees and sky in *Beautiful Wales* is relevant here: 'Tall hedgerow elms and orchard trees held blue fragments of the sky among their leaves and hid the rest.'[91] The sky is not depicted as part of the background. It is foregrounded. It turns into physical fragments outlined by branches. Thus, the perspectives shift, like Wittgenstein's ambiguous duck-rabbit figure, perceived either as a duck or as a rabbit but not as both simultaneously.[92] The branches in *Beautiful Wales* are pushed from their position as figures in the foreground to the background, their main purpose becoming that of marking the divisions between the 'blue fragments' of sky. They are turned into frames for the sky.

4

Gaps

> The best craftsmanship always leaves holes and gaps in the works of the poem so that something that is *not* in the poem can creep, crawl, flash, or thunder in.
>
> Dylan Thomas[1]

Just as the division between ellipses and aporia is not always clear, so it might initially appear that ellipses, aporia and aposiopesis all come under the generic term 'gap' since each of them is marked by forms of absence. However, the term 'gap' in this book is not simply an equation for absence. It specifically denotes shifts in emphasis from what is missing to what is present. This is in accordance with dictionary and etymological definitions, which clearly distinguish the gap from other forms of absence. It is an 'open mouth, also opening, chasm', 'an unfilled space or interval; a blank' and 'a break in continuity'.[2] When a gap forms part of a work, it does not, like ellipses and aporia, signify omission or irresolution. It becomes the omitted thing, appearing as a particular present shape within the work.

GAPS: MIND THE GAP

> a mighty struggle with intangibles
>
> Edwin Morgan[3]

Gaps occur when an absence is framed or outlined. Instead of acting as an elliptic indicator of what is omitted, such absence becomes a physical presence, as in the transformation in *Beautiful Wales* of the background sky into a foregrounded figure framed by branches. The effect is related to the Japanese aesthetic of *ma*, 'space' or 'interval', absence as presence. When *ma* is taken into consideration, the blank spaces surrounding and mingling with the words of a creative piece form as important a part of the completed work as the printed text.

The resonance Thomas felt with this Japanese aesthetic is evident in his description of the last line of 'The long small room': 'The hundred last leaves stream upon the willow.'[4] In the first draft this is the only reference to the willow. The reader needs to make an imaginative leap to link it to previous lines, a link articulated not in the words but by means of the interval, or gap, between them. After receiving Farjeon's response to this draft, Thomas wrote: 'I am worried about the impression the willow made on you', and continued 'I am only fearing it has a sort of Japanesy suddenness of ending. But it is true, whether or not it is a legitimate switch to make.'[5] His awareness of this foreign 'Japanesy' quality for an English readership led him to modify its sudden effect, introducing an earlier reference to willows in the poem.

Similar apparent leaps from one subject to another occur between the refrain and verses in his 'Old Song' poems. 'Cock-Crow', too, switches in its last line from an extended image of cocks as heralds to a description of milkers putting on their boots. The gap between these two images is emphasized with a colon.

GAPS: THAT REALLY EXIST

> I have nothing to say and I am saying it and that is poetry
> John Cage[6]

Thomas's quotations from substantial sections of William James's writings in *The Country* demonstrate his keen awareness of James's thinking on gaps, memory and mental processes, and James's work provides an illuminating approach to Thomas's use of gaps in his composing processes.[7] James wrote in *The Principles of Psychology*:

> Suppose we try to recall a forgotten name. The state of our consciousness is peculiar. There is a gap therein; but no mere gap. It is a gap that is intensely active. A sort of wraith of a name is in it, beckoning us in a given direction, making us at moments tingle with the sense of our closeness, and then letting us sink back without the longed-for term. If the wrong names are proposed to us this singular gap acts immediately so as to negate them. They do not fit into its mould. And the gap of one word does not feel like the gap of another, all

> empty of content as both might seem necessarily to be when described as gaps. When I vainly try and recall the name of Spalding, my consciousness is far removed from what it is when I vainly try and recall the name of Bowles. There are innumerable consciousnesses of emptiness, no one of which taken in itself has a name, but all different from each other. The ordinary way is to assume that they are all emptinesses of consciousness, and so the same state. But the feeling of an absence is *toto coelo* other than the absence of a feeling. It is an intense feeling. The rhythm of a lost word may be there without a sound to clothe it; or the evanescent sense of something which is the initial vowel or consonant may mock us fitfully, without growing more distinct. Every one must know the tantalizing effect of the blank rhythm of some forgotten verse, restlessly dancing in one's mind, striving to be filled out with words.[8]

James's reference to the search for a 'forgotten name', a name now marked by a gap, indicates that this gap in one sense acts as an ellipsis, since it signals the omission of the name. However, it is not a 'mere gap'. It is also an 'intensely active' presence. As well as an ellipsis signalling an omission, it acts as a 'singular gap', a physical presence, containing within it a 'sort of wraith of a name'.

James also discussed the tip-of-the-tongue phenomenon, and the related 'feelings of tendency' or 'sense of the direction from which an impression is about to come, although no positive impression is yet there'.[9] This applies to Thomas's use of spacing in his drafting processes. These spaces act as ellipses which signal that something is omitted, but they also act as gaps framed by words, gaps that provide in their positioning, context and shape the information needed for the later re-drafter or reader to fill them in.

The ease with which James's discussion of the tip-of-the-tongue phenomenon can be interpreted as an account of composing processes suggests close parallels exist between aspects of creative composing and other forms of mental processing. The main difference is that, in the case of a poem, the search is not for 'forgotten' words, but for words that are not yet known. The detail of this search is evident in Thomas's 'April/July/Glory' draft. The ellipses in this draft show that he was not at this point aware of the exact words needed in the poem. However, they also set up patterns of expectation that point to the words' probable rhyme, lexical position and length. Furthermore, they act as physically present gaps, working within the draft to contribute to its poetic effect. James described such gaps as 'singular', distinguished by the 'rhythm of a lost word' or 'the evanescent sense of something which is the initial vowel or consonant [. . .] striving to be filled out with words'. The 'singular', 'intensely active' gap comprises a definite vagueness: 'It is, in short, the re-instatement of the vague to its proper place in our mental life which I am so anxious to press on the attention.'[10] James directly linked this estimation of vagueness as a definite experience, a key doctrine in his theory of psychology, to the perception of sensation. For him, 'pure sensation is the vague'.[11] He did not see vagueness as a signal of something missing, as in ellipses, but of something almost tangibly present and distinct. In these passages, James was developing a concept already present in Wordsworth's experience of specific moments of time and, as Lawrence Kramer has noted, Wordsworth's 'most privileged spots of time [which] are disturbances of its boundaries' are themselves, tellingly, a combination of focused detail and vagueness.[12]

Thomas made use of gaps that possess definite vagueness in his developing drafts. The gaps in some of these drafts are so definite and 'intensely active' that they are left unfilled, as gaps, in the completed works. Near the end of 'Up in the Wind', two 'intensely active' gaps remain present as a line space and indentation, enacting the sudden move in subject from the girl's complaints to the calves drinking outside.

James's conception of vagueness as a definite quality can be seen in action in Thomas's drafting of 'The sun used to shine'. Several images from this poem, composed in May 1916, were foreshadowed in his *English Review* essay in 1914, 'This England':

> The sky was banded with rough masses in the north-west, but the moon, a stout orange crescent, hung free of cloud near the horizon. At one stroke, I thought, like many other people, what things the same new moon sees eastward about the Meuse in France. Of those who could see it there, not blinded by smoke, pain, or excitement, how many saw it and heeded? I was deluged, in a second stroke, by another thought, or something that overpowered thought. All I can tell is, it seemed to me that either I had never loved England, or I had loved it foolishly, aesthetically, like a slave, not having realized that it was not mine unless I were willing and prepared to die rather than leave it as Belgian women and old men and children had left their country. Something I had omitted. Something, I felt, had to be done before I could look again composedly at English landscape, at the elms and poplars about the houses, at the purple-headed wood-betony with two pairs of dark leaves on a stiff stem, who stood sentinel among the grasses or bracken by hedge-side or wood's-edge. What he stood sentinel for I did not know, any more than what I had got to do.[13]

'The sun used to shine' strongly echoes this passage, although the allusions to the struggles in France are more vague, and their distance from the speaker in the poem is described as 'remote' and 'in the east', and is also emphasized by rhyming 'war' with 'afar' (p. 122). In addition, the poem does not spell out the prose speaker's meditations on his role. Such meditations are left to lie, unsaid but implied, in the gaps between the verses. Similarly, the loquacious detail of the betony has been stripped away. Only a hint of the vision of this flower remains. An early draft of the poem shows the deliberate manner in which such detail was deleted. Thomas first inserted 'sentry' above 'few dark wood', and then deleted both 'few' and 'wood'.[14] The lines eventually read:

> sentry of dark betonies,
> The stateliest of small flowers on earth,
> At the forest verge; (p. 122)

However, the increase in vagueness results not in more detachment but in a sharpening of emotion, even though that emotion is not named. The removal of detail and the insertion of gaps between the short enjambed lines that often stretch over stanza breaks have the effect of transforming the vagueness and confusion expressed directly by the speaker in the prose essay into a definite vagueness in the poem. In particular, the series of what James called 'singular gaps' between the stanzas carry an unmistakable and specific charge, alluding to emotion that lies somewhere outside the printed text.

Thomas often made use of line breaks and enjambement in this way: to create gaps that would intensify the printed text. 'Tall Nettles' describes a plough over a line break, using the gap to intensify a sense of tiredness, age and neglect:

> the plough
> Long worn out, (p. 119)

Such gaps allow for and encourage poems to continue to have an effect in the blank spaces between the printed words, lines and stanzas. These gaps are vague in the sense that it is not easy to ascertain exactly what they contain. They do not refer to missing words. However, they are also clear, specific and calculated, their outlines adding definite richness to the printed text, which is rendered sharper and stronger as a result.

Thomas also made use in his poetry of indentations and spacing at the end of lines in order intensify and heighten. The tessellated effect of 'After Rain''s alternate short and long lines, set as ragged right text, reiterates the momentary quality of a pause in rain, just as the first long line stresses the unremitting length of a downpour:

The rain of a night and a day and a night
Stops at the light
Of this pale choked day. The peering sun
Sees what has been done. (p. 38)

Delicate negotiations between voice, person and perception in 'The Other' are reflected in the mid-line placing of the spoken words in lines that are frequently enjambed:

                              But 'twas here
They asked me if I did not pass
Yesterday this way? 'Not you? Queer.'
'Who then? And slept here?' I felt fear.

and

                              Nothing
Told me that ever till that day
Had one like me entered those doors,
Save once. That time I dared: 'You may
Recall' (p. 40)

In 'Old Man', the switch from the speaker's imagined future recollection of himself as he is now, watching the child's interaction with the plant, to a memory of his own first encounter with it, is signified by two unfinished lines and a line space:

A low thick bush beside the door, and me
Forbidding her to pick.

                              As for myself,
Where first I met the bitter scent is lost. (p. 36)

The placing of 'As for myself' and 'and me' in similar positions on the page, at the end of a line, reinforces the return to an awareness of self. This is mitigated, however, by the fact that 'and me' ends a line, while 'myself' is placed after a gap, indented, as if following some unwritten text, and so reflecting the elusiveness of memory. The speaker easily draws on present events to imagine a future memory of the child but the memory of his past experience is severely fragmented. He tells us this and the gap demonstrates it. The gap also heightens tension as focus draws in upon the speaker, upon what is not said or remembered, and upon what is fragmented, missing, lost, suggesting a Romantic sense of identity of things and people as fundamentally insecure.

Paradoxically, the gaps created by line and stanza breaks are what make a poem visible, as is evident in the Cardiff University library collection, digitised in the First World War Poetry Digital Archive. Thomas wrote the first draft of 'The Trumpet' without line breaks in one continuous paragraph in order to disguise his poetic activity: 'You see I have written it with only capitals to mark the lines, because people are all around me and I don't want them to know.'[15] Only when Farjeon typed it out in lines as marked by the capital letters did it become visible as a poem. Without the gaps, it was hardly recognizable as such.

Another use of gaps is to highlight what is tangential while allowing it to remain marginal. Woolf expressed this in the passage in her review of Thomas's *A Literary Pilgrim* where she discerned a vague and yet definite 'something' in the work of Thomas Hardy and Emily Brontë:

> through the half-shut eyes with which we visualize books as a whole, we can see great tracts of Wessex and of the Yorkshire Moors inhabited by a race of people who seem to have the rough large outline of the land itself.[16]

Woolf was evoking the power of the marginal. Clarification of what is perceived is achieved by half-shutting the eyes to increase the vagueness of that perception but also the sense of it as a whole. Like Thomas and James, Woolf emphasized how, although the content of such vagueness may be elusive, its size, outline or frame announces its presence.

Thomas also made use of the way definite vagueness allows a writer to discern what lies on or beyond the margins of words, employing *matryoshka*-like asides to point beyond the main subject of the text to other alternative readings and topics. These asides mainly appear in his prose. Although they surface in his poetry, there is less need for them in a form that already makes generous allowance for the tangential in the physical gaps created by line breaks, enjambements, indentations and line spacing.

Building on James's understanding of vagueness as a definite experience, Thomas differentiated between two forms of vagueness, as in his description of early records of English history as 'a geological picture, something large, clear, architectural', and not as 'a mass of insignificant names'.[17] This distinction is evident in his poetic processes as can be seen in the changes between his 'April/July/Glory' draft and the completed poems. 'April/July/Glory' has the lines:

> Now it is when Kate comes to me _____
> God bless her
> Nightingale's tsoo tsoo tsooed
> Turned in tears back[18]

The typographical ellipsis of an extended dash indicates uncertainty. So many different texts could be inserted here. In the draft, the dash suggests an indiscriminate 'mass' of names. However, at some point during the drafting process this uncertainty is resolved with the result that in 'April', these lines become:

> And sharply the nightingale's 'tsoo, troo, tsoo, troo';
> To say 'God bless it' was all that I could do.
>
> But now I know one sweeter
> By far since the day Emily
> Turned weeping back
> To me, still happy me, (p. 86)

The typographical ellipses have disappeared. The nightingale's song is now sharper, more defined, directly quoted and a more accurate approximation of birdsong. The 'it' of 'God bless it' now refers specifically to the nightingale. However, vagueness still exists, since 'it' also refers to other elements of the natural scene that the speaker has witnessed, and points beyond these to a vaguer sense of the beauty of nature. The scene with Kate/Emily has moved to a separate stanza but the connection between the sections remains, vague, but specific, residing in the spacing that divides and links them.

The defined vagueness in 'April' mirrors *The South Country*'s vague yet specific description of an architectural 'geological picture'. The picture is 'something large and clear', both indefinite and with a defined outline, its framed 'architectural' space rendering it a 'singular gap': empty but particular. The term 'architectural' evokes a concrete physical structure, apt in this search for corporeal or concrete records of what pre-dates or exists at the limits of linguistic records. Mapped onto a completed poem, such a description suggests Iser's 'network of response-inviting structures' at play beneath and behind the printed words.

Freud's work on gaps as specific entities is relevant here. His theories were current in Thomas's literary circles. His writings were translated into English in Thomas's lifetime, and they were also directly accessible to Thomas in the original, since he had good German. They were, in addition, particularly evident in D. H. Lawrence's work, which Thomas read and admired, writing to Emily Bottomley in 1912 that 'I hope Gordon isn't become too classic to like Lawrence' and reviewing Lawrence's *Love Poems* as 'the book of the moment' in 1913.[19] Thomas would also have encountered Freud's theories during his 1912 and 1913 treatment by Godwin Baynes, a nervous disorder specialist who later became the champion and translator of Carl Jung.

Freud's work on dreaming is particularly apposite, given the explicit connections he drew between the activity of dreaming and the composing process. In 'Creative writers and day-dreaming', he compared 'poetical creation with the day-dream', indicating that the processes of composing poetry and shaping dream images operate according to similar principles.[20] Furthermore, in *The Interpretation of Dreams*, he explicitly recognized gaps that remain as gaps, unfilled, like the spaces purposively left empty in the line spacing, indentations, line and stanza breaks of Thomas's poetry. He noted how 'our memory reproduces the dream not only incompletely but also untruthfully, in a falsifying manner', and queried 'whether in our attempted reproduction we have not filled in the gaps which really existed'. He outlined the crucial role such gaps play in dream-work and observed that 'gaps in the dreams are often of the nature of boundary-zones' between different significant areas of the dream.[21] Like James, Freud read such gaps as 'singular' and 'intensely active', but also saw them affecting the fragments that form a dream. They mark the limits of those fragments and, to a degree, also extend those limits.

This relates to the active part gaps play in Thomas's drafting processes and shaping of the text of a completed poem, as in his rearrangement of lines and stanza breaks from the 'April/July/Glory' draft to form part of 'April'; his use of enjambement to break up syntax in 'Tall Nettles'; and the line breaks that transform the one paragraph draft of 'The Trumpet' into a poem. In all these cases, spaces are actively integral to the poems' effects.

GAPS: AS MARKERS OF RHYTHM

> I passed the horizon ridge
> To a new country, the path I had to find
> By half-gaps that were stiles once in the hedge,
> Edward Thomas (p. 52)

Thomas's use of physical gaps when writing is most obvious in the peculiar gap-ridden orthography of his handwritten letters and signature. Newlyn has claimed that poetry gives Thomas 'an opportunity not afforded by prose, for experimenting with the shape of sentences on the page, so as to create a subtle visual complement to sound-patterns'.[22] However, uneven spacing proliferates in Thomas's letters and prose too. Some evidence of this remains in the handwritten copies of his poems, although it is less apparent in his published work.

Thomas never referred to his orthographic spacing directly, but it is clear that he employed it to mark the limits of what is actually written and extend expression beyond that point. He often bunched groups of words together or separated them with gaps that bear little relation to grammatical groupings. Frequently, full stops or commas are preceded and followed by significant gaps , like these .[23]

In a handwritten note he sent to de la Mare dated 10 March 1907, the words act as frames for the spaces that juxtapose them:

> if possible stay one night , since
> a day with a long uncomfortable
> railway journey at each end is nothing
> at all but an interval.[24]

The word 'long' is framed by two spaces but, equally, 'long' and 'uncomfortable' also frame a space. In a similar fashion, the comma in 'if possible stay one night , since' marks a pause in the text, but also closes a previous pause suggested by the space between 'night' and a comma: 'night ,'. The space after 'night' becomes part of 'stay one night', which then reads as 'stay one night '. Similarly, the space after the comma becomes part of the following phrase 'since a day' so that it reads as ' since a day'. Just as branches frame and foreground the sky in *Beautiful Wales*, so this extended spacing between words and punctuation pushes gaps from background to foreground. They become an important part of the content of the note. They also directly reflect content, visually and rhythmically representing the 'interval' visit de la Mare had proposed, as well as evoking its discomfort.

Less obvious but still significant examples occur in the handwritten manuscripts of some of Thomas's poems. R. G. Thomas noted that the manuscript of 'Some eyes condemn [Sonnet 4]' is a good

> example of Thomas's use of rhetorical spacing in manuscript. (In Bod [the manuscript held in the Bodleian Library, Oxford] in the octet, there are spaces before and after the colons, for instance. Line 14 has a large space after *flamed* into which EE [*Poems* published by Selwyn & Blount in 1917] has inserted a comma.)[25]

In this manuscript version, the printed words frame spaces that signal and offer possibilities not recorded in ink. Contrasting ligatures highlight these spaces, as when the cross of a 't' joins two separate words together, so covering or filling what would otherwise be a space. In the following lines, the handwritten ligatures are marked with asterisks:

> Some eyes condemn the*world they gaze upon :
> Some wait patiently till they*know far*more
> Than earth can teach them : some laugh at*the*whole
> As*folly of another's making : one ,

I knew, that laughed because he saw , from core
To rind , not one thing worth the*laugh his soul
Had ready at waking : some eyes have begun
With laughing : some stand startled at the door.

Others , too, I have seen rest , question , roll,
Dance, shoot . And many I have loved watching . Some
I could not take my*eyes from till they turned
And loving died . I had*not*found my goal .
But thinking of your eyes , dear , I become
Dumb. For they*flamed & it was me they burned.[26]

The gap after the ligatured 'flamed' at the end of the sestet briefly allows prominence to that infinitesimal moment before the eyes' flame burns the speaker. This moment occurs in the physical blank space between the flaming and burning sections of the last line. Similarly, the more conventional use of gap at the end of the octet helps build a sense of summation and pregnancy. Such gaps strengthen effects already present in caesurae, line endings and enjambements, but they have a further purpose. They reflect difficulty of thought, encouraging the reader to move with the exploratory narrative voice and to search out truth contained not just within the words but within the gaps.

Attempting to interpret Edward Thomas's use of spacing for the *Collected Poems* (1978), R. G. Thomas admitted defeat: 'I have tried to discover a fixed principle behind this habit and failed to do so'.[27] Nevertheless, R. G. Thomas did allude to emphasis on progression, search and movement, relating these spaces to the rhythm of the text in which they lie, and seeing them as acting like 'almost a kind of guide to the way in which a passage or a sentence could be read. (Spacing played a key part in the notation of sol-fa which Thomas used in transcribing songs.)'[28] P. J. Croft, too, discerns a connection with rhythm in Edward Thomas's 'highly flexible spacing, both within and between words. This rapid and spontaneously variable hand is held together by the writer's instinctive sense of rhythm and possesses a vivid individuality.'[29]

R. G. Thomas's and Croft's readings resonate with Charles Olson's 'post-modernist' interpretation of spacing in the 1950s. Olson saw e. e. cummings's use of spaces as representing 'that time to pass that it takes the eye – that hair of time suspended – to pick up the next line'.[30] Olson's correlation of space with the breath and performance of the poet does not fully map on to Edward Thomas's more approximate use of space as a rough indicator of rhythm, speed, content, emotion and atmosphere. However, the differences can be related in part to variations in technical media. For Olson, the advent of the mechanical typewriter afforded him the opportunity to exploit spacing in the way he wished. In his view, the exactness and specificity of the spaces that the typewriter produces make it possible to incorporate the body, voice and performance of the poet in the spaces of the printed poem. For Thomas, the reverse is true. His idiosyncratic use of spacing is most endemic in his handwritten letters. In handwritten versions of poems it is beginning to disappear, present only subtly, and, as R. G. Thomas observed, 'Thomas himself substitutes ordinary punctuation practice when he comes to type his own poems and, in the poems that he passes for printing, there is no attempt to deviate from common practice.'[31] One explanation is that other people were involved in the typing of his manuscripts and production of the printed versions. However, there is no record of Edward Thomas asking for spaces to be reinserted. He simply allowed the precision in spacing demanded by the typewriter and printing machine to iron out the more fluid indeterminate use of gaps of his handwritten work.

GAPS: AS A 'SOB-FILLED PAUSE'

What was hard to understand –
the holes
in everything, the held wings
broken.
Gillian Allnutt[32]

In his prose book, *In Pursuit of Spring*, Thomas referred to an imaginary writer's note-taking, a writer whose writing habits were clearly similar to Thomas's. He carefully emphasized the risk note-taking poses: of obstructing access to what the writer 'truly cared for', of covering the gaps and not allowing the important, the emotional, to survive:

> He said that they [notebooks] blinded him to nearly everything that would not go into the form of notes; or, at any rate, he could never afterwards reproduce the great effects of Nature and fill in the interstices merely – which was all they were good for – from the notes. The notes – often of things which he would otherwise have forgotten – had to fill the whole canvas. Whereas, if he had taken none, then only the important, what he truly cared for, would have survived in his memory, arranged not perhaps as they were in Nature, but at least according to the tenderness of his own spirit.[33]

This description of note use and misuse in creative composition echoes Freud's employment of patchwork imagery in *The Interpretation of*

Dreams. Describing the function of secondary revision in dream-work, Freud wrote that 'with its rags and tatters it stops up the breaches in the structure of the dream'.[34] Initial fragments of a dream may revolve round painful emotional material, but the act of patching that occurs in secondary revision represses this material. Patches obscure emotional content by covering the gaps in the dream's structure that contain such emotion.

Thomas, too, saw gaps as containers of emotion. His 'An Unpublished Author' refers to the loss of emotional import in the even spacing of print, suggesting its previous presence in the irregular spacing of a handwritten text. This unidentified 'unpublished author', once again, closely resembles Thomas:

> It is true that his was a calligraphy as terrible as ever beatific printer changed into decent type; but is the printer indeed beatific? 'Did you,' writes he himself, 'ever consider how much of *l'homme même* goes into an author's handwriting, how much is abstracted by that plaguey modernism – printing? Take, for example, the wine-bibber who sits down to write verses. Splendid visions he has; chance words of his are divine; but on the chill day following how little that is divine and bacchic remains, if the memorial scrawl is lost and only a *fair* copy lives. It would scarce be worse if a painter bade his lackey put in such or such a line.'[35]

Conversely, a lack of gaps reflects a lack of emotion. Thomas's *Walter Pater* describes Pater's closely written prose as stacked with words 'like bricks' with little or no space between them. They refuse 'to fall into the rhythms which only emotion can command'.[36]

As biographer and critic, the comparative irregularities and consequent gaps of handwritten script held important clues for Thomas. In *Richard Jefferies, his Life and Work*, which includes a facsimile of a handwritten letter from Jefferies, he made several interpretations of Jefferies's handwriting, examining it for emotional import. He noted how it 'varied very much at this period [as a schoolboy], showing self-consciousness' and 'as a youth is a slight indication of his uncertainty and confusion; for a time it was back-handed, and again it was a compromise between writing and printing'.[37]

As letter-writer, too, he made expressive use of gaps. Commonly, when referring in letters to his burdensome workload as a reviewer, he heaped titles on top of each other as if to form a pile of books precariously balanced on a desk. In a letter to Bottomley he went further, placing a vertical list of books he had to review over a second horizontal list of other tasks in waiting. This horizontal list apparently ends in a three-point ellipsis, but then continues, as does the sentence, with a reference to a planned walk with a visitor:

> Thank you for your poem. Let me have time. I may not be able to open it for a week, because I have to review
>
> *Thomas More* by Stephen Gwyn
> *The Grey Brethren* by Michael Fairless
> *William Bodham Donne & his friends*
> *Peeps into Nature's Ways*
> *A Country Diary*
> *Travels round our Village*
> *A folio Chaucer*
> *A new Keats*
>
> Also to correct proofs, sow beans, peas, brussels sprouts, leeks, radishes . . . and walk much with a visitor this weekend.[38]

In this letter, the repeated commas of the horizontal list replicate the effect of the spaces dividing each item in the vertical list. Each comma, like each line break, singles out individual words or groups of words, 'beans, peas, brussels sprouts', physically separating them from their neighbours. Nevertheless, as the decision to head this list of vegetables with the vegetable-like occupation of proof correction indicates, the order of the items and, therefore, the connection between them, has been carefully considered. Similarly, the items on the vertical list have been positioned so as to resemble a top-heavy pile of books. Also, the ellipses in the horizontal list reiterate the endlessness of the commissioned tasks. This impression is reinforced by the addition of yet another item after the ellipses. The ellipses apparently conclude and act as a frame for the list, 'leeks, radishes . . .' but are then inverted into a gap, framed by the radishes on one side and the planned walk on the other, 'radishes . . . and walk much'. The result is more than mildly emotional. It verges on the melodramatic.

A more poignant example of space filled with emotion occurs in one of Thomas's last letters to his wife:

> But it
> was dirty & tiring , for I had on
> vest
> shirt
> 2 waistcoats
> tunic
> one Tommy's buttoned waistcoat
> British warm
> & waterproofs
> Only 2 or 3 shells came over & I found

> the telephonists dozing & here in a dry
> corner we dozed or smoked till daybreak [39]

This letter, like others Thomas sent from the front, is in a crowded and close hand, presumably due to the scarcity of paper. Given this context, the relatively generous spacing of a vertical list with its visual depiction of layers of bulky clothing is all the more striking. The list also brings home the physical difficulties of his situation. The spaces surrounding the list and interspersed within it subtly acknowledge the presence of censorship, one of Thomas's military duties. They also suggest self-imposed restrictions on emotional expression. Instead of speaking directly of his feelings, Thomas let the spaces speak for him.

A number of his handwritten poems show the connection between space and emotion. The last lines of the handwritten version of 'In Memoriam (Easter, 1915)', entitled 'Eastertide', has some interesting gaps. The spaces in this version appear closely connected to its emotional charge. An approximation of the handwritten spacing reads:

> Now far from home , who , with their sweethearts , should
> Have gathered them & will do never again .[40]

Each clause is surrounded by gaps replete with the poignancy that the content of the words evokes. The spacing and abbreviation of the ampersand reinforces the sense of a sad pause that allows for no more caveats or additions but a simple lack of result – the sense that there is nowhere else to go – 'never again'.

GAPS: AS SHREDS AND PATCHES

> A wandering minstrel I–
> A thing of shreds and patches,
> Of ballads, songs and snatches,
> And dreamy lullaby!
> W. S. Gilbert[41]

In a letter to Bottomley, Thomas deliberately sculpted out a vertical list:

> The fact is I dislike the book; so I ran dry at once – had to steal from old articles & patch them up – & even then could not cover the space which
> finally
> I covered
> with the help of
> a sonnet by De la Mare

and
a long sentence of prose by W. H. Hudson.[42]

Paradoxically, this list, shaped by gaps, is Thomas's response to one of his own commissioned tasks, the editing of *The Book of the Open Air*. He filled what he saw as inappropriate gaps in this book with patches of words gleaned from friends, requesting Hudson to 'give me leave to use, if necessary, one or two short passages – never more than 200 words – from your books to fill up a page or two of the book which would otherwise be blank?'[43]

In his letter to Bottomley, when describing his attempts to cover apparently inappropriate gaps in his work, Thomas resorted to patchwork imagery. The lines in the letter are also laid out so that the words referring to the act of patching work as apparently ill-fitting patches, emphasized as such by the brief line 'and' near the bottom of the list. The unevenness of the list means that it does not just cover gaps. It also creates them. As in the book to which the letter refers, the words plainly do 'not cover the space' of the page. They are turned into graphic illustrations of their own purpose, deliberately rough, space showing beneath and between them. Perhaps the reason Thomas 'could not cover the space' was not just because of a shortage of material but because for him those gaps 'really existed'. They might be patched over, but they are not completely filled in. The words covering them also highlight their existence. This can be said equally of the patches of words that form the list in the letter and those that cover the first page in *The Book of the Open Air*.[44]

Similar gaps exist in Thomas's prose books. His tendency to write pieces the length of an essay or paragraph often results in a gap between what he has written and what is expected to fill the pages of a book:

> Positively only reviews & nature ever make me think at all & that in a way beyond my control – things occur to me & I think for about the length of a lyric & then down & blank & something new – if the old idea returns it will not grow, but is only repeated.[45]

Many of his prose books are formed by the 'piling-up of landscapes', short sketches and short prose poems.[46] Gaps link and divide these 'landscapes', marking transitions between different significant areas in a way that evokes Freud's 'boundary-zones' of dreams.[47] As on the first page of *The Book of the Open Air*, Thomas often resorted to word-patching to help make up commissioned word counts, although the quotations or long lists he used frequently highlight the very gaps that they appear to cover.

Thomas blamed the patchwork effect of his prose on publishers' demands. Referring to old essays he added to *The Heart of England*, he wrote: 'Dent insisted on 6,000 [words] – & so I had to throw them in. They make a nasty mess.'[48] However, he also appeared to court gaps, even in the act of patching, as in the insertion of extremely long lists in his prose books. His long horizontal lists create metaphorical space by interrupting the main text and the uneven line lengths of his vertical lists also highlight space. At times, these long lists of names, often consisting of place names, almost seem to take on the status of poetry. This is sometimes reflected in the layout. The list of wood names in *The South Country* reproduces 'notices fixed to the doors of barn and shed, with the names of the copses and woods' visually on the page by judicious use of indentations. The space created by the vertical list gives it the shape of a poem and this impression is emphasized by the list's proximity to two separate quotations from Jonson's 'To Penshurst'. The indentations heralding the Jonson quotations are identical to the indentation heralding the wood name list. The judicious placing of these three texts, and the way that they all meditate on the name and place of Penshurst and its woods, reinforces the status of the first list of wood names as poetry, indented, as it is like a poem:

At Penshurst lately, for example, I saw these names:

Black Hoath Wood.
Heronry Pond.
Marlpit Field.
Tapner's Wood.
Ashour Farm.
Sidney's Coppice.
Weir Field.
Well Place.

I was back in Sidney's time, remembering that genial poem of Ben Jonson's, 'To Penshurst,' and especially the lines:

Thy copse too, named of Gamage, thou hast there,
That never fails to serve thee season'd deer,
When thou wouldst feed or exercise thy friends.
The lower land, that to the river bends,
Thy sheep, thy bullocks, kine, and calves do feed;
The middle grounds thy mares and horses breed.
    Each bank doth yield thee conies; and the tops
Fertile of wood, Ashore and Sidney's copps.
To crown thy open table, doth provide
The purple pheasant with the speackled side, . . .[49]

Thomas abbreviated many of his poem titles so that they seem to trail off into blankness. This forms another use of space. So little is given away in the title 'When first' that it verges upon aporia even before the body of the poem, the attempt at articulation, has begun. Thomas's reference to absence in the poem, the memory of what is gone and the attachment to it, 'louder the heart's dance / At parting than at meeting be', is heralded by an absence of words in the title (p. 134). Such unorthodox use of space resonates with the more dramatic experiments of his modernist contemporaries. It also chimes with Japanese use of absence in, as Noguchi phrased it, 'the art [*sic*] how to leave unsung', developed more recently in the work of Steven D. Carter.[50] Carter's translations of Japanese tanka exploit physical spacing, using truncated or indented lines to convey the original Japanese tanka reading experience:

> I have adopted an approach that I hope helps reflect the syntax and image-order of the originals. Each of the five lines that make up a complete *uta* are thus 'anchored' on the left margin, with the syntactic patterns of the originals then represented by 'jogging' of lines to the right, suggesting the way the Japanese poems seem to 'unfold'. [51]

Thomas's 'The sun used to shine' subtly integrates conventional gaps in layout into the poem. The emotional charge of the spaces between lines of this poem has already been observed, but the gaps between stanzas also deserve attention. A number of the printed stanzas start on a negative note but build to a more positive ending. This is then refuted in the next printed stanza which begins negatively once again. These leaps in tone are further highlighted by enjambement between the stanzas. Stanza one's closing light tone in 'cheerfully parted' is darkened by the completion of this phrase with 'each night' in the next stanza. Stanza two's closing 'poetry' is qualified in stanza three by 'to rumours of war'. Stanza four's 'birth' is located in stanza five 'in sunless Hades fields' (p. 122). These shifts in tone suggest something at work in the space that divides the stanzas, something that acts as an invisible counterpart to the worded text. During the gaps the tone of the poem changes direction, shifting from positive to negative, a shift that is then reversed by the printed words that follow. The physical area that the poem covers on the page is therefore larger than the area covered by the printed text. Like the space that precedes the punctuation in Thomas's handwritten orthography, the area outside the printed text in this poem frames, and is framed by, the printed stanzas. In this way, the poem includes the inexpressible as well as what can be expressed. The gap as 'an unfilled space or interval' becomes as much a part of the work as the filled space, with the result that the written text approaches the condition of Noguchi's haiku: 'a tiny star carrying the whole large sky at its back'.[52]

5

Unfinishedness . . .

pictures of perfection as you know make me sick and wicked
Jane Austen[1]

How pleasant –
just once *not* to see
Fuji through mist.
Matsuo Bashō[2]

The term 'unfinishedness' refers to the particular if invisible shape of a work that extends beyond its visible written parts. Thomas's subscription to unfinishedness in poetry is clear in a letter to his friend Jesse Berridge:

> Send the verses back when you have done with them. I fancy they are sufficiently new in their way to be unacceptable if the reader gets caught up by their way & doesn't get any effect before he begins to consider & see their 'unfinish'.[3]

Thomas was influenced by the Romantic poets' appreciation of unfinishedness, evident in their interest in ruins, Wordsworth's and Coleridge's fascination with the overgrown and almost indecipherable lettering of epitaphs, and poems such as Coleridge's 'Kubla Khan', subtitled as 'Of the Fragment of Kubla Khan'. The Romantic doctrine expressed by Wordsworth in the preface to *Lyrical Ballads* (1802) also had a significant effect on Thomas. Wordsworth wrote:

> [A poet] should consider himself as in the situation of a translator, who deems himself justified when he substitutes excellencies of another kind for those which are unattainable by him; and endeavours occasionally to surpass his original, in order to make some amends for the general inferiority to which he feels he must submit.[4]

Thomas recalled this passage in his own reference to poetry as translation in *Feminine Influence*.

John Ruskin mentioned unfinishedness in *The Stones of Venice*, noting, in reference to sculpture, that 'no good work whatever can be perfect, and *the demand for perfection is always a sign of a misunderstanding of the ends of art*' and that 'no great man ever stops working until he has reached his point of failure; that is to say, his mind is always far in advance of his powers of execution.'[5] Thomas, keenly aware of Ruskin's work in this field, named one of his *Oxford* chapters, 'Stones of Oxford'.

Thomas echoed Ruskin's approach to the composition process in *Stones of Venice*, which, for Ruskin, involved looking at it through the lens of architecture. In *The South Country*, Thomas transmuted a description of buildings into a meditation on language. He described religious architecture as 'a dead language, majestic but dead'.[6] Similarly, in his letters he noted his tendency to write about houses, often used as images of self-expression and forming titles of several of his works: 'so far the best things I have done have been about houses. I have quite a long series – I discover, tho I did not design it.'[7]

Thomas's frequent recourse to architectural and building imagery when describing the composing process in his critical and creative work indicates the continuing importance to him of design in a creative piece, and his sense that all works need structure. Even those that sport their own unfinishedness need an incipient structure that they can then refrain from completing. In Thomas's writing, use of imagery drawn from building and architecture encourages the concept of a creative piece as a habitation or space to be inhabited, and also of absence, whether in the composing process, or the completed work, as a physical and inhabiting presence.

UNFINISHEDNESS: BEYOND . . .

> it is better to leave a little imperfection
>
> Kenkō[8]

Adoption of the aesthetic of unfinishedness makes it difficult for an artist to know when to stop working on a creative piece, since the stopping point no longer coincides with an obvious point of finish. Thomas was well aware of this. When the publisher's reader Edward Garnett suggested that Thomas's poetry was in need of 'chiselling', he countered 'it would be the easiest thing in the world to clean it all up & trim it & have every line straightforward in sound & sense, but it would not really improve it'.[9] The poem must either continue beyond the 'straightforward' point or end previous to it.

Ruskin's reference to a great man's 'point of failure' in *The Stones of Venice* alludes to an unfinishedness that results from deliberate continuation beyond the poet's capabilities and point of control. Such unfinishedness occurs in Thomas's poetry too. In 'Beauty', at exactly the moment when the narrator-poet gives up trying to 'frame' or contain the 'epitaph', the composing process starts to move beyond his points of reference, resulting in the discovery of 'Beauty', a word that can, of course, also be read as referring to the whole poem.[10] Thus, the poem becomes a self-reflexive analysis of Thomas's composing processes. The narrator only finds 'Beauty' when he gives up trying to compose and lets his mind slip through the enclosing and limiting world or room in which he is situated. This occurs when his 'heart, some fraction of me' floats through the frame of the window of the room. 'Beauty' is then found in a half-visible 'misting, dim-lit' vale outside. The marginal, not fully seen and outside the poet's control, becomes, paradoxically, essential to the poetic experience. For the narrator, poet and reader, the 'misting, dim-lit' vale is unfinished and only half-visible, but the gaps, silences and obscurities that render it so are integral to any appreciation of it.

These manifestations of absence act like the 'always silent, but never forgotten, the restless, towering outline of a mountain' in *Beautiful Wales*.[11] They also bear similarities to the lack of beginning to a robin's song, as described in Thomas's novel *The Happy-go-lucky Morgans* (1913). The bird 'often rehearses the first half of his song in silence and then suddenly continues aloud, as if he were beginning in mid-song'.[12] It is not only unfinished but 'unbegun'. Similarly, in 'The Cuckoo', the speaker can only remember not hearing the cuckoo's song:

> When last I heard it I cannot recall; but I know
> Too well the year when first I failed to hear it – (p. 54)

The Icknield Way dedication also recognizes the endlessness of experience. Thomas used his inability as walker and writer to 'find a beginning or end' to the ancient Way as an analogy for his composition practices.[13] A similar focus is evident in the choice of a quotation from Yeats's play *Where There is Nothing* as an epigraph to *The South Country*:

> Did you ever think that the roads are the only things that are endless; that one can walk on and on and on, and never be stopped by a gate or a wall? They are the serpent of eternity. I wonder they have never been worshipped. What are

> the stars beside them? They never meet one another. The roads are the only things that are infinite. They are all endless.[14]

This emphasis on the lack of beginnings and ends resonates with Thomas's interest in the vanishing but not completely vanished beginnings of literature, still evident to him in the marks and swellings of the landscape. In *The Heart of England*, a 'dolmen rises out of the wheat in one field, like a quotation from an unknown language'.[15] *Richard Jefferies, his Life and Work* has 'pure down-land: the breasted hills curving as if under the influence of a great melody'.[16] 'England' in *The Last Sheaf* emphasizes the importance of localized features such as the hawthorn and apple tree to records of early English history, landmarks becoming historical records.

Thomas's preference for metaphors such as 'inscription', 'epitaph' and 'languages' when referring to landmarks suggests that he gave landmarks a literary status. For him, landmarks in combination with the records of the human vernacular formed the poetry of place names. In this context, too, he emphasized unfinishedness. In 'Women he liked', the history held by such means continually vanishes from human memory. Thomas's introduction to Isaac Taylor's *Words and Places* stresses and delights in the fact that knowledge of place names tends to be incomplete. A description of how the people he met furnished him with imaginary but vivid explanations of local place names is followed by the telling comment, 'we have need of men like that'.[17]

Historical records are necessarily incomplete. Just as the robin might appear to start singing after its song has already begun, and the writer begins to describe the Icknield Way when already some way along it, so the historian can only record the more recent activities of history. Thomas was very aware of how earlier records of history and, in particular, records of what is overlooked or ordinary, are only accessible through the imagination: 'the historian who has not the extensive sympathy and imagination of a great novelist will have no chance of success'.[18] He applied these observations of history in its unrecorded past and unknown and unpredictable future to oral literature. His *Celtic Stories* 'Note on Sources' refers to the 'twice-told tales' of the Welsh Mabinogion, 'the old tales on which a young writer practised', and Irish tales which storytellers retell 'age after age, adding to them and taking away'.[19] Oral literature is not fixed. It transforms itself at each retelling. It is, as a result, continually in a state of unfinishedness.

In oral literature artists are part of a mutable unfinished process that extends beyond individual creators. The individual artist recedes into anonymity as subsequent 'addings' and 'takings away' occur. Thomas attempted to extend such oral anonymity to written work. This is the case when he decided not to credit Bottomley for his part in arranging Welsh lyrics for *Beautiful Wales*; when he slipped his and others' translations and quotations anonymously into his work; and when he published his poems under a pseudonym. He did not evince an anxiety of influence or sense of indebtedness to the past, but a sense of shared responsibility for a creative piece.

Woolf addressed this subject more directly in *A Room of One's Own*:

> Chaucer [could no more have written] without those forgotten poets who paved the ways and tamed the natural savagery of the tongue. For masterpieces are not single and solitary births; they are the outcome of many years of thinking in common, of thinking by the body of the people, so that the experience of the mass is behind the single voice.[20]

Her words echoed Thomas's dedication to *The Icknield Way*, which clearly links the intertextuality created by a lengthy literary and oral tradition and the consequent unfinishedness of any particular work, set as it is within that tradition. Thomas wrote:

> [It is] another of those books made out of books founded on other books. Being but half mine it can only be half yours, and I owe you an apology as well as a dedication. It is, however, in some ways a fitting book for me to write. For it is about a road which begins many miles before I could come on its traces and ends miles beyond where I had to stop.[21]

Thomas's words accord well with Japanese attitudes towards poetry. As Chamberlain noted in *Things Japanese* in 1902, the Japanese view poetry 'more as the product of an epoch than of an individual', Japanese poetry and poetic devices forming an 'elliptical and enigmatic style, which continually crosses the border-line of obscurity'.[22] Such a description can easily be applied to Thomas's verse. This indicates connections that reach across not only temporal but also cultural boundaries, unfinishedness being an essential element in Japanese aesthetics. Kenkō declared in a passage in *Miscellany of a Japanese Priest* that resonates with Thomas's and Ruskin's relation of creative processes and architecture: 'There are some who say that when a palace is being built, you should never fail to leave one little piece of it uncompleted.'[23]

UNFINISHED: COMING OUT OF FINISHEDNESS . . .

> Of course you always fail, but as Beckett said: 'Fail again, fail better.'
> Carol Ann Duffy[24]

In his writing life, Thomas moved from appreciation of 'finish' to desire for 'unfinishedness' in a creative piece. His initial focus on 'finish' is seen in his admiration of Pater, who 'used to purge my writing of its excess'.[25] His early estimation of polished, finished prose is also evident in a letter to his friend, Harry Hooton, written in 1897. This letter draws on architectural imagery when discussing the use of language in composition:

> there is some sort of morality in strenuously achieving a nearly perfect style, in building, as the Greeks said, ('build the lofty rhyme') the cottage of the temple of living sounds. Pater is, I am sure, the only example of his own theories. Robert Louis S[tevenson] is far below him, though he too consciously builds. I always think style, in its limited point – the perfect sentence, is like the casting by a spider of its thin thread far out from itself towards some remote object, to attain which is its intent, but to fall short of which by a hair's breadth is to fail utterly.[26]

However, soon, as Longley notes, Paterian prose began to represent 'a literariness and wordiness of which Thomas wished to purge himself'.[27] Thomas expressed this disaffection most fully in *Walter Pater* (1913), in which he quoted Oscar Wilde's opinion that Pater's prose is 'often far more like a piece of mosaic than a passage in music'.[28] Thomas then amplified this with his own image: 'On almost every page of his [Pater's] writing words are to be seen sticking out, like raisins that will get burnt on an ill-made cake.'[29]

In the same passage, Thomas described alternative approaches to composing:

> The most and the greatest of man's powers are as yet little known to him, and are scarcely more under his control than the weather: he cannot keep a shop without trusting somewhat to his unknown powers, nor can he write books except such as are no books. It appears to have been Pater's chief fault, or the cause of his faults, that he trusted these powers too little. The alternative supposition is that he did not carry his self-conscious labours far enough.[30]

The reference to the weather in this passage is an indication of the importance for Thomas, when composing, of the uncontrolled influence of the external environmental conditions that remain changeable, unpredictable and so unfinished. In several of his letters, he made close connections between the composition of poems such as 'Words', 'There's nothing like the sun' and 'The clouds that are so light' and outdoor experiences of weather.[31] 'Beauty' refers to the effect of the outdoor environment on composing, contrasting a controlled failed attempt at composition indoors with an unplanned but successful discovery of beauty outdoors. In a sense, Thomas was advocating an 'open air' process of composing, similar to the *plein-air* approach of the Impressionist painters, and similar, too, to his regular practice of researching while travelling the countryside and, later, of drafting poems when on public transport through the countryside. These practices encourage unfinishedness.

Working outdoors ensures that the outcome of a poem is influenced by an environment beyond the poet's control. Thomas could not dictate the weather or the speed of a train in which he was sitting so his completed poems' unfinishedness in part resides in areas outside his jurisdiction. 'Beauty is there' in the countryside, not in the poet's room (p. 58).

In 'Reading out of doors', Thomas discussed how the natural environment could enhance and inhabit completed works. He explained this, once again, in terms of architecture: 'Nature does on their [printed books'] behalf as she does sometimes for cheap architecture. She festoons them with ivy flowers; the birds sing and build close by.'[32]

Wordsworth's and Coleridge's references to the weathering of epitaphs when placed outside in graveyards graphically illustrate the continued effect that an environment can have on a written work. Thomas's epitaph poems also pick up this theme. 'A Tale', 'Tall Nettles' and 'The Cherry Trees' allude to natural processes of change related to seasonal and weather conditions. Falling cherry blossom, weeds, nettles and 'dust on the nettles' strongly affect manmade edifices, artefacts and pathways: hiding, ruining and obscuring cottages, rollers, ploughs and 'the old road' (pp. 73, 119, 120).

Thomas's predilection for epitaphs is unsurprising, since a traditional epitaph makes a good exemplar for the unfinished but completed poem. Using age-old formulae of words, epitaphs pre-exist their carvers, their beginnings lying in oral literature, and have no end, surviving long after their writers have been forgotten. They are, too, separated from their subject matter by time, set up specifically to remember what is gone, and so highlight the belatedness of their composition. This is explored in the naming of 'Bob's Lane' in 'Women he liked'. The name acts as an epitaph. Bob, the namer of the lane, has died and of the lane 'the name alone survives' (p. 127). The lane is named only when it has lost its function.

UNFINISHEDNESS: INTO STRANGENESS AND LOOSENESS . . .

> When I was the age of these children I could draw like Raphael: it took me many years to learn how to draw like these children.
>
> Pablo Picasso[33]

Thomas's increasing preference for unfinishedness in his writing is evident in changes in his work's structure, particularly at sentence level. He observed to Bottomley, 'how careless of the minutiae of form I get – long rambling sentences, which I know to be imperfect. I hope it means that I am getting into a truer method.'[34] Like the 'long' and 'rambling' nettles that later take over the farmyard in 'Tall Nettles', these extended wandering sentences contribute to a sense of unfinishedness.

Thomas's preference for a looser structure is indicated in his appreciation of flexible attitude to form, an unfinished fluidity that is always in flux, just as the oral tradition remembers, or 'misremembers', its literature through generations. He championed old folk songs that 'come to us imploring a new lease of life on the sweet earth'. Much of his mature verse is influenced by balladic tradition and several poems include the word 'song' in their title.[35] 'The Ash Grove' borrows its title from a song, and 'Early one morning', entitled 'Song [3]' in the *Collected Poems* of 1978, was written 'to the tune of Rio Grande'.[36] In *The Heart of England*, Thomas praised in an imagined ballad 'the strangeness and looseness of its framework [which] allowed each man to see himself therein'.[37] The absence contained within the ballad's looseness enhanced its creative potential.

Thomas's admiration of the fluidity and flexibility inherent in folk songs is underpinned by a fascination with rhythm. His observations of his young daughter Myfanwy's impromptu arrangements of songs stress her use of a constant rhythmic core:

> She sang four or five verses of 'John Peel' the other morning without one line of sense, yet using hardly one word that isn't in the song, just transposing and rearranging, retaining only the tune and the metre. Some lines were better than ever but I can't remember one.[38]

In a letter to Helen that alludes to the main source for 'An Old Song II' he noted his own explorations with rhythm, playing around with tunes and words when improvising:

> I liked walking thus, humming tunes and combining or improvising tunes. I remember how I did it when I was most cheerful at Minsmere – often ribald tunes. I was going to write an essay to be called 'In Amsterdam there dwelt a maid' (p. 169)

He also emphasized the importance of rhythm as a base in *Walter Pater*: 'rhythm is of the essence of a sincere expressive style. Pater's rhythm is intermittent, and, except in short passages like that on La Gioconda it is rarely emotional'.[39] In the same passage, his allusion to Oscar Wilde as 'too vigorous to fall into this error', implies that such a core needs to be worked for.

Clearly influenced by Wilde in his own criticism of Pater's 'finished' prose, Thomas quoted directly from Wilde more than once in *Walter Pater*. His reference to Wilde in relation to rhythm is particularly significant, since in 'The Critic as Artist' Wilde argued for a shift away from the written page to the rhythms of speech:

> Since the introduction of printing, and the fatal development of the habit of reading amongst the middle and lower classes of this country, there has been a tendency in literature to appeal more and more to the eye, and less and less to the ear.[40]

Wilde also wrote, 'Yes: writing has done much harm to writers. We must return to the voice.'[41] His views resulted in some extreme experimentation. Dowling records:

> Wilde then experimented with his own speech to test the limits of what could be perfectly said with neither affectation nor the lame gait of ordinary talk. Hence Yeats's astonishment when he first heard Wilde 'talking with perfect sentences, as if he had written them all overnight with labour and yet all spontaneous'.[42]

Dowling points out that such a performative ideal necessitates 'an entire assent to the evanescence and final extinction of the spoken work of art', and produced for Wilde work that was necessarily self-exhausting and could not be secured through written language.[43] As a result, Wilde outlasted his performed work. Yeats noted that Wilde was 'the greatest talker of his time, and his plays and dialogues have what merit they possess from being now an imitation, now a record, of his talk'.[44] Dowling, too, reports: 'It was only when Wilde ceased to speak his tales and elaborated them in print that his style – Yeats and Robert Ross and André Gide all agreed – stiffened into artifice.'[45] Thomas also referred to the artifice of Wilde's writing, criticizing him for his 'decorative instinct'.[46] Wilde's attempts to return to the rhythms of speech were sabotaged by their own extreme and earnest focus.

Although Thomas argued for 'the necessity for the aid of speech in literature', unlike Wilde, he recognized limitations to the artist's control.[47] In the composing process, and in the completed poem, Thomas saw the poet's and the reader's access to a poem as limited, relating to the completed piece's unfinishedness. In contrast to Wilde's attempts at perfection of performance and control of the composing process in his production of what Yeats referred to as 'perfect sentences', Thomas experienced composing 'blindfold', writing to 'dictation'.[48] For him, 'love-poetry, like all other lyric poetry, is in a sense unintentionally overheard, and only by accident and in part understood'.[49] Such an approach to composing prefigures and relates to Olson's later description of gaps on the page as a representation of the process of performance.

When Thomas criticized what he calls Pater's 'tin soldier' words for refusing 'to fall into the rhythms which only emotion can command', he was suggesting that the emotional life of a piece resides not only in its spaces or gaps but in its shifting and unfinished rhythms.[50] His explanations of this resort to the use of a tidal imagery to emphasize the importance of fluidity and tensions between different but simultaneously occurring rhythms: 'the book is a poem; I had almost said a piece of music. The ideas rise up and fall, lose their outlines, and, resurgent again, have not fulfilled their whole purpose until the full-charged silence of the conclusion', and 'poetry in verse is at one with the tides and the pulse'.[51]

Frost approached poetic composition in a similar way. At the time that he was having lengthy discussions with Thomas about poetry, he wrote to John Cournos: 'I like to drag and break the intonation across the meter as waves first comb and then break stumbling on the shingle.'[52] Both Thomas and Frost saw unfinished, breaking, stumbling rhythm as crucial to a poem.

An ambiguous *kakekotoba*-like effect in Thomas's 'The Mill-Water' has the rhythm straining against the sense, as qualifications of what has already been written are suggested and then delayed at each line ending:

> Sometimes a thought is drowned
> By it, sometimes
> Out of it climbs; (p. 98)

The repeated use of 'sometimes' confirms the frequency of both the experience of drowning and of climbing.

Other references to multiple and conflicting rhythms occur in the 'cross breezes cut[ting] the surface' in 'Beauty' (p. 58), and allusions to crossing roads in 'Aspens', 'The Signpost', 'The Green Roads' and 'Up in the Wind'. Conflicting rhythms in these poems tend to occur when speech and metrical rhythms pull against each other in and across the lines, although this intricate interplay between metre and speech is often hidden in an apparently loose rhythmic structure. The result is, as de la Mare observed, that Thomas's poetry 'must be read slowly, as naturally as if it were talk, without much emphasis'.[53]

Peter Levi notes of Thomas that 'the use of an individuated vernacular speech tone [is] in descant with conventional metre and with itself'.[54] Longley records in detail examples of tension between syntax and metre in 'October' and 'Aspens', discussing how 'the metre [in 'Aspens'], veering between iambic and trisyllabic stress patterns, interacts with the syntactical pull between statement and qualification'.[55]

The act of composing such complicated rhythms requires deliberate, sustained effort. Thomas implied this when he criticized Pater for not carrying 'his self-conscious labours far enough'.[56] It is also implicit in an exchange of letters with Garnett, during which Thomas defended himself from Garnett's accusations of 'intolerably affected' and deliberately cultivated 'literary' passages that 'smell of the lamp' in 'The Attempt'. He argued that 'such phrases however bad came to me without thinking or seeking. It is your "simple & direct" phrases that I have to seek for.'[57] Non-closure and simple rough 'unfinish' are skilful manoeuvres, not easily achieved.

There is an echo here of Ruskin's emphasis on deliberate effort when sculpting with a chisel. In accordance with the aesthetic of unfinishedness, Ruskin preferred 'coarse' and 'blunt cutting' over '*cold* cutting – the look of equal trouble everywhere'.[58] In Japanese aesthetics, too, deliberate effort in composing is related to choice of tools. Kenkō wrote: 'I am told that a good craftsman always uses a knife which is the least little bit blunt. Myōkwan's knife did not cut perfectly.'[59] The poet may aim for imperfect finish, but must aim with great care, just like the Japanese tea master, Rikyū, who, according to apocrypha, 'shook the maple-trees to make the leaves fall' on a recently swept path for a more natural look. The 'unfinish' of an area previously 'swept' into neatness resulted from a calculated effort, continuing the process of cleaning beyond the point of neatness and finality.[60]

There is a danger that over-zealous practice of unfinishedness can result in poems that continue for too long, and several of Thomas's letters to Farjeon reiterated, in relation to different poems, his concern about presenting too much information. He worried whether 'Some eyes condemn' offered too obvious a rhythm: 'I am glad you liked the sonnet, I suppose it was one. My fear was that it ended with a click.'[61] He also wrote of 'How at once':

> By the way, you misread that poem you didn't much like – about the swifts – missing the point that year after year I see them, *realising that it is the last time*, i.e. just before they go away for the winter (early in August). Perhaps it is too much natural history.[62]

The letters to Farjeon show how he made use of external readers' responses to his drafts when redrafting. However, his dependence on these responses in the writing of his poetry pales in comparison to his earlier reliance on external readers when redrafting prose. In 1909, he wrote to Garnett: 'Have you time to look at another sketch of mine? [. . .] I am not at all sure that I am on a wise path – far less a profitable one – and you are the only man I can turn to for an opinion.' In contrast, in a letter written in 1915, he dismissed Garnett's criticism of his poetry: 'I don't think I could alter "Tears" to make it marketable. I feel that the correction you want made is only essential if the whole point is in the British Grenadiers, as might be expected in these times.'[63] Passages in his letters to Farjeon also reveal how, once he began to compose his mature poetry, he exhibited a much surer and keener sense of the need for 'unfinish' and of the effects of the network of response-inviting structures in his writing, and consequently was less dependent on the responses of external readers.

UNFINISHEDNESS: SUSPENDED . . .

> Nature has no arrangement, no plan
> Richard Jefferies[64]

Any reader of Thomas needs to pay careful and deliberate attention to his verse. The effect of much of it is tied in with the effort accompanying each reading, both in terms of unravelling and rearranging its complicated syntax, and of registering and accepting its unfinishedness. However, for his contemporary readers the effort demanded was much greater, due to the novelty in his time of such experiments with 'unfinish' in rhythm, rhyme, form and syntax. Thomas shows awareness of this, attributing readers' difficulties with his 'sufficiently new' verse to their inability or reluctance to 'consider and see their [the poems'] "unfinish"'.[65] It is perhaps difficult today to comprehend fully the extent of the unfamiliarity of his poetry to contemporary readers, and of their difficulty in making necessary provisions as they read for unknown elements of suspension or open-endedness. At times unable to pick up the unfamiliar patterns held within in his pieces, contemporary readers had problems gauging their success as pieces of creative art. Thomas's delayed posthumous success as a poet bears witness to this.

Predictably, the unfinished quality present in his poems often relates to their endings, as suggested in Thomas's concern with a possibility of too much finishedness in the 'click' of the ending of 'Some eyes condemn', and too little finishedness in the sudden switch at the end of 'The long small room'. In both his poetry and his prose he aimed for suspended, rather than finished or unfinished, endings. He noted the relation of such endings to the uncertainties of his time: 'perhaps we worry less about conclusions, generalizations nowadays, in our anxiety to get the facts & feelings down – just as science picks up a million pebbles & can't arrange them or even play with them'.[66]

Thomas made a specific link between suspended endings and the contemporary scene when discussing Jefferies's novel, *After London* (1885). The story of *After London*, as Jeremy Hooker has observed, 'replaces the centre with the margins', as it tracks what would happen if nature reclaimed the city, transforming it into a wasteland.[67] The novel ends with Felix, 'absorbed in thought', walking off into the distance, 'still onward; and as the dusk fell he was still moving rapidly westwards'.[68] The 'suspended breath' of this ending, as described by Thomas in *Richard Jefferies, his Life and Work*, continues the theme of the novel.[69] Order reverts to chaos or, more specifically, the structure of urban conglomerates is replaced with the more fluid organic activity of nature, continually in process. In his comments on *After London*, Thomas argued for the general adoption of such endings:

> That is the end. It is a wilful one, as if on a hexameter instead of a pentameter, yet it needs no defence. Others could have been found to conform to the needs of perhaps a majority. But to end with suspended breath is as true to Nature, and in keeping with this age; it might be used as a variation upon 'happily ever after' or 'necessity is great'.[70]

Thomas's preference for suspended endings is also evident in *Feminine Influence*. He qualified Coleridge's definitive statement on the artist in *Biographia Literaria* (the artist 'must imitate that which is within the thing') by adding that 'there are no musts in art, only an infinite may'.[71] He also alluded to an emphasis on 'may' rather than 'must' in *Richard Jefferies, his Life and Work*, relating his appreciation of suspension of a sequential logic in works of art to the aesthetic of asymmetry:

> 'There is,' he [Jefferies] says, 'no design and no evolution.' The sequence from cause to effect does not seem to him inevitable. There is no 'must' – which recalls the brook's 'there is no why.' The balance of logic does not correspond with life, with the irregular human frame, the unbalanced tree.[72]

The reference to the brook is an allusion to Jefferies's *Wood Magic* (1881), in which the natural environment is identified as having 'no design and no evolution'. Thomas cited *Wood Magic* earlier in *Richard Jefferies, his Life and Work*: 'We have been listening to the brook, me and my family, for ever so many thousands of years, and though the brook has been talking and singing all that time, I never heard him ask why about anything.'[73] This resonates with Thomas's approach to the composition of his prose, which often consists of series of prose poems loosely strung together. He wrote to Bottomley, while composing *The South Country*, that '[s]o far I have no scheme, no frame on which to hang my landscapes, etc', and continued in this and subsequent letters to document his search for a frame that would not destroy the fluidity of his work.[74] He likened structure to the flow of a brook, an image that was for him a concrete, if typically free-flowing, expression of the suspended unfinished logic in creative writing.

Thomas's preference for what remains open, unresolved and unfinished makes him an exemplary poet of the absent: of the unfinished, but also of gaps, ellipses and aporia. This is evident in his insistent focus on periods of transition in his choice of titles, *Light and Twilight*; 'Interval', with its 'brief twilight' (p. 39); and 'The Bridge', with its

> moment brief between
> Two lives, when the Night's first lights
> And shades hide what has never been, (p. 66)

However, as the image of the bridge suggests, in this articulation of what is absent and unfinished, Thomas favoured balanced transition, resting deliberately between points of resolution. This preference is combined with an aversion to closed formal composition. He had a 'dread of the sonnet. It must contain 14 lines, and a man must be a tremendous poet or a cold mathematician if he can accommodate his thought to such a condition.'[75] In *Richard Jefferies, his Life and Work*, he connected these feelings about the sonnet form with his aversion to the requirements of commissioned pieces of writing:

> the length of an article demanded by an editor has no necessary connection with the subject of it. In prose such lengths are as destructive to order and beauty as the fourteen lines of a sonnet commonly are to sense.[76]

His preference for a less prescriptive, more open-ended, unfinished form recalls the Romantic value for roughness, variation and asymmetry. It also resonates strongly with Japanese aesthetics, in which the irregular is valued above the regular. Kenkō observed that it is 'better to have dissimilarity', not chaotic dissimilarity but one that has its own balance, and praised a garden with 'its old clump of trees, its garden plants not artificially trained but with a meaning of their own, its bench of bamboo, its well-adapted little hedge and its furniture placed naturally', preferring it to plants and trees 'trained in a meaningless fashion'.[77] The scene Kenkō described is neither of disordered chaos nor of artificial order. Instead, it is a meaningful and considered adaptation of the natural organic processes of nature. A similar balance can be perceived in the carefully judged provisionality of the endings, alternative readings, asymmetry, non-linear sequences and rhythmic tensions of Thomas's mature poetry.

Thomas's poetry also pays particular attention to transition and process, to what is not yet finished and only half-articulated. Many critics have commented on this. Andrew Motion remarks on Thomas's 'genius for producing poems which appear to think aloud rather than be a means of delivering finished thoughts'.[78] In reference to Thomas's use of rhythm, J. P. Ward remarks that 'many lines direct their rhythm to something not finally said, to something half-verbalised and elusive. This has of course been repeatedly noticed about Thomas; it is inescapable.'[79] Balance, however, is still retained in the unevenness of the rhythms, as they first pull towards one pattern and then veer into another. Such compensatory shifts dislocate any tendencies to resolution and finishedness of metre.

One aspect of Thomas's use of absence in composing is that it often occurs as a result of shifts in emphasis and degree of visibility of initial drafts, as is seen in the development of the drafting process of 'The sun used to shine'. Manipulation of rhythm also plays an important part, evident in the shifting but carefully judged 'unfinish', the subtle and exact use of enjambement, and the series of intricately interwoven qualifications and sub-clauses in his completed pieces. This emphasis on movement in the creation of absence in the composing process and completed pieces leads on to the aspect of composing that is the focus of the next chapters – how the shifting movements created by dislocation can be harnessed both to create absence in a piece and also to control its effects, countering tendencies to 'over' finish.

6

Temporal Dislocation

behind us already the green
trees are deserting their leaves
W. G. Sebald[1]

Thomas addressed the subject of poetic composition tangentially. Asides relating to it abound in his travel and country books, critical biographies, reviews of poetry and many epistolary discussions with contemporary poet friends. References also exist, implicitly, in the shifts in content and style between his drafts and completed poetic works. He wrote more directly about it in *Feminine Influence* but this whole book was composed tangentially, without a considered structure: 'I put down all but everything just as it occurred in the few months I was doing it.'[2] Dislocation therefore lies at the heart of his composing processes.

Critics have often emphasized this. Peter Sachs sums him up as a 'tramp in spirit' who wrote with an 'effortless peripheral vision', with 'typically aslope' poems that require the reader to tread a series of paths 'in or beyond the margin of the road'.[3] Motion describes how moods or situations in the poems are 'ambushed and forced into precision by modifiers and conditionals'.[4]

Thomas employed physical and temporal dislocation and other dislocatory effects in the act of naming. Dislocation also forms an essential role in his creative use of ellipses, aporia, gaps and unfinishedness. His composing activity, too, involved temporal dislocation, distraction or dislocation of attention, and dislocated or tangential associative thought processes.

Of all these forms of dislocation in Thomas's composition processes, this chapter will examine in particular temporal dislocation. Temporal dislocation refers to occasions when experiences relating to one period of time affect poetry written at another. It can apply to drafts and to completed works. It influences both readers' interpretation of a piece and, in the case of a writer acting as reader, the way in which a draft develops.

TEMPORALITY: IN THE NAMING OF COMPLETED WORKS

My work is often three steps ahead of me.
Sam Taylor Wood[5]

Thomas's awareness of the effects of temporal dislocation on language is discernible in his choice of poem titles. He used the provisional title 'Bob's Lane' to refer to a poem in a letter to Farjeon on 29 June 1916. This title was later adopted by R. G. Thomas for the *Collected Poems* (1978), R. G. Thomas probably not being aware that Edward Thomas had exchanged it for 'Women he liked' in the *Poems* of 1917, thus indicating a growing preference for dislocation. The title, 'Bob's Lane', refers directly to the poem's subject-matter. The title, 'Women he liked', does not. 'Women he liked' appears as a phrase in the first line. This creates the expectation that it will form the poem's main focus, but the subject is then dropped and never resumed. Using the phrase as the title reinforces both the initial expectation of its importance to the poem and the shock when that expectation is not fulfilled. The effect is to make the poem a work about dislocation and, since it also explores the naming of a lane, dislocation during and after acts of naming.

'But these things also', like 'Women he liked', is a title that also appears in the first line of the poem. It, too, highlights dislocation of subject matter, bringing to the centre of attention what has previously been overlooked, emphasizing items normally lying on the periphery of vision, while also continuing to stress their marginal qualities.

Another act of dislocation occurs in the investigation of naming in 'Women he liked'. By the end of the poem, an unnamed 'track' has been elevated to the status of 'lane' and officially named as 'Bob's Lane'. This progression to named status can be called an act of temporal dislocation, since what is now known as 'Bob's Lane' refers to a function and thoroughfare that no longer exists. The naming of this track occurs as a result of Bob's act of planting elms along it. However, the planting also results in the track's destruction, since the shade provided by the elms renders it too muddy for use as a lane. Concomitant with the track's acquisition of the name 'Lane', therefore, is the loss of its practical use as a thoroughfare. The means by which the track acquires its name are also the means of dislocating the track from the function originally resulting in its name:

> the mist and the rain
> Out of the elms have turned the lane to slough
> And gloom, the name alone survives, Bob's Lane.[6]

The thing named is affected by the process of naming. So, too, is the creator of that name. Farmer Bob not only enabled the naming of the lane through his actions, but is himself named within that name as its creator and owner. When, by the end of the poem, he is dead, the name of the lane becomes an epitaph both to him and the now defunct lane.

The poem too acts as an epitaph, commemorating the act of naming by repetition of 'name' and the rhyme or half-rhyme of 'lane' or 'Lane', 'train', 'blame' and 'rain'. These particular rhyming words also hint at other temporal dislocating processes of movement in 'lane' and 'train'; natural wear and tear in the weathering influences of 'rain'; and guilt, 'blame', – a consequence of destruction. The lane is both linked to an act of destruction and commemorates that act and what has been destroyed: the thing named; the namer or enabler of that name; and the history that lies behind that name. 'Women he liked' suggests, therefore, an inherently destructive element present in the creative process of naming. Both oral and printed acts of naming are implicated, since the road or place name of 'Bob's Lane' was created as part of an oral tradition and then recorded in the poem. At the same time, naming is shown to aid memory. A reminder of the lane survives in its name and, rather than any 'Women he liked', it is this name that remains at the end of the poem.

However, very little of the lane's past remains at the end of the poem, apart from the way the name itself acts as a memory. The elements of the past referred to in the name, the lane and Bob have all become 'slough'. By such emphasis on temporal dislocation Thomas highlighted the dichotomy between the impermanence of natural phenomena and the relative and ultimately futile fixity of language. Just as the lane is temporally dislocated from the nomenclature it receives, so, he implied, any referent is similarly divorced from its name.

In 'Anon', Woolf also investigated this temporal division between the named and the name. Julia Briggs notes Woolf's close connection with Thomas at this time in her life. When discussing Woolf's *Between the Acts*, written concurrently with 'Anon', Briggs observed how Thomas's self-awareness, 'his sense of the loss of the past, and the fragmented nature of consciousness, is especially relevant to a novel that confronts disruption and discontinuity'.[7] She also pointed out Woolf's veiled references to 'Old Man', a poem dealing with naming and the essential inaccuracies, multiplicities and ambiguities inherent in the naming process, in *Between the Acts*, and her more explicit references to it in the initial draft of the novel.[8]

In 'Anon', Woolf emphasized the temporal dislocation that accompanies oral composition. She began by detailing the several acts that occur before a huntsman, inspired by birdsong, begins to sing: he 'rested his axe against the tree for a moment' and then proceeded to fell the tree and make a hut.[9] These individual acts serve as a temporal barrier between the huntsman's eventual song and the birdsong he hears originally. However, Woolf's description of the huntsman's song partly reconnects these separated songs of bird and huntsman as she emphasizes the anonymity of the human singing voice. This anonymity is achieved when the audience joins the huntsman in song, making it a communal rather than an individual performance. In such ways, the human voice, like that of the original bird, is shown to emanate from and so inhabit the environment in which it sings.

Woolf's dealings with birdsong take on further significance when set against Hudson's observations on birdsong in the chapter, 'Bird Music in South America', in *Idle Days in Patagonia* (1893), quoted by Thomas in *The Country*. Drawing on his knowledge as an ornithologist, Hudson provided physiological reasons for the 'aërial quality [of the songs of birds] which makes them differ from all other sounds', attributing this to the birds' highly developed vocal organs, hollow bones and feathers, and the elevation from which they tend to sing. His additional emphasis on the importance of listening to birdsong in its natural environment amongst 'the patter of rain on the forest leaves, the murmur of the wind' suggests that, just as the birds' organic make-up directly affects the 'airy resonant quality' of their songs, so their songs inhabit and are enhanced by the physical location in which they are produced.[10] This emphasis on sound as inhabiting the birds' physical structure and environment forms a parallel with the processes involved in artistic creations. It echoes particularly the tendency in Thomas's and others' descriptions of poetic composition to resort to imagery drawn from activities such as building and architecture, focusing on the provision of dwellings, as if the creator needs to dwell within the environment in which the composition process occurs, or the environment, indeed, needs to dwell within the creator.

Traces of Hudson's physiological explanations of the effect of birdsong surface in Thomas's writing. *The South Country* observes how 'the bird has admitted a larger air' and the powerful effect of birdsong is partly dependent on the listener's distance from the world that birds inhabit, leading to the suggestion that birdsong offers a sound bite of what is otherwise beyond the listener's reach:

> Beautiful as the notes are for their quality and order, it is their inhumanity that gives them their utmost fascination, the mysterious sense which they bear to us that earth is something more than a human estate, that there are things not human yet of great honour and power in the world.[11]

Woolf's description of the origin of human song in 'Anon' provides, with her emphasis on communal participation in the human song, a way of temporarily annulling the potential separation and temporal dislocation that might otherwise occur between singer and audience:

> Thus the singer had his audience, but the audience was so little interested in his name that he never thought to give it. The audience itself was the singer; 'Terly, terlow' they sang; and 'By, by lullay' filling in the pauses, helping out with a chorus. Every body shared in the emotion of Anons [*sic*] song, and supplied the story.[12]

Woolf showed how close correspondence between environment and song, with the audience becoming the singer, is denied to the printed word: 'Caxtons [*sic*] printing press foretold the end of that anonymous world; [*sic*] It is now written down: fixed; nothing will be added; even if the legend still murmurs on.'[13] An act of naming is set and fixed in print. Unlike oral literature, it cannot be altered easily, so the inevitable temporal dislocation that accompanies any act of naming is heightened considerably, the very permanence of the print throwing into relief the original impermanence and changing characteristics of the thing named. The more words are tied to specificities of time and person, the greater their temporal dislocation from the original experience to which they refer.

Paradoxically, although entry into print dislocates a song or place name from the occasion that inspired it and the voice that created or retold it, print also places that song or name firmly in a fixed past which has in some sense now become present: 'The printing press brought the past into existence.'[14] However, this juxtaposition of past and present further emphasizes the distance of the song or name from its reader. The reader looks at the printed song in the present moment, but the very fact that it has been printed means the song is not of the present. It is a fixed record from the past.

Such distancing is brought about through division of a work from the environment in which it was written. Thomas's response to this can be seen when he placed the printed book, symbolized by *Morte d'Arthur*, physically back in the natural environment in 'Reading out of doors'. Such placement results in an invigoration of the text and a return, as 'the wood sorcery catches it', to some of the flexibility of oral literature.[15]

The emphasis in 'Adlestrop' on a detached railway platform place name weaves together many of the effects of temporal dislocation. It reveals not only the division of that name from the place it names but the temporal dislocation between the name and the thing named and, conversely, the powerful relation between the natural environment and place names.

The initial suggestion of a memory of place in the line 'I remember Adlestrop – / The name' is quickly transmuted into the memory of a place name. The peopled village and busy railway station that result in the naming of this place are absent. The station is bare. There is no one there. The name and its referent are out of step. In later lines, the name 'Adlestrop' is almost obliterated by the list of the grasses growing in its natural environment: 'Adlestrop – only the name // And willows, willow-herb, and grass' (p. 51). Consideration of the present sights and sounds of the natural environment overwhelm the previous focus on the place name. Caught up in the present moment, the speaker and the reader are taken far away from the name of a station platform. However, the choice of 'Adlestrop' as title and the identification of the birds at the end of the poem by means of place also suggest an intimate link between named places and their environments. The birds are 'Of Oxfordshire and Gloucestershire', and the repetition and rhyming of the place word and name of 'shire' with the end-rhyme 'mistier' and the following 'Farther and farther' allow birds, poem and reader to go further, beyond the lines and the borders of vision, into the mist, the silent absences of the poem. The rhyme words act almost like *kakekotoba*, as they encourage shifts from one meaning to another and into areas that lie beyond articulated meaning.

As in 'Women he liked', 'Adlestrop' presents naming as a belated act, involving labels that are inaccurate, temporally dislocated portrayals of the named phenomena. The omission in 'Adlestrop' of any clear record of the history or origin of the place name 'Adlestrop' also implies that such belatedness exists not only in the individual named poem but in the more anonymous acts of naming places.

TEMPORALITY: OF BELATED ACTS

> a past charged with the time of the now
>
> Walter Benjamin[16]

'The Work of Displacement', a section of the chapter on dream-work in Freud's *The Interpretation of Dreams*, states: 'The dream is, as it were, *centred elsewhere*; its content is arranged around elements that do not constitute the central point of the dream-thoughts.'[17] This concept of the centre as marginal resonates with Thomas's writing on temporal dislocation in 'But these things also' and his aporetic tale, 'The Castle of Lostormellyn'. Similarly, just as Thomas presented dislocation or displacement in naming as necessarily involving a rewriting of the original source, so Freud presented an equivalent rewriting as the central tenet of his concept of *nachträglichkeit*, translated by Jeffrey Moussaieff Masson as 'retranscription'. Freud wrote to his friend Wilhelm Fliess:

> Our psychic mechanism has come into being by a process of stratification: the material present in the form of memory traces being subjected from time to time to a rearrangement in accordance with fresh circumstances – to a retranscription. Thus, what is essentially new about my theory is the thesis that memory is present not once but several times over, that it is laid down in various kinds of indications. (I postulated a similar kind of rearrangement some time ago [Aphasia] for the paths leading from the periphery . . .)

The letter continues

> I should like to emphasize the fact that the successive registrations represent the psychic achievement of successive epochs of life. At the boundary between two such epochs a translation of the psychic material [takes] place. I explain the peculiarities of the psychoneuroses by supposing that this translation has not taken place in the case of some of the material, which has certain consequences.[18]

Successive acts of memory necessarily involve interaction between different points along a time continuum. *Nachträglichkeit*, also translated as 'afterwardsness' by Jean Laplanche, refers to the effect of such interaction.[19] Nicola King explains how *nachträglichkeit* 'makes explicit the fact that memory, operating as it does in the present, must inevitably incorporate the awareness of "what wasn't known then"'.[20] In other words, in a process of stratification later memories and awareness affect retranscriptions of past events.

The etymology of *nachträglichkeit* highlights the close relation it shares with physical displacement or dislocation, since *träglich* suggests 'carry', while *nach*, 'to' or 'after', indicates movement from or to a fixed point.[21] The concept of *nachträglichkeit* helps illuminate aspects of Thomas's poems. His 'Digging ("What matter makes my spade")' forges a connection between physical positioning and awareness or retranscription of the past. Two pipes from different ages laid close together affect the speaker's awareness of each separate pipe, and also their relation to other possible buried pipes or bones:

The dead man's immortality
Lies represented lightly with my own,
A yard or two nearer the living air
Than bones of ancients (p. 99)

The explorations of naming in 'Women he liked' also relate to the effects of *nachträglichkeit*. The poem posits temporal dislocation as a necessary occurrence when naming. The act of naming the lane in the poem is affected by present memories relating to the lane in the past. Similarly, moving on in time, to when the lane no longer exists as a lane and its namer is gone, memories of the past lane are affected and altered by present knowledge of the lane remembered.

Thomas himself observed *nachträglichkeit* at work in the composing process, as in his acknowledgement of the disadvantages of a 'note-book habit'.[22] He commented on the failure of notes to allow for changes in emphasis over time and stated his preference for '[c]ontinuous letters or journals':

> Notes made on the spot are very likely to be disproportionate, to lay undue stress on something that should be allowed to recede, and would do so if left to memory; and once made they are liable to misinterpretation if used after intervals of any length. But the flow and continuity of letters insist on some proportion and on truth at least to the impression of the day, and a balance is ensured between the scene or the experience on the one hand and the observer on the other.[23]

Nachträglichkeit is also relevant to Thomas's examination of acts of memory not yet written down or named. The line 'Remembering again that I shall die' in 'Rain' revolves around the moment when a memory affects a present thought about a future occurrence (p. 105). A similar example occurs in 'The Unknown Bird':

I cannot tell
If truly never anything but fair
The days were when he sang, as now they seem. (p. 55)

'Home ("Not the end")' circles round a nostalgic longing for a non-existent home: 'That land, / My home, I have never seen' (p. 64). Here, too, as noted by Seeber, 'the past and its ills determine the present like an open wound, its remembrance therefore bringing an "impurer pang / Than remembering what was well"'.[24]

Nachträglichkeit, in its combination of references to the past with present knowledge not known then, is inherently belated. The same is true of acts of naming during which temporalities are both displaced and connected. Thomas expressed this by shuttling between tenses relating to past, present, future and conditional realities in *matryoshka*-like tangles of subordinate clauses. In 'The Unknown Bird', intricate shifts in tense and syntax dislocate the names and words used from any one context. These shifts also, however, connect all the different words and temporal realities to which they refer. 'In Memoriam (Easter, 1915)', a four-line poem presented in the form of a commemorative epitaph, switches tense from past to present to conditional to future, as flowers become both celebration and memorial, mourning the loss of those who 'should have gathered them' and serving as their reminder:

> The flowers left thick at nightfall in the wood
> This Eastertide call into mind the men,
> Now far from home, who, with their sweethearts, should
> Have gathered them and will do never again. (p. 80)

TEMPORALITY: IN THE COMPOSING PROCESS

> [The artist] does not work on himself but on that thing which escapes him in so many ways, and never belongs to him until after the event.
>
> Pierre Macherey[25]

For Thomas, *nachträglichkeit* was essential to the drafting process. He criticizes Jefferies's early work because of its lack: 'the [subject-]matter was not yet digested', and deliberately strove for *nachträglichkeit* in his own writing, consistently returning to pieces at a later date in order to rework them into prose or poems.[26] He deliberately cultivated the effect of delayed influence, writing to an external reader who had responded to a draft of *Feminine Influence* that 'I shall keep your letter by me & reproduce it consciously or unconsciously, literally or in digested form.'[27]

Woolf also showed awareness of the role of delayed influence in composing. 'A Sketch of the Past', written concurrently with *Between the Acts* and shortly after she had recorded her 'gulping up [of] Freud', reflects many of Freud's ideas, including *nachträglichkeit*. Briggs notes the investigation in 'A Sketch of the Past' of 'the nature of consciousness, split between "the platform of the present; and the depths of memory"', Woolf writing how the 'past is much affected by the present moment. What I write today I should not write in a year's time.'[28]

Her *Between the Acts* also highlights the need for a significant time lapse between an original stimulus and a resultant attempt at composition. *Nachträglichkeit* is evident in her overt reference to Thomas's discussion of naming in 'Old Man' in the initial version of *Between the Acts*. It is also discernible in the passages describing Miss La Trobe's act of composing a new play: this act seems to coincide with a moment when a tree is suddenly 'pelted with starlings', the starlings' noise linking human language to the environment. However, a closer reading reveals that the reference to the starlings' noise in fact comprises a memory of an earlier experience. There is a significant lapse in time between the actual bird noise and the onset of the composing process. Woolf emphasized this point by including, shortly after the starlings' pelting of the tree, a failed attempt at composition: 'What would the first words be? The words escaped her.'[29] The successful attempt comes after a clear shift in time and location, when Miss La Trobe has moved indoors to a bar. Drinking there, she hears the first words of her play at the same time as she remembers the noise the starlings made. Woolf thus made clear that it is not the starlings' activity but Miss La Trobe's memory of it that heralds and instigates the first words of her new play.

The choice of activity – starlings pelting a tree – and the link between this and memory, time delay and creative compositions echo elements present in Thomas's 'There's nothing like the sun':

> Yet never shone the sun as fair as now
> While the sweet last-left damsons from the bough
> With spangles of the morning's storm drop down
> Because the starling shakes it, whistling what
> Once swallows sang. But I have not forgot
> That there is nothing, too, like March's sun,
> Like April's, or July's, or June's, or May's,
> Or January's, or February's, great days:
> And August, September, October, and December
> Have equal days, all different from November. (p. 102)

The speaker's attempts to recall and celebrate the sun in the various months of the year evoke the effects of *nachträglichkeit*. Different layers of time interact and affect each other. The sun of March and other months is warmed by the memory of November's starling and 'sweet last-left damsons', the detail of the starling's whistling evoking the earlier song of the swallow.

In the notebook source of 'There's nothing like the sun', Thomas made much clearer observations of the connections between different layers of time. He described his current environment through recollections of sunny intervals in the past, bounded by rain, linked with the starling and damsons, the memory of the swallow. The day was as '[s]weet as last damsons on spangled tree when November starling imitates the swallow in sunny interval between rain and all is still and dripping' (p. 259).

In Woolf's *Between the Acts*, delayed interaction between the natural environment and the creative process is evident in both the composition process and performance of memorized lines. When Miss La Trobe's outdoor play is interrupted by the sounds of nature, lines written in the past are silenced and changed by sounds of the present:

> Then the wind rose, and in the rustle of the leaves even the great words became inaudible; and the audience sat staring at the villagers, whose mouths opened, but no sound came.
>
> And the stage was empty. Miss La Trobe leant against the tree, paralyzed. Her power had left her. Beads of perspiration broke on her forehead. Illusion had failed. 'This is death,' she murmured, 'death.'
>
> Then suddenly, as the illusion petered out, the cows took up the burden. One had lost her calf. In the very nick of time she lifted her great moon-eyed head and bellowed.[30]

Woolf's cows link human language and the sounds of the environment: 'The cows annihilated the gap; bridged the distance; filled the emptiness and continued the emotion.'[31] However, they do this after the wind's interruption of the memorized human performance. Spontaneous completion of the human actors' lines by sounds of nature only occurs after a combative situation in which other spontaneous natural sounds drown out the actors' lines. The act in the past, recalled by the memorized lines of the play, is affected by the situation in the present, the actions of the wind and the cows. This prefigures the way the starlings' original act of pelting the tree is affected by Miss La Trobe's memory in the bar. At each stage of the process, there is a significant temporal delay. First, the wind's interruption renders the actors 'inaudible'. Time passes. Then, once 'the illusion [has] petered out', the cows 'continue' the play, acting like Thomas's 'landscape and the air', thinking his thoughts for him.[32]

Miss La Trobe's experience of the starlings, and the similar emphasis in Thomas's 'There's nothing like the sun' on memory's role in creative articulation, suggest that the influence of initial writing conditions tends to be belated. The creative process surfaces only when the initial experience has moved to the peripheries of attention and memory. The image of the starling in 'There's nothing like the sun' hovers above a four-line litany of months' names in which the sun at other times of the year is recalled. There is no need to isolate and illustrate each with a separate image. The memory of the starling in sun in November, itself an imitator of the swallow, although tangential to the sun of March or June, can be linked to them even while it is temporally dislocated from them. In this way it provides a sufficient image that encompasses them all. This effect pulls in more than one temporal direction, since the starling vignette not only recalls and encapsulates the sun of November, but also lends its warmth to the succeeding lines and months.

Thomas's use of provisional, unfinished or peripheral phrases in his titles is striking. Even though, as Longley observes, 'the few poems printed elsewhere in his lifetime prove that Thomas came up with titles when publication loomed' (p. 27), these, too, frequently consist of a fragment of a phrase pulled from the first line of the poem. As a result, while naming the poem, the phrase also creates dislocation between this almost provisional title and the poem itself, as in 'Women he liked'. Perhaps Thomas desired the poem to retain some provisionality and sense of disjuncture or temporal dislocation beyond the end of the composing process, for the completed poem to remain, in other words, as a continuing draft.

While the possibility of redrafting remains open, so does the possibility that dislocation of a draft will result in bringing it closer to the unwritten and unfolding pattern it contains, but of which the writer may not yet be fully aware. A poem not yet identified as a poem allows the writer to continue altering it. Once fixed and viewed as finished, either as a draft or final poem, further changes become difficult and the writer or reader is less able to envision what is not yet written down: the pattern hidden in the burgeoning poem's 'network of response-inviting structures'.[33]

Such a desire to delay recognition of a poem as a poem would necessarily affect the timing of its exposure to a public readership. This occurred with drafts of 'The Trumpet' and 'Lights Out' when Thomas disguised the fact that he was working on poems by running the lines together on the page, thus delaying or even avoiding altogether public recognition of them as poems in his military camp. Thomas was also wary of showing his work to his literary peers: 'I didn't really mean anyone to know about my verses. I have shown them to a few only. But I was keeping them rather secret.'[34] Keeping a developing poem secret, by alteration or rearrangement of parts within it, whether from others' eyes or from the poet's own, not only facilitates the possibility of further redrafting but reduces the loss concomitant with the final completion of a creative act as played out at the end of 'Women he liked'.

Woolf's 'Anon' illustrates this point. The opening lines refer to successive time delays between the huntsman's originating impulse to sing and its linguistic expression. These delays are created by his acts of felling a tree and building a cottage. Further delays are then mentioned as the text charts the history of the progression of literature from bird-song to printed text: 'the silent centuries before the book was printed' and the word is 'later written down, beautifully, on parchment'. Woolf observed that 'Anon is losing his ambiguity. The present is coming visible. Harrison [a contributor to Holinshed's *Chronicles* (1577)] sees the present against the settled recorded past.'[35] Her words are equally applicable to the process of composing an individual poem and the resultant increase in distance between the original referent or impulse and successive drafts.

Woolf's analysis in 'Anon' is useful in understanding Thomas's desire to delay recognition of his poems as completed works. Delay means that the poem not only remains in process but also stays closer to its origins. Similarly, his emphasis on 'unfinish' in his poetry, and his preference for a 'slight something absent' in completed work, represent decisions to remain nearer the source and in process.[36]

An examination of Thomas's drafts shows how a developing poem can first move away from an earlier draft and then, in later drafts, draw nearer to it and, therefore, to the poem's origins. One such instance is evident in the return to a deleted line in the reworking of 'April/July/Glory' into 'July'. Another is evident in the draft of 'A Tale', dated 28 March 1915, printed as an alternative 'Cancelled version' in the *Collected Poems* (1978). 'A Tale' contains the lines:

> In flowerless hours
> Never will the bank fail,[37]

Deletions show that in the line 'In flowerless hours', Thomas previously favoured 'The' and then 'On' over 'In'.[38] Also, placed under the line 'In flowerless hours' is the deleted line: 'Of winter never fail'. Three days later, some of these deletions were reinstated. These are printed as the 'Revised version' in *Collected Poems* (1978):

> The flowerless hours
> Of Winter cannot prevail[39]

In these examples, later drafts act in retrospect as measures of earlier drafts. It is as if the fitness of certain words is best discovered after they have been dropped. The gap these words leave behind serves to ascertain whether or not their presence is necessary.

The first version of a poem, like 'a new art', has no measure. Judgement of it can only occur when it has become past. This will happen either when it has been succeeded by another draft or as a result of temporal dislocation, as when Thomas recorded: 'I roughly finished a book on Pater last Sunday: am keeping it by me to tone it down for a few weeks.'[40]

Woolf described this process in a passage on the history of literature:

> A new art comes upon us so surprisingly that we sit silent, recognising before we take the measure. But, while we have a measuring rod handy, our past[, and] a press that at once applies a standard, the Elizabethans had no literature behind them with which to compare the play, and no press to give it speech.[41]

7

Dislocating Thought

> Time like a lake breeze
> Touched his face,
> All thought left his mind.
> Shinkichi Takahashi[1]

Dislocation of thought can interrupt, interfere or pause sequential thought processes by distracting attention or offering tangential non-logical sequences of thought. It is a distinguishing feature of Thomas's style, which builds on Wordsworth's practice of composing while walking and Keats's open flexible state of negative capability, 'taking hints from every noble insect that pays us a visit'.[2] As Newlyn notes, Thomas 'understood how a relaxed walking pace can stimulate the thinking process' and 'saw analogies between the movement of roads and the way thoughts branch sideways, or pause to take in random and fleeting associations, without losing their sense of direction'.[3]

Like temporal dislocation, dislocation of thought occurs in works in progress and completed pieces. It also affects both writer and poem's eventual readers, and an examination of Thomas's critical observations of the effects of dislocatory elements in poetic composition in other poets shows how his understanding of this helped prepare for his mature poetic attempts.

DISLOCATING: UNTROUBLED BY THOUGHT

> Moment of beauty
> full stopped in its track
> down the exact time is now
> an autumn evening
>
> Motokiyo Zeami[4]

At the time when Thomas was writing, cubist approaches to perspective and modernist writers such as Joyce, Stein and Woolf developed an appreciation of the importance of recognition before judgement into an emphasis on multiple ways of seeing. Stein wrote:

> The need that a picture exist in its frame, remain in its frame was over. A picture remaining in its frame was a thing that had always existed and now pictures commenced to want to leave their frames and this also created the necessity for cubism.[5]

A similar awareness is evident in Wittgenstein's later utilization of the ambiguous duck-rabbit picture as an illustration of aspect perception or interpretive 'seeing as'.[6] Wittgenstein contrasted this with viewing that only emphasized one perspective, 'like a pair of glasses on our nose through which we see whatever we look at. It never occurs to us to take them off.[7]

Woolf's description of encountering a new art by sitting 'silent, recognising before we take the measure' emphasizes how, during this pause of recognition, the process of reading and considered judgement of what has been read is briefly arrested.[8] Pausing allows the reader to take in the network of response-inviting structures embedded in the work of art. Once this pattern has been absorbed, the reader can 'take the measure', assessing how far the completed work fits the pattern it suggests.

This form of dislocation surfaces in the Impressionist and post-Impressionist theories of painting, current in Woolf's and Thomas's time. Monet's painterly advice resonates with Woolf's awareness of the need to recognize 'before we take the measure'. Lilla Cabot Perry recalls:

> I remember his [Monet] once saying to me: 'When you go out to paint, try to forget what objects you have before you – a tree, a house, a field, or whatever. Merely think, there is a little square of blue, here an oblong of pink, here a streak of yellow, and paint it just as it looks to you, the exact color and shape, until it gives your own naïve impression of the scene before you.'[9]

Similarly, Cézanne said to Émile Bernard: 'we must render the image of what we see, forgetting everything that existed before us.'[10]

Woolf's keen appreciation of the new approaches to perception in art is evident in her comment in 'Mr. Bennett and Mrs. Brown' on the post-Impressionist exhibition in 1910: 'In or about December, 1910, human character changed.'[11] Thomas also showed awareness of different ways of seeing. In 1909, he refers in *The South Country* to clarity obtained by recognition without judgement:

> The eye untroubled by thought sees things like a mirror newly burnished; at night, for example, the musing man can see nothing before him but a mist, but if he stops thinking quickly the roads, the walls, the trees become visible.[12]

An ambivalent reference to his 'notebook habit' in a letter to de la Mare dated 9 October 1909 also indicates Thomas's wariness about taking measure too precipitously.[13] 'How I Began' connects this 'notebook habit' to his great self-consciousness regarding his readership. Thomas dated this back to his youth when he 'had in view not the truth but the eyes of elders'.[14] An early letter to Helen also shows his awareness of how self-consciousness when composing encourages judgement before recognition to take place: 'I even think of how I could describe it [a scene in nature], actually while I gaze! how mean! how ridiculous! what prose fancy!'[15]

Hooker connects Thomas's self-consciousness with difficulties found in his prose rhythms: 'Time and again in his prose, self-consciousness breaks in, interrupting its rhythmic movement and concentration. It is at the roots of his problems as a prose writer.'[16] Thomas, too, wrote: 'I am only just learning how ill my notes have been making me write by all but destroying such natural rhythm as I have in me. Criticising Pater has helped the discovery.'[17] Thomas thus clearly depicted self-consciousness as a hindrance to the composing process. He saw it as obscuring the clarity obtained by recognition without judgement and interfering with the 'natural rhythm' of a state 'untroubled by thought'.[18]

In typical dislocatory fashion, Thomas's focus on the creative processes of others reveals much about his own creative processes. As Longley observes, his criticism, 'unusual in being before the poetic event, survives as its best interpreter'.[19] His comments on writers such as Coleridge, Hardy, Pater and Hudson confirm his growing preference for methods of composing involving states 'untroubled by thought'.

In a discussion of Coleridge's theories of composition, Thomas introduced the concept of an 'infinite may' of alternatives in which no single definitive view predominates.[20] Hardy's 'spectatorial position' in 'the increasing abstractness of his style' is criticized: 'if men and women are performing for the entertainment of a god, Mr. Hardy has a seat.'[21]

Thomas's attack on Pater, he told Bottomley, 'helped the discovery' of his own weaknesses as a writer. He saw himself like Pater in his 'self-conscious and mechanical' labour of composition and failure to make room for the indirect non-deliberate influence of 'unknown powers' on his composing processes.[22]

In contrast, Thomas singled out W. H. Hudson as one of the best writers of his age. Hudson's writing gave Thomas 'perfect pleasure, with its edge perhaps a little keener for the faintest touch of envy'.[23] In *The Country*, which Thomas was typing up for publication in the summer of 1912, he discussed Hudson's experience of a 'noon-day pause' from thought, making extensive use of quotations from an essay on the limits of perception by William James, 'On a Certain Blindness in Human Beings'.[24] James had suggested, and Thomas subsequently implied, that the effect of replacing thought with what Hudson had termed a state of '*suspense* and *watchfulness*' inevitably involved a focus on the physical senses.[25] The passage Thomas lifted from James's essay is a quotation James had himself taken from Hudson's *Idle Days in Patagonia* account of days in remote solitude in the country, when, as Thomas put it, 'thought was impossible', Hudson living, as he described it, in a state 'of *suspense* and *watchfulness*'.[26]

As passages are dislocated from Hudson's work to James's essay and then from James's essay to Thomas's book, recontextualizing layers are created. The effects of *nachträglichkeit* are inevitably invoked, 'what wasn't known then' in Hudson's work informing the lifted passages that appear in the writing of James and Thomas.[27]

In *The Country* Thomas also referred to James's emphasis in 'On a Certain Blindness in Human Beings' on the physical base of such experiences. They reside in 'this mysterious sensorial life, with its irrationality'.[28] Earlier, in the same essay from which Thomas was quoting, James wrote: 'The intense interest that life can assume when brought down to the non-thinking level, the level of pure sensorial perception has been beautifully described by a man who *can* write – Mr W. H. Hudson.'[29] The conclusion drawn by both Thomas and James is that a focus on the senses or the 'non-thinking level' is a desirable and even necessary part of the composing process. They also both suggested that interruption of the 'thinking level' or any other activity in the mind facilitates focus on the sensations.

Closer to home, Thomas investigated the effects of focusing on the 'non-thinking level' in the 'Insomnia' passage on composition. He prefaced the account with an emphasis on the senses of sight and sound: 'when the light began to arrive' in 'the song in the enclosed hush, and the sound of the trees beyond it'.[30] In context, this description forms an analogy for falling asleep, the aim of the insomniac narrator. This aim is achieved only in the last lines of the essay, at which point the description of sleep acts, in turn, as an analogy for composition. Crucially, when the writer tries to fall asleep he cannot. When his focus is placed elsewhere, he is successful. This success is accompanied by an awareness of and focus on sensation: 'Gradually I became conscious of nothing but the moan of trees, the monotonous expressionless robin's song, the slightly aching body.'[31] The part played by the physical senses and perception of sensation is key.

A similar trajectory occurs in *The South Country*. Investigations into the language of the land make frequent use of images of physical contact. Marks on the land are 'scars' carved deep within it.[32]

In 'Roads', too, the relationship between hill road and traveller is centred on the experience of being seen and touched. The poem details the perception of light on the wet road and the physical contact between feet and road: the road will not gleam '[i]f we trod it not again' (p. 106).

Thomas was deeply in tune with his physical senses. J. W. Haines recorded:

> [H]e seemed to me to be able to use all the senses more acutely than most people use a single one. The colour of flowers, the form of trees, the tints of dead leaves were no more and no less to him than the sound of water falling or the song of birds. Further they were no more and no less than the scent of newly turned earth, of the wild rose, or the bitter-sweet garden herbs, the grass after rain, or indeed of the taste of an apple. In truth his sensations were sometimes too much for him. [. . .] [T]he flowers, the weeds, the undergrowth, the soil beneath all, he heard every sound and every silence nor could he detach himself from what he saw and heard. Poetry and only poetry could fuse all these sensations[33]

Thomas cultivated this keen sensory awareness as a writer. His notebooks record the sounds, smells and sights of nature. His revelation in a letter on 10 June 1914 to John Freeman that 'I have a crude plan of turning sensations, etc., straight into prose' is played out in his poetry.[34] 'March', which strongly recalls the robin of 'Insomnia' with its invocation of the thrushes' unthinking, 'earnest' production of '[t]heir unwilling hoard of song', begins with a focus on bodily sensation:

> While still my temples ached from the cold burning
> Of hail and wind, (p. 35)

The thought processes of 'Old Man' revolve around the scent of a plant. 'Digging ("Today I think")' opens with 'Today I think / Only with scents –' (p. 79).

Sensory perception occurs in the present, as the first line of 'Digging ("Today I think")' declares. Such focus distracts the mind from past and future eventualities and issues of purpose, aim and intention. Thomas showed awareness of this when he wrote to Bottomley of

> [the] degree of selfconsciousness beyond the dreams of avarice (which makes me spend hours, when I ought to be reading or enjoying the interlacing flight of 3 kestrels, in thinking out my motives for this or that act or word in the past until I long for sleep).[35]

The focus on sensation and the present moment is often accompanied or followed by a sudden realization of thought. This occurs in 'Gone, gone again', where prolonged focus on the physical image of the house results in an almost Joycean epiphany, which, nevertheless, retains a grounding in physical observations, as the qualities of the house, 'Outmoded, dignified, / Dark and untenanted,' are attributed to the 'writer' or speaker. J. P. Ward notes of the crucial line, 'I am something like that:' (p. 132), that 'the writer seems suddenly to surprise and sober himself with his abrupt recognition that he is himself like the old house he is talking about'.[36] The dislocation involved in the formation, recognition and sudden application of an unfamiliar metaphor to a hitherto apparently unrelated object is accompanied by surprise, the metaphor being an apt device with which to create dislocation given its dependence on transport of qualities from one object to another.

'Like the touch of rain' also deals with unexpected realization connected to dislocation of thought. The first verse re-enacts the shift from a focus on the senses to a disjointed and surprised reawakening into thought processes as the subject moves from a physical description of the experience of rain falling on skin to an expression of the writer's relationship with a woman. The realization is stimulated by physical sensation, in this case the sensation produced by the physical 'touch of rain' while on a walk:

> Like the touch of rain she was
> On a man's flesh and hair and eyes
> When the joy of walking thus
> Has taken him by surprise: (p. 118)

'The Word' re-enacts a similar experience. The 'pure thrush word' in the poem 'suddenly is cried out to me' when the speaker's attention is not focused on the song but is 'thinking of the elder scent' or is 'content / With the wild rose scent that is like memory' (p. 93).

'Gone, gone again' and 'Like the touch of rain' make use of deliberations and perspectives that simultaneously undercut and confirm each other. The description of rain in 'Like the touch of rain' and the joy resulting from the unexpectedness of the rain's physical touch also refer to the woman. The speaker talks about the house in 'Gone, gone again', but, equally, the house 'talks', or provides information, about the speaker, who becomes both object and subject.

Since many of Thomas's poems were written very rapidly, often in the space of a day, and their arrival tended to be unexpected, it seems quite obvious that accounts of dislocation in his poetry are likely to involve an element of surprise. However, earlier records show him working hard to reach such a point of surprise. As early as 1909, he exhibited a preference for states conducive to surprise, lack of explanation, unfinishedness and states of mind 'untroubled by thought'.[37] Punning 'mystery' with 'mist', he wrote: 'It is not for me to be "concise, carven, jewelled", my dear Gordon! Mistery is mine.'[38] He confessed his preference, in the opening pages of *The South Country*, to walk without maps, and implied an almost deliberate cultivation of disorientation and surprise in relation to the discovery of place names: 'On a dull day or cloudy night I have often no knowledge of the points of the compass. I never go out to see anything. The signboards thus often astonish me.'[39] In 1910, surprise formed a crucial element in his appreciation of the writing of Noguchi, for a phrase that, making use of 'simple and familiar words [. . .] combines them in a way that gives a shock of astonishing loveliness'.[40] Produced in the same year, 'Mother and Sons', from *Rest and Unrest*, a story collection title that suggests a moment between settled states, also makes strong connections between physicality, a thought-free state and a surprised creativity:

> For the most part I saw nothing and thought of nothing. I was well and warm and pleased by the ring of my shoes upon the rocks of the wild roadways. I was living that deep, beneficient, unconscious life which is what after all we remember with most satisfaction and learn, often too late, to label happiness when the pleasures have all fallen away.
>
> [. . .] I was astonished as perhaps a poet is when he has wrought something lovelier than he knew out of a long silent strife.[41]

DISLOCATING: TOO GREAT DELIBERATION

> If he had one great fault as a poet, it was that he always knew, too well indeed, what he was going to write
>
> Yone Noguchi[42]

In *Feminine Influence*, Thomas developed the point made in 'Women he liked' about failed composition, where the deliberate act of naming results in the failure of that act. He observed how Drayton's composing process suffers from too immediate a state of great deliberation, a state that makes no provision for Hudson's 'noon-day pause', lacks temporal dislocation and bears too great a proximity to its subject.[43] He continued:

> The failure of Drayton's verses directly inspired by his mistress and actually addressed to her, [*sic*] may perhaps be put down to the too great deliberation of his attitude. He was setting out to do what Shakespeare and very few others have done, to make poetry straight out of experience, not merely upon an impulse due to experience. This seems almost to forbid that unconscious ripening of the idea which Keats knew and wished always and exclusively to obey.[44]

Thomas noted 'the superiority of Drayton's poems which either profess to express another's love or deal artificially with his own' and argued for the need to distance the composing process.[45] This keen awareness of the consequences of a lack of 'unconscious ripening' when composing chimes with Thomas's frequent denigrations of excessive self-consciousness, equating his self-consciousness, manifested in a dependence on notes when writing, with obstruction in the composing process. The self-consciousness that note-taking fosters risks destroying his 'natural rhythm'.[46]

In 1913, in response to this awareness, Thomas initiated a method of distancing or dislocating himself as a writer from the composing process. During the composition of what he termed his 'literal matter of fact absolutely unrhetorical autobiography', *The Childhood of Edward Thomas*, he practised deliberate restraint from intellectual interference.[47] R. G. Thomas in *A Portrait*, Andrew Motion in *The Poetry of Edward Thomas* and David Wright in *Edward Thomas: Selected Poems and Prose* have all observed how this actively harnesses Edward Thomas's introspective tendencies, a development that plays a significant part in the onset of his mature poetry.

Thomas explained his method thus:

> I am reconstructing my life from the age of 4 to 16 without using any documents or any other person's recollections. It will depict simply what I *know*, hardly at all what I *think*, of myself, without explanations, or interpretations, or inventions. So far I think it [. . .] is just to record what has not perished. Later on I may get beyond it, but it will become more difficult.[48]

In one paragraph in *Childhood*, successive sentences begin with simple statements drawn from memory: 'Swindon was', 'It was', My aunt was', 'My uncle was', 'He was' and 'I was'.[49] The action stays within the past, uninfluenced by the present perspective. By so doing, Thomas escaped the hierarchy that a qualifying temporal or causal conjunction would have imposed, and avoided the dislocatory intervention or interference of hindsight, reflection or explanation. However, this method circumvents some of the enriching effects of *nachträglichkeit*. The evocation of his childhood is to a large extent devoid of present knowledge of 'what wasn't known then'.

Although intrigued by this experiment, he found the result unsatisfactory. His letter to de la Mare dated 29 May 1914 described *Childhood* as 'a very bald thing in which I have not attempted to do more than record facts. No atmosphere, no explanation. Only the typist has read it & it is not a thing I want seen.'[50] More is needed than simple restraint from thinking. He abandoned *Childhood*, but the lessons learnt play an important role in his later work.

The illuminating investigation in 'Insomnia' of what obstructs and what perpetuates the composing process resonates strongly with aspects of the composition of *Childhood*.[51] The insomniac would-be poet, attempting to fall asleep by making his mind a blank and so escaping from awareness of the dawn and the robin's insistent song, is pushed, unintentionally, by 'an impulse due to experience' into poetic composition: 'Gradually I found myself trying to understand this dawn harmony.' He does not deliberately set out to compose a poem, but is ambushed into a state of mind conducive to composition. Only once the composing process is underway does he focus upon it.

Ambush into creativity, involving dislocation and surprise, surfaced earlier in Thomas's writing, in *The South Country*. In ambulatory prose Thomas noted the value of wandering in a non-linear fashion without maps, 'taking a series of turns to the left or a series to the right, to take much beauty by surprise'.[52] This passage also provides the frame for the poem 'Beauty', where surprise accompanies the discovery of beauty, unexpectedly, at a slant, out of the window of the room in which the poet sits.

In 'Insomnia', the detailed description of the process by which the poet-narrator reaches a state of mind conducive to poetic composition is followed by a demonstration of how such a process can be aborted. As the narrator becomes more intent upon composing and less dislocated from it, 'too great deliberation' sets in. This results in the poem's demise. Thomas emphasized the gradual intensification of deliberation in verbs of successively increasing strength of determination: 'I vowed', 'to make sure' and 'I was resolved'. Untill this point, the narrator's effort of thought, focused on composing, produces the result he intends, but as his effort increases verbs of strong determination are replaced by four successive verbs of compulsion:

> The first line had to be;
>
> nor could I escape from this necessity;
>
> the third and fourth lines, it seemed, were bound to be;

and finally

> I was under a very strong compulsion.

At the point of 'strong compulsion', the composing process suddenly peters out: 'I could do no more; not a line would add itself.' The point is made emphatically. Continuation of fixed focus of thought brings the composing process to a halt.

The fixed rhythm and rhyme of these lines matches the fixed focus of the narrator and reflects the mechanical rhythm of the apparently automatically generated robin's song that inspires the narrator to compose in the first place. The initial lines of the poem are produced in a mechanical manner, but such rigidity fails to sustain the impetus to compose. Unlike the bird, the narrator cannot generate further lines automatically. He also lacks the bird's advantages, as itemized by Hudson, of an aerial stance and hollow bones, which allow its song to dwell physically within the environment from which it emanates. The narrator has to find another way of allowing his own burgeoning song to dwell in the environment. Crucially, in 'Insomnia', after the creative flow runs dry, the narrator, 'as a man, if not as an unborn poet', succumbs to sleep. This eventual success in his original purpose is accompanied by awareness of physical sensations, his 'slightly aching body', implying the importance of dwelling within the body, rather than in a deliberating mind. Once the narrator sets aside his aim of returning to sleep, and is dislocated from it, he achieves it. As with entry into a state of sleep, at the crucial point of the onset of composition, dislocation occurs. Deliberate attentive effort is focused elsewhere. The implication is that the poet, or narrator, will be successful in his initial purpose if he turns his thought away from the process he wishes to initiate or prolong. This can be achieved through focus on physical sensation.

Romantic poets such as Keats and Coleridge evinced a similar interest in composing on the borders of sleep, as in Coleridge's record of composing 'Kubla Khan'. At first sight, Coleridge's experience seems different from that of the poet in 'Insomnia'. Coleridge attributed the halt to his creative flow to the distraction of being woken from sleep and interrupted by a visitor. As a result, the original dreamed poem fragmented into 'Kubla Khan'. However, Elisabeth Schneider points out that 'Kubla Khan' depends on its dislocated fragmented status. The dislocation or distraction

Coleridge reportedly experienced during its composition is crucial to it. Coleridge suggested as much by highlighting the interruptions in composition in a lengthy preface. The content of the preface and the emphasis on dreams and fragments in the title, 'Kubla Khan: or a Vision in a Dream', and subtitle, 'Of the Fragment of Kubla Khan', also indicate an intention to dislocate the piece and broadcast that dislocation. A further consequence is to dislocate Coleridge as writer from the piece, diminishing his responsibility for it and ownership of it, and Schneider's exposure of the unreliability of the 'Kubla Khan' preface as regards information on its composition process in *Coleridge, Opium, and Kubla Khan* further dislocates the writer of the preface from the piece. The effect is not dissimilar to that occurring in Thomas's creative work as a result of his predilection for anonymity.[53]

Coleridge seemed to be playing out the effects of *nachträglichkeit* on himself as well as his work. This is strongly suggested in his unpublished notebooks, where he wrote of a viewer's experience of visual images, supported 'by *the images of memory flowing in on the impulses of immediate impression*', and of how, in relation to nightmares, when an impression is incomplete, '*the imagination . . . the true inward creatrix, instantly out of the chaos of elements or shattered fragments of memory, puts together some form to fit it*'.[54]

Thomas repeatedly emphasized the apparently paradoxical centrality of dislocation in the composing process in his indirect approach to subject matter, as in the remove of the subject of poetic composition from the title of 'Insomnia' and from a large proportion of the essay's content, or as in the apparent lack of relevance of the title of 'Women he liked' to the poem's main subject matter.

In 'Insomnia', the account of composing is squeezed into a few paragraphs near the end, at a point when the subject of insomnia seems firmly established as the main focus. The subject of poetic composition is broached indirectly with a description of successive distractions of attention. This re-enacts the unexpected, interrupting, invisible force of the onset of composing, as well as the dislocation that accompanies it. As a result, the actual onset of the process hijacks not only the narrator but the reader, and the subsequent sustained focus on the progress of composition, its premature demise, the concluding return to the subject of insomnia and the narrator's literal movement into sleep, all reinforce the impression of the marginality of the composing experience both to the narrator and to the essay. Distraction or dislocation of attention is thus shown to be an essential condition of composing, not too focused but not too absent: a principle that can also be applied more widely to computer-generated poetry today or, in Thomas's case, found poetry, as in his approach to the found poem in the valley in 'Beauty', his use of wood names and signs in *The South Country*, and his ubiquitous lists. Marginality is required.

DISLOCATING: DISTRACTION

> as one can see when one has not the habit of knowing what one is looking at
>
> Gertrude Stein[55]

Working under William James in the 1890s, Leon Solomons and Gertrude Stein carried out self-experiments in automatic writing at the Harvard Psychological Laboratory in tandem with James's studies of thought processes. Their findings provide illuminating explanations for the creative effects of dislocation of attention. They also put into context Thomas's uses of dislocation in his poetry, given his interest in James's work and Stein's subsequent focus as pivotal figure, poet, writer and philosopher in the development of literary modernism. Stein's later interests, at the centre of a circle of artists in Paris seeking to develop a fragmented presentation of reality in their writings to parallel effects in Cubist painting, coincided with Thomas's focus on dislocated attention on creativity. They help confirm the modernist tendencies in his writing as identified by critics like Stan Smith in *Edward Thomas* and Stuart Sillars in *Structure and Dissolution in English Writing*.[56] Thomas's focus on dislocated attention and related shifts in spatial and temporal perspectives also prefigured post-Impressionist experiments in this field.[57]

Solomons and Stein's main difficulty when attempting automatic writing lay in the suppression of deliberate writing. Like Thomas defending Garnett's criticism of passages that smelt 'of the lamp', they discovered that premeditated writing is easier to achieve than less deliberate writing:

> there is a general tendency to movement from purely sensory stimuli, independent of any conscious motor impulse or volition. This tendency is ordinarily inhibited by the will, but comes out as soon as the attention of the subject is removed. This tendency to stop automatic movements and bring them under the control of the will is very strong. Nothing is more difficult than to allow a movement of which we are conscious to go on of itself.[58]

They located this difficulty as that of too much attention: 'Our trouble never came from a *failure of reaction*, but from a *functioning of the attention*. It was our inability to take our minds off of the experiment that interfered.'[59]

James had already written on the obstructive effects of too great a deliberation in 1890: 'the object must change. When it is one of sight, it will actually become invisible; when of hearing, inaudible, – if we attend to it too unmovingly.'[60] Solomons and Stein echoed James's stress on movement, or otherwise, of attention in their report: 'these phenomena [of automatic writing] occurred in us whenever the *attention* was removed from certain classes of sensations. Our problem was to get sufficient control of the attention to effect this removal of attention.' Crucially, 'real automatism' or the state in which automatic writing occurs 'comes *whenever the attention is sufficiently distracted*'.[61] This resonates with the composing experience of Thomas's narrator in 'Insomnia'. It begins when his attention is focused elsewhere, on trying to sleep.

James noted the necessity of expending effort when attempting a degree of inattention, observing that the latter can be achieved if attention is continually shifted from one object to another. If the object remains vague and marginal rather than central, then, even if awareness of it is intensified, the attention can escape subjection to what James called the 'lapse into unconsciousness of any too unchanging content'.[62]

Solomons and Stein found achieving inattention in their practical experiments a tricky, skilful manoeuvre. It involved the creation of an artificial division in attention that required the subject of each experiment to attend simultaneously to more than one task. James, too, referred to the need for such a division and the labour involved: 'Practice, however, enables us, *with effort*, to attend to a marginal object, whilst keeping the eyes immovable.'[63] Awareness must remain, or feel as if it remains, focused simultaneously on the central and on the marginal object.

Solomons and Stein also observed the phenomenon of awareness after the event, writing that 'a very distinct stage in the process of becoming unconscious [i.e. able to write automatically] is where we find the word started before we are conscious of having heard it'.[64] James, too, noted in his chapter on attention in *The Principles of Psychology* that

> I myself find that when I try to simultaneously recite one thing and write another that the beginning of each word or segment of a phrase is what requires the attention. Once started, my pen runs on for a word or two as if by its own momentum.[65]

This is similar to Thomas's insomniac narrator's unexpected start to his composing process in 'Insomnia' and to Thomas's own composition experience in 1904, which he described with the word 'blindfold', only seeing a glimpse of what he had written after the event.[66]

Thomas quoted from James's 1901–2 Gifford lectures, to describe, in reference to Jefferies's composition of *The Story of My Heart*, how mystical states of mind 'cannot be sustained for long'.[67] These lectures examine the powerful effect produced by a division in attention in the context of the process of religious conversion. James wrote:

> All the while the forces of mere organic ripening within him are going on towards their own prefigured result, and his conscious strainings are letting loose subconscious allies behind the scenes, which in their way work towards rearrangement; and the rearrangement towards which all these deeper forces tend is pretty surely definite, and definitely different from what he consciously conceives and determines.[68]

Thomas later echoed James's phrase, 'mere organic ripening', as 'that unconscious ripening' of the process of poetic composition.[69] The balance that James described is delicate and easily destroyed. James also wrote:

> It [the 'mere organic ripening'] may consequently be actually interfered with (*jammed* as it were, like the lost word when we seek too energetically to recall it), by his voluntary effort slanting from the true direction.[70]

James was asserting that 'voluntary effort' is a distraction from the process described. In order to continue in a 'true direction', it is necessary to interfere with the interference produced by 'voluntary effort'. This is achieved by dislocating that effort, by slanting attention away from its mistaken trajectory – in other words, by hijacking attention.

A number of Thomas's completed creative pieces hijack the attention in this way. These include the sudden move from the image of cocks as trumpeters to that of the milkers lacing their boots at the end of 'Cock-Crow'; from the subject of women to the naming of a lane in 'Women he liked'; and from insomnia to composing in 'Insomnia'.

James's description of the detrimental effect of voluntary effort can also be applied to Thomas's attempts to articulate marginal or liminal areas of expression. As the trajectory of 'Insomnia' suggests, liminality can only be articulated indirectly, like Solomons and Stein's attempts at automatic writing experiments. This is expressed in many of Thomas's poems. In 'But these things also', line endings split the 'mite / Of chalk', so that the two halves of the phrase are placed, divided, at the extreme ends of succeeding lines (p. 67). 'Beauty' tracks in detail the process by which division of attention furthers the poetic flow during composing. The would-be poet initially attempts to compose an epitaph, a song for the dead, in a stationary fixed position when '[t]ired, angry, and ill at ease' (p. 58). A verb of containment, 'frame', refers to this act, emphasizing the deliberate attempt to enclose the incipient poem inside known boundaries. The epitaph is then abandoned. This is the point reached in 'Insomnia'. However, in 'Beauty', the would-be poet concurs with, rather than struggles against, the demise of the composing process. This leads to success, but only once the aim of writing a poem has been set aside and the attention is no longer focused upon it, expressed with the use of a physical image of divided attention:

> some fraction of me, happily
> Floats through the window even now to a tree
> Down in the misting, dim-lit, quiet vale,
> Not like a pewit that returns to wail
> For something it has lost, but like a dove
> That slants unswerving to its home and love. (p. 58)

The vale, outside the enclosed room, offers an alternative to the initial creative failure. 'Beauty' is out 'there', divided from the poet's physical body in the room:

> There I find my rest, and through the dusk air
> Flies what yet lives in me: Beauty is there.

Significantly, the demonstrative 'there' opens and closes this concluding rhyming couplet, denoting a distant position and also emphasizing the division in the poet's attention, part of which remains in the room and part of which, a 'fraction', is directed towards the vale.

Dividing the attention, therefore, allows the creative process to continue, not lost in too much dislocation and not destroyed by too much concentration. The poet both is and is not involved in the act of creation, surprised by the composing process but also participating in it, an experience Thomas described, in reference to the onset of his mature poetry, as 'this unexpected ebullition'.[71]

Woolf brought this investigation of the subtle interplay between composing, inattention, concentration and dislocation firmly down to the physical level in *A Room of One's Own* with an image of physical movement: 'What idea had it been that had sent me so audaciously trespassing [on a lawn in an "Oxbridge" college].'[72] The physical dislocation enacted by such inadvertent trespassing does not simply reflect the mental dislocation and inattention accompanying the formation of a new idea. The act of trespass occurs because attention is ambushed from the process of walking. Woolf was absorbed, concentrated and, at the same time, distracted from the walk by the idea, and from the idea by the walk. The attention shifts between them, providing no opportunity of focusing for a prolonged period on either.

The relevance of this to Thomas is expressed neatly in Frost's 'The Road Not Taken', which offers a thinly veiled portrait of Thomas hesitating between paths, a characteristic he exhibited both as walker and writer. A semi-colon and stanza break signal the moment at which he is distracted from taking one path by the opportunity presented by the other:

> Two roads diverged in a yellow wood,
> And sorry I could not travel both
> And be one traveler, long I stood
> And looked down one as far as I could
> To where it bent in the undergrowth;
>
> Then took the other,[73]

James also showed awareness of a link between mental and physical activities, suggesting that meaningless movements when thinking in transit possibly 'draft off the stimulations that interfere with thought'.[74] Thomas enacted this in his frequent practice of note-taking and drafting poems in transit. His physical movement as a walker or on a train was a form of dislocation. Even poems written during physical incapacitation did not preclude travel, as exemplified by the imagined swoop to '[t]he tops of the high hills' in 'The Lofty Sky' (p. 53). Thomas experienced the process of poetic composition as both driving and ambushing trains of thought and, crucially, as occurring when he was in physical transit: 'It [composing poetry] has perhaps become a really bad habit as I walk up the hill [from his home to his study] and I can sometimes hardly wait to light my fire.'[75]

The fact that the only comments he appended to poem drafts relate to dates of composition, modes of transit, starting points and, most often, destinations of journeys on which the drafts were composed indicates his awareness of the significant influence of dislocatory conditions on his work. This dislocatory influence is revealed in the composition conditions of his poems alluding to the subject of war. They were all created while he was still in England. In contrast, when at the front and no longer physically separated from the action and effects of war, he recorded that 'I doubt even if I can write – I am practically certain I can't, except a brief diary.'[76]

DISLOCATING: TANGENTIAL AWARENESS AND THE READER

> Digressions, incontestably, are the sunshine; – they are the life, the soul of reading! – take them out of this book, for instance, – you might as well take the book along with them.
>
> Laurence Sterne[77]

In 1897, Freud wrote of the difficulties he encountered when researching his own dreams: 'my self-analysis remains interrupted. I have realized why I can analyse myself only with the help of knowledge obtained objectively (like an outsider). True self-analysis is impossible.'[78] He dealt with this by distancing himself from the dream and writing about it 'like an outsider', dislocating himself as observer from himself as dreamer.

Woolf picked up on Freud's approach in 1939, noting, 'Began reading Freud last night; to enlarge the circumference. [*sic*] to give my brain a wider scope: to make it objective; to get outside.'[79] She also referred, in 1940, to a practice that echoes Freud's 'outsider' stance. She called it a 'sidelong approach', writing, in reference to her literary articles, that the 'surface manner allows one, as I have often found, to slip in things that would be inaudible if one marched straight up and spoke out loud'.[80] This approach dislocates the reader from parts of the piece. This could be an external reader or Woolf herself looking back on earlier work, like Freud when researching his dreams. The parts from which the reader is dislocated slip neatly past any censoring eye straight into awareness.

Coleridge adopted a similar 'sidelong approach' in his titling of and preface to 'Kubla Khan'. The way he presented this dream-inspired piece encourages what Schneider calls an 'impressionistic approach', in which readers 'are apt to read it with but half-conscious attention'.[81] As Jack Stillinger has observed:

> It has persuasively been argued that, were it not for this introductory prose, we would never know that the poem ['Kubla Khan'] was a fragment. The introduction controls our reading from beginning to end: without it, the poetic lines emphasize creativity and inspiration; with the introduction, contrariwise, the lines emphasize the poet's *failure* at creativity.[82]

Stillinger suggests that the emphasis on '*failure* at creativity' is deliberate.[83] Coleridge's 'purposeful authorial intertextuality' results from a shift in role from writer to 'critic *and interpreter* of what he had initially created without a plan, and now, in these subsequent pages of writing, *added authorial intention* that was not consciously present in the original composition'.[84]

Thomas parodied such shifts of role in *Feminine Influence* when he qualified and reinterpreted Coleridge's definition of the artist as one who 'must imitate that which is within the thing'. His initial apparent endorsement of Coleridge, then immediately destabilized by replacing the original authoritative 'must' with 'infinite may', ensures that readers experience, as they read, the dislocating uncertainty that he was propagating.[85]

The passage quoted in *Feminine Influence* is preceded in *Biographia Literaria* by a reference to the 'process of desynonymizing words originally equivalent'.[86] In a sense, Thomas, in his use of Coleridge in *Feminine Influence*, was also practising desynonymization, exposing the 'infinite may' of possibilities behind Coleridge's apparently singular 'must'. Similarly, in his own work, Thomas's sidelong, desynonymizing *matryoshka*-like asides ensure that what might otherwise appear homogenous is seen as actually and perhaps essentially unstable. His use of multiple personae, reported speech within reported speech, narrators retelling stories told to them by others, also result in multiple printed versions of the process of regeneration that occurs in oral literature. These devices add further levels of complication to his work, desynonymizing or de-simplifying their structure.

Another effect of Thomas's use of series of reported accounts is to distance him as writer from the content of his prose. Accounts of what has occurred in the past are retold in the present, subject to the vagaries of memory. This contributes to the effect of *nachträglichkeit*, making Thomas into an external reader of his own work, as if coming new to it.

Such dislocation of creator from created piece, whether poetry or other artistic media, and the consequent effects of *nachträglichkeit*, were examined by Woolf: 'word conscious; an artist; aware of his medium; that words are not paint, nor music; but have their possibilities; their limitations. To be thus aware the writer must have a past behind him.'[87] Her use of 'past' refers to a writer's literary printed heritage, but her comments are also applicable to a writer's relation to past drafts of a particular poem.

Thomas viewed such dislocation of the writer from the work as necessary for its development. In a letter to de la Mare dated 21 March 1915, he referred to himself in the third person as if an external commentator, and as if preparing himself to be his own reader by proxy on receipt of the anticipated feedback from de la Mare:

> I am sending you some verses by a very young poet (not a young man) who desires to remain anonymous except to you & one or two other people. Don't mention them anywhere, as they are to be published (if at all) under a pseudonym. He is coming to town next week & hopes to see you & remains Yours ever E.T.[88]

For feedback to be of value to Thomas, his external readers also needed to retain distance from the text. He helped them achieve this by withholding information on the poems he sent to them: 'I will not instruct you further. I am keen to know just how they come to you.'[89] He also used pseudonyms when publishing his poetry to ensure that previously known information about him would not impinge on reactions to the poems. A similar motivation helps explain his reluctance to title poems with words indicating their subject matter.

Woolf saw it as crucial that an artist has awareness of her material as separate from her so as to provide a measure of the work. She also saw such a method of achieving a measure of a work as important for that work's critics: '[disengaging] the song from the effect of the audience becomes as time goes on a task for the critic'.[90]

In 'The Brook', as in 'Old Man' and 'The Mill-Pond', Thomas delved deep into the writer's experience of dislocation from a developing work by exploring the contrast between adult and child perspectives on a scene. A child's unconsidered response allows for an illumination that otherwise evades the more self-consciously aware and linguistically articulate adult (pp. 96–7). In contrast, the adult narrator names with deliberation and is detached, 'watching' the child and the scene. Crucially, he is 'thus beguiled', a description that implies both entertainment in his activity as observer of the scene and deception resulting from that entertainment. The child, however, paddling and in motion, speaks from no motive. Her act of naming is not differentiated from her experience but comes from within it. The effect is very powerful. The adult narrator's musings on physical and sensorial perceptions such as the sound of running water, the child paddling, birdsong, the silence of a flycatcher and the awareness of the bodies buried in the nearby barrow are all dislocated by the child's voice, which is both 'raised' and also 'raised the dead'.

This dislocation does not merely halt the adult narrator's attempts to compose a description of the scene. By offering a fresh perspective it furthers the adult's composing process. The child's interruption allows the adult to share in a perspective that he could not form alone. Crucially, she brings illumination not for herself but for him, since he is able to observe the perspective knowingly in a way that she cannot. The power of her perspective resides in its lack of knowingness. Unlike her, the adult narrator can dislocate himself from his process of observation and observe it. This allows him to recognize what her voice articulates in a way that she cannot. His facility for great deliberation, self-consciousness and awareness of physical sensorial perceptions, combined with the dislocation her voice provokes, result in a further development of perspective and continuation of the composing process, to encompass, in the final lines of the poem, all the perspectives tracked so far:

> And what I felt, yet never should have found
> A word for, while I gathered sight and sound. (p. 97)

The effect the child's remarks have on the natural scene, raising 'the dead', are echoed in the effect that they have on the narrator. They also re-enact a reader's response to a poem, which can raise or unearth hitherto unrecognized levels of meaning.

In the case of the child, her 'unself-consciousness' comes from her total immersion in the scene. Unlike the narrator, she is not trying to articulate it. Readers other than the writer are of course already detached from the drafting process. As a result, they can more easily immerse themselves in the poem and let go of their awareness of its craft, whereas the writer, often acutely aware of the need for further amendments, finds such immersion difficult. Thomas recognized this in 'The Brook', addressing the final lines, which deal directly with the process of finding words, to the readers of the poem. The speaker admits to them not only his lack of all-knowingness, since he 'never should have found /A word', but also suggests that they, his readers, know at least as much as he does.

As 'The Brook' demonstrates, the very difficulty of a writer's position, caught in the tangle of past and present knowledge, can also enrich a poem. Thomas implied this in a letter to Farjeon in November 1915 in his reference to a sense of gradual rejuvenation: 'By the time I am a sergeant I shall be really young I suppose. I wish I had gone on where the Proverbs left off. Probably I never shall, unless "Lob" is the beginning.'[91] These words encompass Thomas's indulgence in ludic experimentation with shifts and dislocation of conventional expectations and adaptations of the vernacular in *Blackbirds* and 'Lob' and his aim of acquiring a more childlike 'really young' attitude of mind with its concomitant permission to play. This is reflected in his personal delighted observations of his youngest daughter's experiments with language, song and rhythm in 1914 and his persistent critical appreciation of such qualities in other poets, writing of Noguchi in 1910: 'He was foreign as a child is. Indeed, his poetry had much of the quality of children's speech, in its freedom from rule and its inaccuracy.'[92] The words in the letter to Farjeon also point to his discovery of the enriching if dislocatory effects of *nachträglichkeit*, played out in the letter in his use of the future tense, which connects the reference to a 'really young' approach, as if a child, with hopes of promotion to the responsible adult position of sergeant.

This letter to Farjeon also confirms his recognition of dislocation as a crucial creative force throughout the composing process. This clearly stems from his absorption of the discoveries made by James, the concomitant explorations of Freud and developing changes in perception of the modernist era. He saw dislocation to be as necessary to the composing process as focused self-aware deliberation, whether such dislocation is produced by shifts of attention and the 'time lag' effects of *nachträglichkeit*, the influence of writing conditions and readers' feedback, or the awareness of the present moment and immediate physical sensation.

8

Divagations

> I am going to try and be just about the lines you have marked in 'Pewits', though I am not sure whether you question the form of them or the 'divagations' of the idea, but probably the latter – if only I could hit upon some continuous form as you suggest! I doubt if it will come by direct consideration.
>
> Edward Thomas[1]

The frequent incidence of dislocation in Thomas's poems is accompanied by a focus on physical sensations and movements in the present moment, and also on the movements of thought, of expatiation. He called these movements 'divagations', and made use of them to achieve a sense of resolution in his work.

FOCUS ON: DEVELOPING DIVAGATIONS

> One is unable to notice something – because it is always before one's eyes.
>
> Ludwig Wittgenstein[2]

Tracking divagations in thought requires sustained and flexible attention – what Andrew Motion calls 'open-minded wariness'.[3] 'Insomnia' provides a useful exploration of the issues involved, showing how lack or excess of attention halts the composing process. Thomas possibly wrote this essay while he was working on his *Keats*, and certainly the influence of Keats's theory of negative capability is palpable in it. As for achieving and retaining the delicate balance of control and flexibility of attention necessary to continue the composing process so abruptly halted in

'Insomnia', Thomas showed that this required effort and skill, working at it throughout his life.

His fondness for divagatory thought is possibly rooted in his walking habits, particularly his propensity for sauntering, as explored by Newlyn in her essay in *Branch-lines: Edward Thomas and Contemporary Poetry*. When walking, he let environmental conditions lead him, 'guided by the hills or the sun or a stream'.[4] He valued Jefferies's work for resembling 'the record of an actual walk, closed up so as to avoid barren stretches, and of whatever is seen and thought in the course of a walk.[5]

This predilection for divagations comes to the fore in his critical writings. A note to his anthology, *This England*, states that 'indirect praise is sweeter and more profound'.[6] A letter to Frost, criticizing an early version of 'The Road Not Taken', runs: 'There. If I say more I shall get into those nooks you think I like.'[7]

His criticism also makes practical use of divagatory techniques. He referred frequently in the review of one writer to the work of another. While praising Frost's *North of Boston*, he criticized other writers for their 'old-fashioned pomp and sweetness' and 'the later fashion also of discord and fuss'.[8] Even when addressing the intended subjects of a review, his approbatory comments often centre on their propensity to wander:

> Messrs Davies and de la Mare alone have penetrated far into the desired kingdom, and that without having been certain of their goal or of their way, or possessing any guide or talisman known to anyone but themselves,

and, with regard to Pound's *Personae*:

> part of our pleasure in reading the book has been the belief, in which we are confident, that the writer [Pound] is only just getting under sail, that he will reach we know not where; nor does he, but somewhere far away in the unexplored.[9]

Thomas's poems, too, are built up out of divagations. His words track the multiple possible extensions and reversals of thought processes, repeating and circling round an idea, and resisting logical or sensory heuristic leaps.

Critics recognize these qualities as characteristic of his work. Longley names Thomas the 'master of inversion'. She lists at length the qualifiers and negatives in his writing as it moves through a 'complicating resistance of clauses that begin "Even", "At least", "And yet"'.[10] Smith refers to his 'labyrinthine syntax', describing him as looking 'Janus-faced at every threshold in opposite directions'.[11]

Thomas's deliberate cultivation of divagations in order to circumvent the detrimental effects of too great deliberation in creative composition becomes particularly evident in the writing of *Childhood*. His approach here has many connections with Freud's writings on divagations of thought. Freud wrote, when looking at dreams, of

> trains of thought which proceed from more than one centre, but which are not without points of contact; and almost invariably we find, along with a train of thought, its contradictory counterpart, connected with it by the association of contrast.

These words from the *The Interpretation of Dreams* (1899) can easily and usefully be applied to Thomas's writing style, and very appropriately so since the composition of *Childhood* coincided with Thomas's most probable exposure to Freud's ideas as a patient of Baynes in 1912 and 1913. Certainly, the approach Freud adopted when analysing dream thoughts bears startling similarities to Thomas's approach to thought processes. Freud described his method as 'dropping all the directing ideas which at other times control reflection, directing our attention to a single element of the dream, noting the involuntary thoughts that associate themselves with this element'. In his 'Recommendations to Physicians Practising Psycho-Analysis' (1912), he explained this practice further:

> It consists simply in not directing one's notice to anything in particular and in maintaining the same 'evenly-suspended attention' (as I have called it) in the face of all that one hears [. . .] the rule of giving equal notice to everything.[12]

When writing *Childhood*, Thomas, too, veered away from 'directing ideas' to highlight involuntary and associative thought patterns, his aim being 'daily to focus on some period and get in all that relates to it, allowing one thing to follow the other that suggested it'.[13]

FOCUS ON: MECHANICAL PROCESSES

> I am but mad north-north-west: when the wind is southerly I know a hawk from a handsaw.
>
> *Hamlet*, Shakespeare[14]

Describing *Childhood*, Thomas emphasized focused attention and restraint: '[It is] the briefest quietest carefullest account of virtually everything I can remember up to the age of 8.'[15] Control is most carefully controlled – present but not excessive. Such balance is in stark contrast to the debilitating effects of over-control described in 'Insomnia' in its exploration of the risks of inflexibility, resistance to change and a mechanical 'great deliberation' when composing creatively.[16] It contrasts, too, with

Pater's 'self-conscious and mechanical' work with 'nothing in it which was beyond his control', and Hardy's 'spectatorial position' as a writer.[17]

The balanced control aimed at in *Childhood* is also distinct from the unself-conscious acts of birdsong of Thomas's poetry and 'Insomnia'. The birds in 'She dotes' show no emotional engagement with a 'loverless' woman. They 'sing and chatter / Just as when he [her lover] was not a ghost', crying their song '[o]ver and over'.[18] In 'The Green Roads', while an old man, a child and the poet-speaker give detailed views of the forest, the 'thrush twiddles' in mid-poem and is then seen to 'repeat his song' in the last stanza (pp. 128–9). This act of birdsong is key to 'The Green Roads', as Longley observes when she interprets the poem as enquiring 'of itself whether it parallels the thrush's repetitive 'twiddle', or whether it evinces a finer capacity to see, hear and remember'.[19]

'Insomnia' clearly links the narrator's over-focused attempt at poetry composition with the robin's unself-conscious act of song. They share a rigidity of rhythm. Both are described as mechanical products, suffering from over-repetition, fixed rather than free expressive acts, and ultimately detrimental to the composing process. The repetition of lines from the narrator's attempted poem, which 'return again and again to my head', hinder poetic progress, even while they enable sleep: 'It was fortunate for me as a man, if not as an unborn poet, that I could not forget the lines; for by continual helpless repetition of them I rose yet once more to the weakness that sleep demanded.'[20] Similarly, the robin's song, accompanied by a complete lack of deliberation, is habitual, bound, fixed in time, and unchanging. Like Caxton's printing press fixing 'the voice of Anon for ever', the mechanical acts of song and failed poetic attempt block further creative development.[21] Later, in his war diary, Thomas extended this suggestion of birdsong as mechanical to bird flight, using it to evoke the flight paths of war-planes: 'four or five planes wheeling as kestrels used to over Mutton and Ludcombe'.[22]

Thomas's emphasis on the mechanical quality of bird song is accompanied by descriptions of the birds' limited perception of their song and lack of focused engagement with it. Just as the thrush might 'twiddle' and 'repeat' in 'The Green Roads', so the sedge warblers are heard 'reiterating endlessly' in 'Sedge-Warblers', while in 'Roads' the thrush cock sings '[b]right irrelevant things' as the dead return from France (pp. 128–9, 91, 107). Similarly, in 'March', the thrushes 'cared not what they sang or screamed', and in 'If I were to own' the 'proverbs untranslatable' of birdsong are as untranslatable for birds as for humans (pp. 35, 115). In 'The Word', birds sing 'an empty thingless name', and in 'The Unknown Bird', birdsong is empty, intangible and inaccessible, the speaker recording that the bird's 'La-la-la! was bodiless sweet' while the bird itself remains 'wandering beyond my shore' (pp. 93, 55).

These evocations of birdsong stress the distance between maker and product, but also between product and listener, evoking Thomas's reference in his letter to Helen on 21 June 1897 to his own difficulties in engaging with birdsong. 'The Unknown Bird' also highlights the physical dislocation between bird and human listener, and shows how the listener's distance from the world that birds inhabit and their song can contribute to the song's powerful effect. The bird sings high in the trees, the air, or across a lake, far away, often singing where a human listener cannot follow physically. Possibly alluding to Hudson's analysis of the aerial quality of birdsong in *Idle Days in Patagonia*, the birdsong is described as 'bodiless', thus distinguishing it from human song (p. 55). It offers a precious glimpse of what is otherwise beyond the listener's reach, of what cannot be articulated.

The implied analogy with poetic composition in 'The Unknown Bird' is spelt out more plainly in 'Insomnia'. The narrator's difficulty with composing, and his previous reluctance to participate in the experience of dawn, are paralleled with the robin's relation to his song: 'I was an unwilling note on the instrument; yet I do not know that the robin was less unwilling.' The successive emphases placed on the mechanical quality of birdsong, on the difficulty of reinterpreting it as a poem, and on the tendency to adopt fixed rhyme and rhythm can be read as explorations of the inaccessibility of poetry, and the extent to which the responses of those hearing or reading songs or poems depend on the singer's or poet's engagement with their work.

In 'Home ("Often I had gone")' the listener 'and the birds that sang' are momentarily and, unusually for Thomas, united. They share '[o]ne memory'. However, they also share a lack of awareness of or distance from the passage of time: 'they knew no more than I / The day was done' (p. 81). The listener only exits the continual cycle of birdsong when another perspective is introduced: his perception of a labourer walking past with 'tread / Slow'. This labourer is unlike the birds and the listener. Less absorbed in but more careful of his surroundings, he is very aware, 'half with weariness, half with ease', that '[t]he day was done' (pp. 82, 81). Also, he is more engaged than the careless birds with the sound he makes. The description of his sawing emphasizes the passage of time and, in contrast to the birds and their listener, of actions brought to a completion:

> The sound of sawing rounded all
> That silence said. (p. 82)

A specific adverb of time, '[t]hen', marks the transition in this poem from the listener's absorption in the birds' mindless song to the more detached observation of the labourer working attentively at his craft. The detailed physical perception of the solitary labourer's movements and particulars of his external environment as he treads slowly 'past his dark white cottage front' are written in the simple past tense, which, like 'then', attaches the experience to one period of time. In contrast, the listener's description of birdsong is redolent with shifting tenses, indicating the hindsight and confusions inherent in *nachträglichkeit* rather than a direct focus upon present birdsong:

> now it seemed I never could be
> And never had been anywhere else;
> 'Twas home; one nationality
> We had, I and the birds that sang,
> One memory. (p. 81)

The listener, when with the birds, participates in their absorbed experience of their song, but can only describe it at a later point in time. He is more detached when he is observing the labourer. He is also more immediately aware of the labourer's movements and environment. His detachment reflects and is reflected in the labourer's specific awareness of his craft as he plies it. It is in fact the labourer's present awareness of his actions that draws the attention of the listener. It startles him from absorption in the birdsong and enables him to break out of the impasse in which he is caught as the ever-revolving cycle of birdsong is followed and completed with the sound of the labourer's sawing.

The sound of the labourer's craft begins, ends and works with a silence that denotes its absence. This silence is crucial, denoting the absence of sound, which comes 'through the silence from his shed' and also rounds 'all / That silence said', both shaped by and shaping it, carving out an end or coda to the birdsong, the day and the poem. The 'sound of sawing' encompasses the silence that surrounds it and, it is implied, silence encompasses the poem, forming a setting for the words presented on the page. The labourer's engagement with the sound he makes and his aware, controlled attention to every movement of his sawing affect the perceptions of the poem's audience. His attention to every moment, including the beginning and the end of the sound and movement of sawing, allows the poem, the birds, the listener, and the poem's eventual reader, to move out of an apparently endless cycle of birdsong into a conclusion of silence. In contrast to the apparently endless and overwhelming absorption in birdsong experienced by the listener, the labourer, through attentive focus on the particular activity of sawing that 'rounded' the poem, encompasses all perspectives, as the use of 'rounded' suggests. This focus is not however simply set in opposition to the birdsong. The repetition of 'silence' in the third last and last lines, surrounding and penetrating the sound of sawing, indicates the need for obliqueness in this form of attention, for lack or absence, if completion is to be achieved.

The etymological antecedent of 'saw' is saying, story or saga. This possible reference to oral storytelling, which depends upon the storyteller's vivid fluid engagement with the performed story and listening audience, reinforces the implication that, unlike birdsong, the labourer's immediate non-mechanical control of his saw represents the equivalent of a flexible creative act.

Like Thomas, William James contrasted directed specific and flexible attention with chain-like mechanical habit. Using italics to emphasize the effect of habit on attention, James drew on the image of a monotonous and repetitive 'chain of little thin notes':

> *habit diminishes the conscious attention with which our acts are performed* [. . .] habit soon brings it about that each event calls up its own appropriate successor without any alternative offering itself, and without any reference to the conscious will, until at last the whole chain, *A, B, C, D, E, F, G,* rattles itself off as soon as *A* occurs, just as if *A* and the rest of the chain were fused into a continuous stream.[23]

Thomas resorted to a similar image when describing birdsong in 'Insomnia'.

Later in *Principles of Psychology*, James prefigured, in his italicized phrase 'things are *really being decided*', Thomas's depiction of the labourer actively sawing in the moment in 'Home ("Often I had gone")':

> The whole feeling of reality, the whole sting and excitement of our voluntary life, depends on our sense that in it things are *really being decided* from one moment to another, and that it is not the dull rattling off of a chain that was forged innumerable ages ago.[24]

Parallels to James's 'sting and excitement of voluntary life' are also present in Thomas. In 'The Brook' and 'The Mill-Pond', Thomas described the effect of unique perceptions and actions of specific moments in time on experiences of absorption in the natural environment and birdsong. Individual and non-mechanical child and girl voices have a startling effect on a narrator's experience of an apparently idyllic scene. The scenes that they interrupt involve a blend of the natural environment and birdsong. In 'The Mill-Pond':

Less than the cooing in the alder
Isles of the pool
Sounded the thunder through that plunge
Of waters cool. (p. 56)

and in 'The Brook':

I was thus beguiled.
Mellow the blackbird sang and sharp the thrush
Not far off in the oak and hazel brush,
Unseen. (p. 96)

Sharp or mellow, the birdsong inhabits its environment, beguiling its listeners and recalling Hudson's emphasis in *Idle Days in Patagonia* on the importance to birdsong of details of the environment in which it is sung: wind, trees, height and air.

In contrast to the songs of birds, the voices of the young people in 'The Brook' and 'The Mill-Pond' are directed to particular occasions. They are specific, exact, focused. Detailed, timely and striking, they have an interruptive effect on the speakers and poems, paralleling the effect produced by the labourer's sawing in 'Home ("Often I had gone")'.

The sharp effect of the individual and non-mechanical human voices of a child and a girl in Thomas's poems evokes Nietzsche's distinctions between the 'not-striking' quality of 'purity' and the 'impure' in language in lecture notes first published in the Kröner edition of his works in 1912. Nietzsche referred to 'pure' as 'positively the customary usage', where 'the "impure" is everything else which attracts attention in it. Thus, the '*not-striking*' is that which is pure.'[25] For Thomas, too, what is pure is 'not-striking'. Birdsong is an 'empty thingless name', a 'pure thrush word'(p. 93), whereas, as in the effect of the humanly crafted sound of sawing in 'Home ("Often I had gone")', the exactness and specificity of human voices in 'The Brook' and 'The Mill-Pond' are striking, and therefore 'impure' in Nietzsche's terms. They do not blend and inhabit. They are not blithely at home. They jar, strike or jolt awake, heralding changes in pace, mood and direction that help form the resolution to each poem. They also mark an end to the absorbing experiences of the natural environment and birdsong recorded in each poem, shaping them and bringing them to a close.

FOCUS ON: DIRECTED ATTENTION

> I don't pretend not to have a regular road and footpath system as well as doing some trespassing.
>
> Edward Thomas[26]

'Home ("Often I had gone")', 'The Brook' and 'The Mill-Pond' show the power of an exact focused and directed attention in the process of composition. Thomas extended this in 'The Gypsy' to the tracking of divagatory thoughts, exploring and openly acknowledging the limits of a writer's abilities, rather in the manner of the *matryoshka*-like asides in works such as *The South Country*. By means of divagatory techniques, he celebrated the gypsy's superior powers of articulation, teasing out the effects on the composing process of retaining close connections with the land.

The gypsies inhabit their environment by living close to land that has been discarded by modern civilization. Their '[v]ans were drawn up on wastes' (p. 58). Their itinerant way of life, contrasting with the changing effects of civilization and less nomadic styles of living, is presented as relatively permanent: the gypsy musician's 'glance / Outlasted all the fair, farmer and auctioneer' (p. 59). Unlike the poet, who is 'a ghost new-arrived', the gypsy musician's sparkling eyes and noisy music dominate the scene. Modern civilization, with its fairs, sovereigns and Christian religion, seems comparatively insipid: 'Not even the kneeling ox had eyes like the Romany' (p. 59). When one of the gypsies barters with the poet, she prefers to trade with things rather than with money, accepting 'half a pipeful of tobacco' in exchange for her vivid conversation, her 'grace / And impudence in rags' (p. 58). As Longley observes, quoting Peter Howarth on 'the possibility of hearing Thomas's hexameters as having four or six stresses or both', the resultant 'stumble in this transaction [. . .] is as if, the gap between price and value thus exposed, dealings with nomadic people can never be commensurable on both sides' (p. 189).[27]

The poet cannot keep up with the gypsies. His attempts to 'translate to its proper coin / Gratitude for her grace' are cut short as the gypsy darts 'off and away', and the words that issue from the poet's 'dipping' pen are, it is implied, a poor alternative to the rich vernacular of the gypsy sister, the folk song or the drumming and stamping of the gypsy brother as he plays on a folk instrument, the mouth organ:

> I paid nothing then,
> As I pay nothing now with the dipping of my pen
> For her brother's music (p. 58)

However, the admitted inadequacy of the written word can be seen also as a mark of its success. It allows Thomas's work to retain an impression of absence. The fullest possible representation in words of the 'grace' of the gypsy involves and includes an acknowledgement of the inevitable failure of such an attempt. Such honesty makes room for the gypsy to act as the writer's amanuensis, peopling the landscape for him. As a result, despite the poet's admission of the shortcomings of his divagatory explorations of the gypsies' creative prowess in conversation, the poem still holds its own vigour, drawn from what John Lucas calls the 'dancing measure' of the gypsies' song.[28] As Longley phrases it, the poem's 'climax of liberating abandon' combines hexameter couplets with 'folk verses' and 'gypsy idioms' (p. 189):

> That night he peopled for me the hollow wooded land,
> More dark and wild than stormiest heavens, that I searched and scanned
> Like a ghost new-arrived. The gradations of the dark
> Were like an underworld of death, but for the spark
> In the Gypsy boy's black eyes as he played and stamped his tune,
> 'Over the hills and far away', and a crescent moon. (p. 59)

The reference to the folk song, 'Over the hills and far away', evoking the gypsies' own itinerant lifestyle, is then followed by the arrival of 'a crescent moon', as if the gypsies move in melodic counterpoint to a lunar or seasonal cycle in lines that declare through their rich and powerful use of rhythm, imagery and rhyme the successful result of Thomas's directed attention to negative as well as positive aspects of the composing process.

Both 'Home ("Often I had gone")' and 'The Gypsy' invert Thomas's 'Reading out of doors' (1903) vision of the writer's environment playing a dominant role in the creative experience of reading a book. In these two poems, the labourer's craft and the gypsy's song act upon the environment, silencing the birdsong and peopling for the writer 'the hollow wooded land' (p. 59). In contrast to the experience of reading, the poems show how the experience of composing involves a symbiotic relationship between the environment and the human voice or craft, each modulating the other.

This modulation is also present in the allusions to negative and positive aspects of composition. In 'The Gypsy', negative remarks about the writer's abilities are accompanied by exact attention to detail. In 'The Child on the Cliffs', a precise image: 'the grasshopper works at his sewing-machine / So hard' questions and mocks the writer's powers of articulation (p. 65). In both poems, these negative references are swiftly followed by very powerful expressions of energetic articulation and successful imaginative renderings. 'The Gypsy' ends with an ecstatic dancing rhythm that evokes the music the poet could not otherwise fully describe. 'The Child on the Cliffs' sees the child leave the 'book to the grasshopper' and move on to interpret the 'more strange' invocatory sounds and sight of the sea – the beckoning foam that 'curls / And stretches a white arm out like a girl's'. Then, with a beautiful suggestion of the power of multiple perspectives, the loving mother's voice responds to the child, pointing out the sweet call of the bell from the buoy to the boy.

The trajectories in 'The Gypsy' and 'The Child on the Cliffs', from the effort and discomfort of initial negative experiences of composition to triumphant creative success, resonate with Solomons and Stein's experiences in initiating automatic writing. Although they reported it as being very difficult to attain, they also wrote that, once successful, 'the first thing to disappear is the feeling of effort'.[29]

While composing requires the exactness of a directed attention, it also involves an attention that undergoes successive breaks in flow. Such breaks are created in 'The Gypsy' and 'The Child on the Cliffs' by the sudden switches from negative to positive. They are also evident in the curious enjambment shifts in mood in 'The sun used to shine'. In 'Insomnia', too, the onset of the composing process, when the narrator's focus switches from attempting to fall asleep to attempting to compose, is marked by a paragraph break, a clear indication of disconnection:

> But as fast as I made my mind a faintly heaving, shapeless, grey blank, some form or colour appeared; memory or anticipation was at work.
>
> Gradually I found myself trying to understand this dawn harmony. I vowed to remember it and ponder it in the light of day[30]

The simple past of '[g]radually I found myself', the phrase after the paragraph break, shows that at this point creative activity has already started. However, the reflexive 'found myself' suggests that the narrator has only now become aware of his creative activity. Its initial onset has passed him by. There has been a break in the flow of attention. Other breaks in attention are indicated in the oscillation, before the paragraph break, between 'I' and 'memory or anticipation', and between a 'grey blank' to 'some form or colour'. Despite the apparently divagatory description of thought processes, breaks in thought still remain, the attention leaping continually from one point to the next.

Thomas observed a similar phenomenon in the conclusion of his essay, 'This England', later subtly reworked into the structure of 'The sun used to shine', in which the rough junctures in thought processes or series of disconnected 'strokes', as they are described in 'This England', become the enjambement shifts in tone between stanza breaks in the poem. 'This

England' also suggests other conflicting processes: 'at one stroke, I thought' and 'I was deluged, in a second stroke, by another thought, or something that over-powered thought.'[31]

Although, unlike the fixed deliberation that brings the composing process in 'Insomnia' rapidly to a halt, an associative divagatory flow instigates or furthers the process of creative composition, this is not to be confused with the smooth run of words that occurs in automatic writing. Divagatory techniques embrace disconnections, leaps and switches in subject matter and mood. Thomas made this clear in the last lines of 'The long small room'. The image of a hand crawling like a crab over the page is strongly suggestive of Solomons and Stein's description of automatic writing as 'not he but his arm that is doing it'.[32] However, 'The long small room' swiftly leaps from this 'crab-like' continuous writing activity to an apparently unrelated image of falling leaves:

> this my right hand
> Crawling crab-like over the clean white page,
> Resting awhile each morning on the pillow,
> Then once more starting to crawl on towards age.
> The hundred last leaves stream upon the willow. (p. 137)

A flexible and open divagatory tracking of thought moves the poem on from the smooth continuity of 'crab-like' writing to the unexpected and powerful image of the willow. This divagatory tracking is framed by abruptness: a quick turn in thought introduces it and the poem's ending silence completes it. Thomas was keenly aware of this effect, referring in a letter to Farjeon to a 'switch' and 'sort of Japanesy suddenness of ending', and concluding with words that indicate his awareness of the need for breaks in attention and a sense of absence of self when composing: 'I will think of it as much like somebody else as possible.' His crucial revelation to Farjeon that he actually began composing the poem by working backwards from the powerfully and creatively vibrant concluding line turns the whole composition process of this poem into an exploration of the creative quality of disconnected associative thought: 'I started with that last line as what I was working to.'[33]

In Thomas's work, sudden reversals from negative to positive tones are often accompanied by a sense of release, freedom, intense thrill or joy. The subject of this joy tends to be the composition process.

Joy is not a word usually associated with Thomas, but it is clearly present in his letters in the gleeful delight with which he recorded the immediacy of his poetic compositions after twenty years of failing in and believing he was incapable of writing verse. It also occurs in his poetry. In

'Like the touch of rain', a feeling of joy is accompanied by surprise and by exact flexible attention on the present and on physical perceptions. This attention is focused by and on the touch of rain. Intense awareness of physical senses and physical sensations are bound up with a release of joy:

> On a man's flesh and hair and eyes
> When the joy of walking thus
> Has taken him by surprise: (p. 118)

This connection between joy and physical sensation, a delighted alertness in the physical present in a state of heightened awareness, contrasts sharply with the trance-like state associated with Solomons and Stein's 'definite motor reactions unaccompanied by consciousness' – in other words, automatic writing. James made the connection in his emphasis on the importance of sensuous experience, accompanied by alert attention, which then results in a feeling of happiness: 'this mysterious sensorial life, with its irrationality, if so you like to call it but its vigilance and its supreme felicity'. Woolf's *Between the Acts*, too, shows awareness of the power of strong physical sensation when composing, as revealed in Miss La Trobe's ambitions for her outdoor play: 'She wanted to expose them, as it were, to douche them, with present-time reality.'[34]

FOCUS ON: CONTROL AND FLEXIBILITY

> The flickering, fickle mind, difficult to guard, difficult to control – the wise person straightens it as a fletcher straightens an arrow.
>
> Gautama the Buddha[35]

The need for flexible present awareness when composing suggests an a-hierarchal a-chronological approach that, in Thomas's case, bears relation to the fragmentation of contemporaneous modernist writers and what they saw as the invigorating and new aesthetic of Japan. Such writing can be said also to have come out of a response to a sense of general malaise in a time of waning religion and of political and social uncertainty, when in literature, as in other disciplines, old sureties were being questioned and found wanting. As Stan Smith points out, it also connects with the effect of depopulation of rural areas:

> A displaced mass, dislocation of the old culture, the restructuring of social life demanded by the town, the decline in real wages and the growth of unemployment during the first decade of the century ushered in an epoch which Thomas

> described, in a review in the *Daily Chronicle* on 13 January 1908, as 'a centrifugal age, in which principles and aims are numerous, vague, uncertain, confused, and in conflict.'[36]

However, it would be misleading to tie such an approach to composition too definitively to the conditions of a particular period or the personal composing habits of a particular poet. Thomas's reference to 'a centrifugal age' looks back to Coleridge's *Biographia Literaria*, part of which is quoted in *Feminine Influence*. Coleridge wrote:

> If in the midst of the variety there be not some fixed object for the attention, the unceasing succession of the variety will prevent the mind from observing the difference of the individual objects; and the only thing remaining will be the succession, which will then produce precisely the same effect as sameness. This we experience when we let the trees or hedges pass before the fixed eye during a rapid movement in a carriage, or, on the other hand, when we suffer a file of soldiers or ranks of men in procession to go on before us without resting the eye on anyone in particular. In order to derive pleasure from the occupation of the mind, the principle of unity must always be present, so that in the midst of the multeity the centripetal force be never suspended, nor the sense be fatigued by the predominance of the centrifugal force. This unity in multeity I have elsewhere stated as the principle of beauty. It is equally the source of pleasure in variety, and in fact a higher term including both.[37]

This passage seems to inform Thomas's 'Tears', where a day when 'twenty hounds streamed by' and are 'made one, like a great dragon', succession becoming sameness, is juxtaposed with 'that other day' and a more precise evocation of the weather, 'an April morning, stirring and sweet / And warm'. Similarly, a description of '[s]oldiers in line' takes the time to detail their hair, complexion, clothing and the music that has the startling effect of 'piercing that solitude / And silence' (p. 52).

Similarly, Coleridge's 'unity in multeity' foreshadowed James's reference to things '*really being decided* from one moment to another'. For James, each moment has its particular and individual focus but is also linked to other points in time through continual temporal progression and human beings' sense of this, which provides 'the whole sting and excitement of our voluntary life'.[38]

Coleridge's 'unity in multeity' also steered Thomas's interest in fragmented work. Discussing *The Happy-go-lucky Morgans* with de la Mare, Thomas stressed the importance for each 'fragment' in a work to play a part also in contributing specifically to that work, actively shaping it:

> I should like to know if you think there are cul-de-sacs or broken threads which could be opened out or joined up. I hope it was not a collection of

> shapeless fragments tho I know they were fragments – a not impossible compromise between a continuous fiction and a Leftaineronish group. However, the point is that I don't want to leave in things that are useless in their place.[39]

The letter continues with an extraordinary passage that holds within its words and orthographical layout the substance of Thomas's poetics. By enumerating the qualities he was attempting to avoid in his writing, he elucidated his intention to create both fragmentation and firmness of shape and form:

> Of course I should like to
> know just what you think
> useless
> incomplete (excessively)
> obscure
> inconsistent
> Has it in places a private
> character in a bad sense ,
> preventing readers from sharing
> my knowledge , real or pretended?
> Does the tendency to be continuous
> in the last few chapters (about
> Philip) only show up the
> //
> mass without that tendency? [40]

The list of items to avoid, and in particular the bracketed 'excessively', reflects Thomas's appreciation of balanced, tempered and not too 'incomplete' use of 'unfinish'; of not 'inconsistent' dislocation; of not 'obscure' elliptic and aporetic obliquity and absence; and of definite vagueness that does not simply 'show up the mass'. All these qualities are informed by his sensitivity to the need for reader-accessibility, which, of course, motivates the whole import of this passage to de la Mare, a regular reader of Thomas's draft works. Thomas emphasized that to achieve such accessibility requires care, steering clear of 'a private character in a bad sense' and avoiding shapelessness when binding fragments loosely together with associative logic. In addition, he was wary of his own 'tendency to be continuous'.

The balance he was working towards is evident in the structure of the 'Insomnia' essay. Unlike the mechanical works of the insomniac narrator and the robin, the essay appears loosely woven, even as it skilfully links the two subjects of entry into poetic composition and into sleep. *Matryoshka*-like, the essay shifts the focus between topics while also connecting them. At times a topic seems tangential to the main text, tentative and marginal. At times it appears to usurp it. Mutual validation is achieved by means of interconnecting allusions, creating a sense of complex rootedness as the divagations become an indirect description of the process of attempting to fall asleep, while also tangentially and astutely forming an observation of the composing process. By indirection, directions are found out.

Freud's reference in *The Interpretation of Dreams* to an attention both directed and 'dropping all the directing ideas' bears a similarity to the emphasis Thomas placed on balance between control and flexibility. Freud also discussed the importance of the associative and converging qualities of dream-thoughts. The former constitute 'a real point of intersection, where very many trains of thought contributing to the dream converge', while offering multiple possibilities of interpretation. Freud expressed this by drawing on an image from Goethe's *Faust* that combines elements of constancy and change with connectedness and shifts in movement:

> This is where we find ourselves in the middle of a thought-factory where, as in the weaver's masterpiece,
>
> Ein Tritt tausend Fäden regt,
> Die Schifflein herüber, hinüber schiessen,
> Die Fäden ungesehen fliessen,
> Ein Schlag tausend Verbindungen schlägt.
>
> ('One thrust of his foot, and a thousand threads
> Invisibly shift, and hither and thither
> The shuttles dart – just once he treads
> And a thousand strands all twine together.')[41]

These thoughts had powerful currency among writers in the early twentieth century. In her novel-biography, *Orlando* (1928), Woolf drew on the same passage in *Faust* to explore the associative qualities of the mind and memory, rewording as if describing the stitching movements of a needle. She prefaced this with an image of the mind as a patchwork of fragments and hiatuses, 'a perfect rag-bag of odds and ends', which, in its turn, evokes Yeats's 'foul rag-and-bone shop of the heart', and Thomas's reference to patching up old articles when working on *The Book of the Open Air*.[42] Woolf wrote:

> [Nature] has contrived that the whole assortment shall be lightly stitched together by a single thread. Memory is the seamstress, and a capricious one at that. Memory runs her needle in and out, up and down, hither and thither. We know not what comes next, or what follows after. Thus, the most ordinary

> movement in the world, such as sitting down at a table and pulling the inkstand towards one, may agitate a thousand odd, disconnected fragments, now bright, now dim, hanging and bobbing and dipping and flaunting, like the underlinen of a family of fourteen on a line in a gale of wind. Instead of being a single, downright, bluff piece of work of which no man need feel ashamed, our commonest deeds are set about with a fluttering and flickering of wings, a rising and falling of lights.[43]

Woolf's 'in and out, up and down, hither and thither' emphasizes the multi-directional but seamless movement of Goethe's 'one thrust of his foot' and 'a thousand threads'. Goethe's 'thousand strands all twine[d] together' was for Woolf not one 'single, downright, bluff piece of work' but disjointed, accompanied by 'a fluttering and flickering of wings', the 'thousand odd, disconnected fragments' of associative links that each movement may 'agitate'. She hinted at the importance of rhythm as a constant core, holding together multiple divergent movements to form a contrapuntal whole. This resonates with Thomas's delighted observation of his young daughter Myfanwy's complete transposition and rearrangement of the words and notes of 'John Peel' in which some lines 'are better than ever', while Myfanwy retained 'only the tune and the metre'.[44]

Thomas used sewing imagery in 'The Child on the Cliffs' but, unlike Woolf, he stressed mechanical rather than hand-driven sewing. The duty-bound grasshopper's toil at the sewing machine expresses not the multiplicity of thought processes but the diametrically opposed movements of too great deliberation. Nevertheless, this image indicates, as do the images of Woolf, Freud and Yeats, the specific resonances of this view of mind processes in the early twentieth century, resonances that were far-reaching as indicated by the way that the highly regarded Japanese poet, Shinkichi Takahashi, born in 1901, wove Goethe's image into his poem 'Stitches':

> With that bamboo needle
> She knits all space, piece by piece,
> Hastily hauling time in.[45]

Lucien Stryk's decision to translate 'Stitches' and publish it in 1997 is an indication of how this image also appeals across time.

Closer to the present day is my own use of the same image in *The Drier the Brighter* poem 'patched work'. This poem, consciously inspired by Woolf's use of Goethe, was, like all *The Drier the Brighter* poems, composed as part of the practical research that underpinned the writing process of the present book, acting, therefore, as additional proof of the powerful influence of environment and tangential dislocatory activity on composition processes, particularly since the poem was written before I had realized the significance of the re-use of Goethe's image to this present discussion of composition:

> was it at that point that the seamstress was asked
> to line language with things?
>
> her needle ran hither and thither
> with no time to cut patterns
> sewing whatever was nearest to hand.[46]

The reappearance of Goethe's image across cultures and periods suggests the high importance of the ideas it holds about control and flexibility or sameness and variety in composing and related thought processes, and the high importance also of rhythm. Thomas's description of *The Happy-go-lucky Morgans* as 'fragments' and Woolf's emphasis on the disjointed quality and the wealth of associations that accompany even the 'pulling of the inkstand towards one' serve as indicators of the literary cultural context in which they both wrote. However, like other poets' reworkings of Goethe's images, these passages also demonstrate the delicacy required in the interplay between control and flexibility in poetic composition, best achieved through continual readjustments of attention rather than the unmoving attention that James warned against or the too great deliberation that Thomas deplored.

FOCUS ON: BEATING THE BOUNDS

> As he listened,
> Mindlessly,
> The eavesdrops entered him.
> Zenji Dogen[47]

At the heart of Thomas's use of divagations in composing is a process of continual readjustment of attention. This involves a shifting perception of the framework of a developing poem. It also consists of an awareness of boundary, of the effects of single, multiple, enveloping and blurred perspectives and of exactness of attention.

Thomas particularly used repetition to beat the bounds within which the exact attention of the writer, and reader, is set. J. P. Ward notes how such repetition tests the limits, not only of intellectual thought, but also of language:

> To repeat is to return and find it surviving.
>
> I take it that these repeats express the finitude of a man's reaching and accepting the bounds of his own thinking, in a way analogous to repeat-phrases like 'a sociology of sociology' and 'the meaning of meaning' in more explicit disciplines. A barrier in intellectual penetration is reached so that, with nothing further to add, we start using the same words again, as though someone were to bump into an invisible perspex frame and begin to notice the doubling-up of his or her own footprints.[48]

Such 'doubling-up' occurs in the repetition of place names in 'Lob': ''Twas he first called the Hog's Back the Hog's Back' (p. 77). It surfaces, too, in the meditations on plant names in 'Old Man'. Simultaneously they move on from a citation of different names of a plant and return to them, as if beating the bounds of humanly achievable knowledge and articulation:

> Old Man, or Lad's-love, – in the name there's nothing
> To one that knows not Lad's-love, or Old Man, (p. 36)

Thomas also used this kind of repletion to extend the boundaries of language. In 'October', the second 'day' in the line 'Some day I shall think this is a happy day' is distinct from the first, and yet each informs the other (p. 101). The vague 'some day', located at an indeterminate point in the future, is contrasted with the more specific 'happy day' of the present moment, but that 'happy day' is only considered happy in hindsight. Thus, the repetition contributes to a reinterpretation and redefinition of what has already been said, shifting the boundaries established by the previous use of 'day'. The altered position and context of the word when repeated provides a new perspective from which to view its twin. Each mutually qualifies the other. No one perspective suffices.

Longley observes how Thomas's multiple rhythms of metre redefine the boundaries of his divagations, transforming and complicating 'traditional metres by feeding them the roughage of speech', as in the 'swinging speech rhythms of "The sun used to shine"'.[49] A similar phenomenon is at work in his aporetic *matryoshka*-like syntax. In 'Out in the dark', what Ward terms the poem's 'invisible perspex frame' and the area that is framed both shift in the last line when the aside '[i]f you love it not' switches the focus of the poem from fear to love of dark (p. 139).

Multiple perspectives also have the effect of blurring exact boundaries of interpretation. In 'Beauty', the area focused upon moves from the room to the valley. The perspectives from which these two locations are viewed parallel two possible approaches to composition, while the poem in its entirety comprises a third approach. Each measures and redefines the others, just as the poem's title, 'Beauty', is used in the piece to refer to the 'poem' found in the valley. Such shifts in perspective and plays on words evoke the ambiguous Japanese *kakekotoba*, a prime device for expressing the indefinite and inconstant nature of boundaries. Paradoxically, however, the blurring of boundaries is only effective if accompanied by exactness. This could include the precise definition of the sawing of the labourer in 'Home ("Often I had gone")' that 'rounded' the silence and the poem (p. 58), or the eventual sharpened awareness of the narrator at the end of 'The Brook' that interweaves the previous perspectives of child and adult narrator with the perspective of the reader.

Inversions of perspective or shifts in frames of reference offer the potential for further readjustments beyond the perspectives directly accessible to the writer. In 'Out in the dark', in the line, 'Stealthily the dark haunts round', the darkness becomes the subject of the poem instead of, and as well as, the area beyond its boundaries (p. 138). There is a sense of bounds being beaten from without as much as from within. This is drawn out more explicitly in Thomas's earlier work, *Oxford*:

> Underneath the shrubs the gloom is a presence. The interlacing branches are as the bars of its cage. You watch and watch – like children who have found the lion's cage, but the lion invisible – until gradually, pleased and still awed, you see that the caged thing is – nothingness, in all its shadowy pomp and immeasurable power. Seated there, you could swear that the darkness was moving about, treading the boundaries.[50]

The content of the dark, which he deliberately resisted naming in this passage, is invisible. Consisting of unperceived and unarticulated areas of 'nothingness', it is inaccessible and its boundaries can only be framed from the outside, by the naming of areas that the writer and reader can perceive. In a manner similar to the effect created by shifts of tone in the stanza breaks of 'The sun used to shine', the focus on shifting perspective makes the gaps and absences in and around the printed text as important as the printed text.

FOCUS ON: ENVELOPING PERSPECTIVES

> the subject advances into utterance through certain precautions, repetitions, delays, and instances whose final volume (we can no longer speak of a simple line of words) turns the subject, precisely, into a great envelope empty of speech
>
> Roland Barthes[51]

In 'On a Certain Blindness in Human Beings', James wrote:

> Neither the whole of truth nor the whole of good is revealed to any single observer, although each observer gains a partial superiority of insight from the peculiar position in which he stands. Even prisons and sick-rooms have their special revelations.[52]

Thomas echoed James's sentiments, using a physical image to represent an isolated man's mind and so suggesting that the limitations resulting from a single perspective connect as much with physical as mental perceptions:

> Everyone must have noticed, standing on the shore, when the sun or the moon is over the sea, how the highway of light on the water comes right to his feet, and how those on the right and on the left seem not to be sharing his pleasure, but to be in darkness.[53]

However, such a statement is tempered by his admission in *Walter Pater* of the superficiality that can come with a multiplicity of views and widening of perspective in relation to articulation and communication:

> [M]en understand now the impossibility of speaking aloud all that is within them, and if they do not speak it, they cannot write as they speak. The most they can do is write as they would speak in a less solitary world. A man cannot say all that is in his heart to a woman or another man. The waters are too deep between us. We have not the confidence in what is within us, nor in our voices. Any man talking to the deaf or in darkness will leave unsaid things which he could say were he not compelled to shout, or were it light.

Earlier in *Walter Pater*, he alluded to the rapid increase in audiences for printed material, referring to John Earle's discussion on the effect of newspapers on prose. Thomas's awareness of this new and diverse audience was also informed by his contribution of several volumes to the popular Modern Biographies Series, People's Books and Traveller's Library. In *Walter Pater*, he suggested that a wider audience rendered prose more superficial and limited the extent to which the writer could 'say all that is in his heart'. He reinforced this with a subsequent reference to the possibility of a more select audience of 'one or two', a limited few 'who can enter that solitude and converse with him' of all that is within.[54]

His exploration of multiple physical and spatial perspectives in 'The Watchers' implies an awareness of such diverse audiences but also a refusal to simplify because of this. The poem, as the plural 'Watchers' indicates, experiments with several perspectival shifts between multiple viewers. The man who watches his horse down in the water is watched by a watcher, himself watched by the eye of a stuffed fish in the inn. At the start of the poem, the perspective of a conventional external narrator appears to act as the dominant view, but this is then undercut with a series of perspectives, triggered in the fourth line by the word '[w]atching' (p. 119). Once the initial external viewpoint is abandoned, the poem never returns to it, leaving it hanging and undermined.

It is unusual for Thomas to establish an authoritative point of view in his poetry and this is possibly why he chose not to include 'The Watchers' in his *Poems* (1917). Most of his poems avoid adopting privileged external narratorial positions or undermine them more directly. Instead, each poem, or the areas the poem borders but does not articulate, provides several points of reference for the various exploratory journeys that occur. 'Thaw' contains dizzyingly complicated perspectival shifts from the writer to the birds and back, and from spring to winter to spring, but it is held as one, bound by strong irregularly placed rhythms and rhymes.[55] The uncertain seasonal transition, the 'speculating rooks' and the multiple perspectives offered all combine in the end-, mid- and part-rhymes of 'half-thawed', 'cawed' and 'saw'. A disorientating switch in height is also encapsulated in rhyme, the poem moving from its starting point in the 'snow' on the land up to the rooks and then looking down on 'we below' (p. 114). The readers are guided to view the scene from two perspectives: the perspective of the elevated rooks but also, because of the first person plural, the perspective of the people below. A similar effect occurs in 'Fifty Faggots', where, as Smith puts it, the speaker 'occupies no privileged position outside the narrative. Rather he is situated within it, aware that he shares this situation with other creatures.'[56] No one perspective dominates. All affect each other. It is impossible to disentangle them.

This predilection for multiple perspectives is also evident in Thomas's complicated textures of tense, in his disquisition on the effects of naming in 'Women he liked', and in his description of overwhelming absorption in birdsong in 'Home ("Often I had gone")'. It occurs, too, in his presentations of kinetically experienced events, an approach that seems to reflect the burgeoning medium of film at that time, proleptically foreshadowing the possibilities offered by digital, animated and interactive poetry. The speaker in 'The Barn and the Down' walks through the poem, 'the great down in the west / Grew into sight' and 'the barn fell to a barn' (pp. 68–9). Smith articulates the effect as follows: 'The landscape is no mere canvas against which to parade a self-contained passion, but a three-dimensional space into which the speaker moves.'[57]

There is no record of Thomas's direct contact with Paul Cézanne's work. However, the continually shifting ground created by his divagations and the resulting blurring of specific linguistic and semantic boundaries and single perspectives parallels Cézanne's and the Impressionists' approach to ways of seeing, as in Cézanne's use of the image of an all-encompassing envelope in his advocation to Émile Bernard in 1905 to 'draw; but it is the reflection which *envelops*; light, through the general reflection, is the envelope'.[58] Joyce Medina describes Cézanne's approach as an effacement of 'the hard distinctions between inside and outside', writing of Cézanne's still-life objects that

> by drawing the oscillating ellipses of the rims with multiple contours, he blurred the exact boundary between the object and the space surrounding it. Thus, within the 'halo' of outlinings, a shape emerged from, and at the same time merged with, the spatial envelope in which it was in flux.[59]

In another letter to Bernard, Cézanne referred to the importance of the unfinished quality of his 'envelope' approach:

> Now, being old, nearly 70 years, the sensations of colour, which give the light, are for me the reason for the abstractions which do not allow me to cover my canvas entirely nor to pursue the delimitation of the objects where their points of contact are fine and delicate; from which it results that my image or picture is incomplete.[60]

This encourages further parallels with Thomas, both artists perceiving the result in creative work of blurring and unfinishedness to be a more accurate and fuller rendering.

The post-Impressionist Camden Town Group was active in London between 1911 and 1913, at a time when Thomas made frequent visits to the capital. It is not clear whether Thomas ever met them, but his approach to perspectives and boundaries resonates with contemporary post-Impressionist extensions of Impressionist ways of seeing to conflations in the realm of time and abolitions of traditional presentations of multiple perspectives.[61]

Woolf's discussion of different approaches to novel-writing in 1919 is very pertinent here. She not only made use, like Cézanne, of the image of an envelope, but her reference to a chain-like 'series of gig-lamps' bears strong similarities to James's and Thomas's images of habitual attention as a chain, thus suggesting that her envelope represents the same flexibility of directed attention as that seen in Freud's analysis of dream-work, James's analysis of thought processes and Thomas's writings on poetic composition. She writes: 'life is not a series of gig-lamps symmetrically arranged; life is a luminous halo, a semi-transparent envelope surrounding us from the beginning of consciousness to the end.'[62]

FOCUS ON: SPIRALLING

Turning and turning in the widening gyre
William Butler Yeats[63]

When Thomas focused in his poems on an 'envelope' approach of multiple temporal and spatial perspectives, he placed emphasis upon process. In accordance with this, despite constantly shifting divagations, his poems rarely strain for conclusions. Exact reference points remain, but he exploited the limited perspectives of his individual speakers, moving beyond them. He placed fragmented visions firmly within a fragmenting world, showing acceptance of multiplicity and an ability and willingness to relax into indeterminacy. Divagatory movements confidently inhabit the poems. In their multiple exploratory journeys, they offer one certainty: that nothing is certain. This unhurried and open acceptance of alternatives evokes Thomas's earlier work with place names in *Richard Jefferies, his Life and Work*, where names are used both temporally and geographically in a spiralling recitation that approximates the physical positioning of the places that they denote on the landscape. As the recitation continues, the names move in ever-widening spirals around Jefferies's childhood home, recreating for the reader in the present an imaginative landscape of the past. Such an approach contrasts strongly with the difficulties Thomas identified in *Exaltations of Ezra Pound* where he saw Pound being 'pestered with possible ways of saying a thing'.[64]

Spiralling movements from exact physical or personal reference points out into indeterminacy were endemic in literature and literary composition in the early twentieth century. Writers of this time exhibited fascination with the flexible open-endedness that spirals offer. They seemed also, proleptically, to anticipate impending chaos, very apposite in the run-up to one or other of the two world wars. Woolf used them, not only in her re-evocation of the fluttering movements around the fabric of Goethe's 'Weaver' and 'surrounding' envelope, but in her diary, written while absorbed in reading Freud in 1939: 'Ideas pullulate, but escape when I try to catch them here. Freud is upsetting: reducing one to whirlpool, & I daresay truly.'[65] Similar images appear in Wyndham Lewis's pre-First World War whirling vortices and Yeats's post-First World War 'widening gyre'. Looking further afield and further back in time, spirals were also identified by Pound in 1914 in the traditional medieval Japanese Noh dramas to which he himself, Yeats and Thomas's friend and collaborator, Bottomley were so strongly drawn:

> I am often asked whether there can be a long imagiste or vorticist poem. The Japanese, who evolved the hokku, evolved also the Noh plays. In the best

> 'Noh' the whole play may consist of one image. I mean it is gathered about one image. Its unity consists in one image, enforced by movement and music.[66]

Earlier still Jefferies made use of a quasi-spiral in *Wild Life in a Southern County*, published in 1879. He wrote in the preface of his difficulty in separating the lives of the different animals and birds he wished to write about from each other and from their habitats. To solve this he arranged the chapter titles and content so that they correspond in some degree to the contours of the country described: 'commencing at the highest spot, an ancient entrenchment on the Downs has been chosen as a starting place from whence to explore the uplands'. The chapters then follow a stream downhill, past a village, a solitary farmhouse and 'finally come the fish and wild-fowl of the brook and lake; – finishing in the Vale'.[67]

Thomas's spirals in the first chapter of *Richard Jefferies, his Life and Work* can be seen as a considered response to Jefferies. Jefferies moved simply from the highest to the lowest point in the land that he covered. Thomas, when retracing Jefferies's physical and imaginative homeland, intensified Jefferies' movement into a spiral, adding extra dimensions. He spiralled round from west to east, up north and down south, and then into an inner circle from west to east again. While Jefferies traced the interconnectedness of the various living beings and the land on which they live, Thomas also highlighted the space that divided them, referring, at the end of a list of geographically connected villages, to the vast tracts of downs and anonymous 'scattered' farms that lie between the spiralling lines that he has recorded. Thomas's movements thus result in an open-ended, unfinished journey: 'the villages of Wanborough, Liddington, Badbury, Chisledon, Wroughton, Broad Hinton, Ogbourne, and Aldbourne, with the downs and scattered farms between.'[68]

The trace of a spiral also appears in Thomas's 1914 and 1915 poems, as in the downward movement of 'The Lofty Sky':

> The tops of the high hills,
> Above the last man's house,
> His hedges, and his cows, (p. 53)

and in the speaker's oscillating reflections on the plant in 'Old Man' as he whirls through conflicting emotions: 'The herb itself I like not, but for certain / I love it' (p. 36). It is evident, too, in the expansion in 'Adlestrop' from the single point of the station name and the linear line of a platform on a railway line to the spiralling flight through 'Oxfordshire and Gloucestershire' (p. 51). Highlighting this deliberate cultivation of spirals, John Bayley notes how in the final version of 'Adlestrop', Thomas 'abandons the short choppy sentence structure' of the two first stanzas to create the smoother movement of a spiral heralded by a moment that seems to emulate the eye of a storm: the 'enveloping stillness which succeeds the contrasts. The full stop is taken out; the grass, flowers and hay united, as it were, with the stillness of "the high cloudlets in the sky".'[69]

Seeber, too, observes how in 'Adlestrop', an 'expanding circle' connects 'the observing speaker with a place', showing the poet 'engaged in a conscious act of bridging the gap between himself and an imagined rural community which is here present in names and unseeable birds'.[70]

FOCUS ON: LACK OF CONCLUSIVENESS

> The imaginary recreation and the trace on the sand which is all that remains of the wind itself
>
> Jonathan Bate[71]

Spirals are repetitious but not exactly so. They evoke seamlessness and continuity, but also suggest a lack of conclusiveness. They are, therefore, a very apt form of movement for Thomas, allowing him to express his acute awareness of the overwhelming amount of material available to him, material that does not fit into any ordered manmade structure. This is an awareness that several Thomas critics have commented on. Longley reads the list in the poem 'November' as showing 'Thomas's anxiety to fill in the whole picture: "Twig, leaf, flint, thorn, / Straw, feather, all that men scorn"'.[72] Smith notes how 'A Tale' is 'replete with history, offering everywhere fragments'.[73] Smith also interprets a passage from the opening chapter of *The Heart of England* as presenting 'the paradoxical fullness of meaning which turns into emptiness'.[74] This passage, discussing the way streets evade taxonomy, shows Thomas clearly recognizing the potentially obliterating effects of an abundance of new material:

> Streets are the strangest thing in the world. They have never been discovered. They cannot be classified. There is no tradition about them. Poets have not shown us how we are to regard them. They are to us as mountains were in the Middle Ages, sublime, difficult, immense; and yet so new that we have inherited no certain attitude towards them, of liking or dislike. They suggest so much that they mean nothing at all. The eye strains at them as at Russian characters which are known to stand for something beautiful or terrible; but there is no translator: it sees a thousand things which at the moment of seeing are significant, but they obliterate one another.[75]

Smith also emphasizes the impression of emptiness or obliteration in the 'series of self-cancelling voices' in 'The Signpost', and notes, when discussing 'It rains', that 'a large number of Thomas's poems open thus, with a negative construction in the first sentence which inserts absence right into the heart of an achieved and actual world'.[76] Bayley, in his discussion of 'Adlestrop' and 'Old Man', talks of the 'diminishing of perspective into nothing'.[77] Hooker refers to Thomas's italicized phrase '*There is nothing left for us to rest upon*' in *The Country* as support for a view that resonates with Longley's interpretation of 'November'.[78] Hooker writes: 'Finding nothing to rest upon, in a decaying rural culture, and with a language of Nature from which a sense of the sacred was evaporating, Edward Thomas attempted to supply the lack.'[79]

However, the passage on strange streets in *The Heart of England* shows that Thomas's attitude to emptiness, lack and absence was more complex than his critics suggest. While he explained how the 'thousand things' an eye sees can 'obliterate one another', he also lamented the lack of a translator.[80] The reference to a translator is significant, given that his judgement of a good translation rested on its ability to contain absence and so acknowledge the existence of the source text. He was therefore alluding to the process of retaining and expressing absence rather than to the urge to make everything visible. What Hooker sees as Thomas's desire to 'supply the lack' and Longley as his urge to 'fill in the whole picture' was a deliberate attempt to resist such impetuses. Instead, by concluding the list in 'November' of '[t]wig, leaf, flint' with the generalization, 'all that men scorn', he preserved the quality of overlookedness with which the list began: 'Few care for the mixture of earth and water' (p. 34). He not only recognized the impossibility of completing such a list but the importance of resisting the urge to complete it. A similar resistance of the urge to name is manifest in *Oxford*. The phrase 'you see that the caged thing is –' is completed with the word 'nothingness'.[81] Only by including 'nothingness' within the picture can the picture be really complete.

The statement that '*there is nothing left to rest upon*' is easily misread. The narrator is here quoting from a story told to him by a previously encountered 'country-bred man with a distinct London accent', but since these words come a few pages into the story, there is a tendency to read them as the narrator's or even Thomas's opinion. A reminder of who is really speaking comes some pages later, when, after closing the country-bred man's recital with a tale of the endurance of an old man met in the woods, the narrator comments that

> I have given it [this story] because unintentionally it refutes his [the country-bred man's] statement that there is nothing left for us to rest on. There was something firm and very mighty left even for him, though his melancholy,

> perverse temper could reach it only through memory. He had Nature to rest upon. He had those hills which were not himself, which he had not made, where were not made for man and yet were good to him.[82]

By deliberately misleading his readers in this passage Thomas forced them to revise their understanding of the narrator's standpoint and so experience a shift in vantage point. He encased the statement that there is something left to rest on in 'those hills' not possessed by man in a web of different points of view. This parallels the effect of complex rootedness he created elsewhere with his use of *matryoshka*-like asides. Such rootedness also strengthens the statement's claim and allows it to act like the central point of a unicursal maze or spiral, from which ever-widening circles emanate.

The multiplicity and strangeness of urban streets offered an equivalent for Thomas in his modern urban world of the power of hills or mountains. They, too, can offer rest. This is reiterated in *The Heart of England*, itself an interesting choice of title in terms of this discussion of the core point of a spiral, where the description of streets concludes with powerful images drawn from nature: 'their surfaces hand the mind on to the analogies of sea waves or large woods'.[83]

In his work, streets, roads, lanes and paths are emblems of transitoriness, dislocation, going on, never stopping, representations of movement between destinations, towards unknown or no destination. It seems paradoxical that he also saw streets as a point of rest. However, streets are physically located and geographically traceable. They are easily able to act as fixed points of navigation, as is graphically illustrated by the twinning of his verbal mapping of roads and trackways at the start of *Richard Jefferies, his Life and Work* with a physical map at the back of the first edition.

The dual emphasis he gave to streets, as indicators of movement and fixed geographical markers, reflects the dual characteristics of spirals: an indeterminate movement outwards and a fixed centre-point. By containing both in one symbol, Thomas could articulate and yet preserve a sense of absence and uncertainty. The words, the symbols and the streets resist attempts to attach to them one single way of seeing, movement or fixity. Another option always hovers in the margins.

Crucially, absence, in the features of the land that 'were not himself' and in the lack of knowledge about streets in *The Heart of England*, provides stability.[84] Such absence offers an external measure of what is present. This stability is dependent on absence remaining outside the control of the writer, as expressed in the last line of 'The Glory', 'I cannot bite the day to the core' (p. 87). What seems to be an expression of impotence is powerful and affirming exactly because the strong, tangible, sensory image while expressing a lack of core also provides a substantial core. It fulfils its own lack.

Thomas came to terms with the overwhelming wealth of material he traced, and his translation of it into poetry, by resting within its multiplicity, staying on this side of determinacy, in the process of making and seeing, remaining on the thresholds that feature so much in his work as crossroads, ridges, stiles, doorsteps and bridges. As Smith puts it, 'for Thomas "meaning" is just irrefutably *there*'.[85] The strangeness of the streets that threaten, like Russian characters, to 'obliterate one another' in *The Heart of England* and the 'cul-de-sacs or broken threads' of his prose that, in *The Happy-go-lucky Morgans*, he feared were 'shapeless fragments' left 'useless in their place', become sources of richness.[86] Typically, and generously, the 'labyrinthine syntax' of the divagations in his poetry bestows shape and purpose on these 'broken threads'.[87] The experimentation in *Childhood* with a composing process promoting sustained but flexible attention allowed him to see streets as offering infinite possibilities, possibilities that were exactly applicable to the divagatory threads of his poems: 'The labyrinth of them, all running at right angles and parallel to one another, with some *culs de sac*, could be mastered but indefinitely extended.'[88]

CONCLUSION

> It was the most roundabout and kindly way towards our end, and so disguised our purpose that we forgot it.
>
> Edward Thomas[89]

The areas that Thomas mapped out in his poetry are 'indefinitely extended' to an ever-receding threshold. What is presented as text is always unfinished or penultimate, focusing, as he expressed it in 'The Mill-Water', on the moment before or after '[a]ll thoughts begin or end' (p. 98). His poetry resists conclusions. Instead, it constantly returns to the subjects of twilight, dawn, the edge of a forest, resorting frequently to qualifiers such as 'nearly' and 'almost'.

His poems reflect and turn upon the process of composition. By dynamically recording and re-enacting the composing process within his work, he encouraged other writers to reconsider and refine their approaches to poetic composition. His ability to re-stage the composing process in his writing, staying within that process even when his poems are complete, indicates why, as Vernon Scannell puts it, his best work 'has always attracted an admiring and devoted readership, especially among other poets'.[90] This also suggests that the aspects of poetic composition he explored form more general principles of poetic composition, resonating with other poets as well. Proof of this is evident in the writings on him by twelve poets in Pear Tree Press's volume *These Things the Poets Said* (1935), and is also seen in the proliferating number of 'Edward Thomasy' poems, an epithet coined by W. H. Auden in reference to his own poem 'Rain', which, he said, was 'the Edward Thomasy poem I can't recall writing'.[91] Anne Harvey's *Elected Friends: Poems for and about Edward Thomas* (1991) contains seventy or so of such poems. Twenty-three poets read their 'Thomasy' poems at the Oxford University Edward Thomas and Contemporary Poetry conference in 2005, and, springing from this conference, over fifty Thomas-inspired poems and essays are contained in *Branch-lines: Edward Thomas and Contemporary Poetry* (2007). There is a particular influence on Welsh poets. Gillian Clarke features in *Branch-lines*. Alun Lewis and Leslie Norris address several poems to Thomas, who was a figure of great importance in their development as poets. Tacit testimony to Thomas's continuing importance to creative artists is also resoundingly demonstrated in the remarkable number of poets who 'write back' to him. The proliferating rewrites of 'Adlestrop' alone is remarkable, whether this creative engagement with Thomas occurs with awareness or, in true Thomas style, is inadvertent.

In the mid-twentieth century, Thomas's work also played a central part in English poets' reaction against Dylan Thomas, neo-Romanticism and the 'Americanization' of English verse. To admire Thomas as a poet was then, and at times still is today, seen as a clear and pointed aesthetic choice, although what that choice represents varies according to the time and context. Thomas was, and is, often cited as heading a line of poets who embrace oral tradition and songs of nature, and also central to discussions of eco-poetry. However, appropriately and unsurprisingly, given his interest in contradiction, openness and flexibility, it is just as feasible to argue that his connections with experimentation, fragmentation and interest in absence, the not said and the peripheral, as indicated in this monograph, imply a strong lead into the experimental work of modernist writers and beyond, as when Donald Davie sets 'Cock-Crow' alongside the work of T. E. Hulme and Pound: 'if Imagism means anything, it surely means a small impersonal masterpiece like this'.[92] Any attempt to pin him down to a particular creed or approach is risky. The slippery character of his syntax, poetic force and creative approach makes him, in more ways than one, less than amenable to the 'high-level exegesis' of any particular school.[93]

Thomas's explorations in the field of poetic composition also inform poets' critical writings on the practice of poetry. Although W. N. Herbert and Matthew Hollis's *Strong Words* does not explicitly include Thomas, his influence is subtly but unmistakably present in the choice of title for the introduction, 'Writing into the Dark', a distinctive echo of the title of his poem 'Out in the dark', which itself can be read as a meditation on the composition process. Herbert and Hollis's replacement of 'Out in' with 'Writing into' extends Thomas's emphasis on inaccessibility from the composing process to the compositions produced and, by implication, to the experience of reading them. As Herbert and Hollis put it, the 'dark' is 'a necessary space in which the poem can do its work', since 'no good poem ever steps fully into the light or becomes completely accessible, but remains, instead, almost infinitely approachable'.[94]

A more immediate and personal example of Thomas's influence on other poets, and of the validity of his explorations in the field of poetic composition, is provided by my poetry collection, *The Drier the Brighter*. As the introduction to this monograph indicates, the environment in which this collection was composed was excessively 'Thomasy'. This comes through in many of the poems in the collection. Because they were all composed between 2002 and 2005 in tandem with research on Thomas's composing processes, they inevitably reflect and build on many of the qualities observed in his processes. As a result, *The Drier the Brighter* poems and their related drafts form specific practical evidence for the arguments of this book. This is documented in detail in the thesis, entitled 'Out in the dark', which provided the basis for this monograph. This thesis shows how, exploiting my privileged access to my composing processes, I used *The Drier the Brighter* poems to confirm, initiate, guide and explore many of the aspects of composing discussed in this monograph.[95] My research into Thomas's idiosyncratic orthography and use of spaced punctuation coincided with experimentation in spaced punctuation in *The Drier the Brighter*, although, crucially, my first use of spaced punctuation in a poem entitled 'unfamiliar' occurred without any overt awareness of Thomas's similar use of it. I only made the connection two days later, as revealed by a note on the composing of the poem: 'I had the idea of "/ , less". And then, of course working on it now, I think of ET.'[96] This delayed discovery of the Thomas influence on my piece subsequently contributed to its redrafting and to the development of other poems dealing with effects of spaced punctuation.

Conversely, however, the research that informs this monograph has had a strong effect on the subject matter, style and form of *The Drier the Brighter* poems, as well as on the process of selecting and ordering the collection. The creative explorations of spaced punctuation in the poetry, initially inspired by Thomas, also had the effect of deepening my understanding of his use of space and gaps, contributing significantly to the discussions of these topics in the monograph. Other areas where a mutual influence can be seen at play include the importance of the environment, both physical and mental; the roles of control and flexibility of attention, indirection, inattention, hindsight and successive memories of an event; and the contribution of Japanese aesthetics of absence to my own critical and creative work after a seven-year stint at a Japanese university, and to Thomas's composing processes in an era which remained very open to Japanese approaches to literature and art. In all these cases, a dynamic process of exchange occurs in which points drawn from one area of research and composition have been applied to another. It is fitting, therefore, that this study of Thomas's composing processes should end as it began, by alluding to its conditions of inception and to other publications that have sprung from the research for it. In true 'Thomasy' style, the spiralling exploration of composing processes widening beyond the printed pages of any one particular volume, chapter or epigraph, enacts one of the crucial findings of this study. What is and appears to be tangential is often of central importance to the composition process, but only for as long as it remains tangential, half-unseen, hovering in the margins.

Appendix 1

DIFFERENCES IN POEM TITLES

Collected Poems (1978), edited by R. G. Thomas	*Annotated Collected Poems* (2008), edited by Edna Longley
'November Sky'	'November'
'Home [1]'	'Home ("Not the end")'
'Digging [1]'	'Digging ("Today I think")'
'Home [2]'	'Home ("Often I had gone")'
'Song [1]'	'Song'
'Digging [2]'	'Digging ("What matter makes my spade")'
'Song [2]'	'The clouds that are so light'
'P.H.T.'	'I may come near to loving you'
'M.E.T.'	'No one so much as you'
'"Home" [3]'	'"Home" ("Fair was the morning")'
'Household Poems':	
1 Bronwen	'If I should ever by chance'
2 Merfyn	'If I were to own'
3 Myfanwy	'What shall I give?'
4 Helen	'And you, Helen'
'Go Now'	'Like the touch of rain'
'Bugle Call'	'No one cares less than I'
'The Pond'	'Bright Clouds'
'Song [3]'	'Early one morning'
'Bob's Lane'	'Women he liked'
'The Swifts'	'How at once'
'Blenheim Oranges'	'Gone, gone again'

Appendix 2

Extract from the end of 'Insomnia' in *The Last Sheaf* (London: Jonathan Cape, 1928).

> Outside, in the dark hush, to me lying prostrate, patient, unmoving, the song was absolutely monotonous, absolutely expressionless, a chain of little thin notes linked mechanically in a rhythm identical at each repetition. I remained awake, silently and as stilly as possible, cringing for sleep. I was an unwilling note on the instrument; yet I do not know that the robin was less unwilling. I strove to escape out of that harmony of bird, wind, and man. But as fast as I made my mind a faintly heaving, shapeless, grey blank, some form or colour appeared; memory or anticipation was at work.
>
> Gradually I found myself trying to understand this dawn harmony. I vowed to remember it and ponder it in the light of day. To make sure of remembering I tried putting it into rhyme. I was resolved not to omit the date; and so much so that the first line had to be 'The seventh of September', nor could I escape from this necessity. Then September was to be rhymed with. The word 'ember' occurred and stayed; no other would respond to all my calling. The third and fourth lines, it seemed, were bound to be something like–
>
> The sere and the ember
> Of the year and of me.
>
> This gave me no satisfaction, but I was under a very strong compulsion. I could do no more; not a line would add itself to the wretched three; nor did they cease to return again and again to my head. It was fortunate for me as a man, if not as an unborn poet, that I could not forget the lines; for by continual helpless repetition of them I rose yet once more to the weakness that sleep demanded. Gradually I became conscious of nothing but the moan of trees, the monotonous expressionless robin's song, the slightly aching body to which I was, by ties more and more slender, attached. I felt, I knew, I did not

think that there would always be an unknown player, always wind and trees, always a robin singing, always a listener listening in the stark dawn: I knew also that if I were the listener I should not always lie thus in a safe warm bed thinking myself alive . . . And so I fell asleep again on the seventh of September.

Appendix 3

Extract from a letter from Edward Thomas to de la Mare with approximation of the spaced punctuation of the original (Bodleian, MS Eng lett c 376, fol. 221).

Page two

> This address will most likely
> find me till Saturday morning ,
> tho it is not the time & place to
> do nothing in , which is all I have
> to do , except that in sleepless
> hours this morning I found
> myself (for the first time) trying

Page three

> hard to *rhyme* my mood &
> failing very badly indeed , in
> fact comically so , as I could
> not complete the first verse or
> get beyond the rhyme of ember &
> September . This must explain
> any future lenience towards the
> mob of gentlemen that rhyme
> with ease .

Appendix 4

Second two pages of the original letter (Bodleian, MS Eng lett c 376, fol. 221).

of myself. I am very sorry to have kept you expecting me vainly. However, I have written to my wife about next Sunday, & we will let you know as soon as we can what can be done. I hope your wife has got over the packing & the return without too much trouble.

This address will most likely find me till Saturday morning; but it is not the time & place to do nothing in, which is all I have to do, except that in sleepless hours this morning I found myself (for the first time) trying hard to rhyme my mood & feeling very badly indeed, in fact comically so, as I could not complete the first verse or get beyond the rhyme of ember & September. This must explain any future lenience towards the mob of gentlemen that rhyme with ease.

Yours ever

Edward Thomas.

Appendix 5

The opening page of Thomas's introduction to *The Book of the Open Air*.

INTRODUCTION

I saw sweet Poetry turn untroubled eyes
  On shaggy Science nosing in the grass,
  For by that way poor Poetry must pass
On her long pilgrimage to Paradise.
He snuffled, grunted, squealed; perplexed by flies,
  Parched, weatherworn, and near of sight, alas!
  From peering close where very little was
In dens secluded from the open skies.
But Poetry in bravery went down,
  And called his name, soft, clear, and fearlessly;
Stooped low, and stroked his muzzle overgrown;
  Refreshed his drought with dew; wiped pure and free
  His eyes: and lo! laughed loud for joy to see
In those grey deeps the azure of her own.

WALTER DE LA MARE.

The blue sky, the brown soil beneath, the grass, the trees, the animals, the wind, and rain, and sun, and stars are never strange to me; for I am in and of and one with them; and my flesh and the soil are one, and the heat in my blood and in the sunshine are one, and the winds and tempests and my passions are one.

W. H. HUDSON.

MATTHEW ARNOLD was, I think, the first English critic to point out the importance of the interpretation of Nature in literature. "The grand power of poetry," he says, "is its interpretative power; by which I mean, not a power of drawing out in black and white an explanation of the mystery of the universe, but the power of so dealing with things as to awaken in us a wonderfully full, new, and intimate sense of them, and of our relations with them." In the same essay, and in "Celtic Literature" and elsewhere, he quotes passages which show more or less precisely what he means by interpretation and especially by interpretation of Nature, and he coins the phrase "natural magic" for this element in literature at its highest power. But it is noticeable that he cannot illustrate his point from English prose, for it was not until some time after his essay was written that any men, except Shelley in "The Coliseum" and De Quincey and Coleridge in a few passages, had dealt with Nature in prose and in a spirit that was not simply observant. If we look farther back, we shall be disappointed if we expect to find an English prose

v

Notes

Notes to Note on the Text and Abbreviations

1. P. J. Croft, *Autograph Poetry in the English Language*, 2 vols (London: Cassell, 1973), I, p. xxi.

Notes to the Introduction

1. Bach, complimented on his organ playing, cited in Karl Geiringer, *The Bach Family* (London: Allen & Unwin, 1954), p. 145.
2. Many of Thomas's letters relating to the composing process are compiled in *Edward Thomas's Poets*, ed. Judy Kendall (Manchester: Carcanet, 2007).
3. *LFY*, p. 237 (27 December 1916).
4. Chris B. McCully (ed.), *The Poet's Voice and Craft* (Manchester: Carcanet, 1994), p. 84. From Manchester Poetry Centre 1988–91 lecture series.
5. Edwin Morgan, in ibid., p. 56: Anne Stevenson, in ibid., p.123.
6. W. N. Herbert and Matthew Hollis (eds), *Strong Words: Modern Poets on Modern Poetry* (Newcastle: Bloodaxe, 2000), p. 11; Bishop, in ibid., p.105; Kennelly, in ibid., pp. 213–14.
7. Judy Kendall, *The Drier the Brighter* (Blaenau Ffestiniog: Cinnamon Press, 2007).

Notes to Chapter 1

1. *Riddley Walker* (London: Jonathan Cape, 1980; repr. Picador, 1982), p. 6.
2. Andrew Motion, *The Poetry of Edward Thomas* (London: Hogarth Press, 1991), p. 22.

[3] Julia Briggs, *Virginia Woolf: an Inner Life* (London: Allen Lane, 2005), p. 383.
[4] *PW*, p. 47.
[5] D. J. Enright, *The Oxford Book of Contemporary Verse* (Oxford: Oxford University Press, 1980), p. xxviii.
[6] John Lucas, *The Radical Twenties* (Nottingham: Five Leaves Publications, 1997), p. 203.
[7] Thomas to Bottomley, *Bottomley*, p. 166 (19 July 1908).
[8] Eng lett 376, fol. 66.
[9] *Sheaf*, p. 16.
[10] *CP*, p. 443.
[11] *ANCP*, p. 149. Further references to this volume will be included in parentheses in the text.
[12] *Bottomley*, p. 158 (26 February 1908); NLW, MS 22915C, folio 198 (11 February 1913). See *Letters to Helen*, ed. R. G. Thomas (Manchester: Carcanet, 2000), pp. 63, 66, 69, 73.
[13] *The Woodland Life* (London: Blackwood, 1897), pp. 157–234; see *Portrait*, pp. 46–7. R. P. Eckert writes that Ashcroft Noble suggested that the diary be 'published as a part of *The Woodland Life*': R. P. Eckert, *Edward Thomas: a Biography and a Bibliography* (London: Dent, 1937), p. 20.
[14] *CP*, p. 460, n. 1.
[15] Ibid., pp. 460–1.
[16] *The Icknield Way* (London: Constable, 1913), pp. vi–vii.
[17] Thomas to Frost, *Elected Friends: Robert Frost & Edward Thomas to One Another*, ed. Matthew Spencer (New York: Handsel Books, 2003), p. 119 (30 January 1916); *LFY*, p. 220 (postmarked 12 November 1916).
[18] *Portrait*, p. 275.
[19] *LFY*, p. 217 (postmarked 2 November 1916).
[20] See Bodleian, MS Don d 28, pp. 2, 17, 20, 22, 27, 32, 37, 50, 60, 64, 69; see *LFY*, p. 110 (10 January 1915).
[21] *A Literary Pilgrim in England* (London: Methuen, 1917; Oxford: Oxford University Press, 1980), p. 176.
[22] Review of *Biographia Literaria*, *DC*, 8 June 1908, 3.
[23] See *LFY*, p. 150 (29 June 1915).
[24] Guy Cuthbertson and Lucy Newlyn, *Branch-lines: Edward Thomas and Contemporary Poetry* (London: Enitharmon, 2007), p. 73.
[25] Ibid., pp. 68, 71, 75.
[26] George Borrow, *The Zincali: an Account of the Gypsies of Spain*, ed. Edward Thomas (London: Dent, 1914), p. vii.
[27] Ibid., p. 165.
[28] Thomas to MacAlister, *Selected Letters*, p. 27 (1 November 1903).
[29] See R. G. Thomas's notes to 'Old Man', 'The Other' and 'The Mountain Chapel' in *CP*, pp. 18, 381–2, 383, 443–4.
[30] *LFY*, p. 150 (postmarked 29 June 1915).
[31] 'Where the wood ends', *The Guardian*, 6 November 2004, 25.
[32] Quoted in *Garnett*, p. 34, n. 21. Thomas sent out his poems under the pseudonym Edward Eastaway.

[33] *LFY*, p. 124 (12 March 1915).
[34] Ibid., p.133 (postmarked 5 May 1915).
[35] Ibid., p. 154 (26 July 1915).
[36] *Independent*, 13 August 2005, 10.
[37] Thomas to Ian MacAlister, *Selected Letters*, p. 27 (1 November 1903).
[38] 'Reading', p. 276.
[39] Eng lett 376, fol. 221.
[40] 'Insomnia', in *Sheaf*, pp. 39–43. See Appendices 2 and 3.
[41] *ETF*, 52 (August 2004), p. 11 (18 March 1915).
[42] Theresa Whistler, *Imagination of the Heart: the Life of Walter de la Mare* (London: Duckworth, 1993), p. 220.
[43] Ibid., p. 280; see Edward Thomas, 'The time deposit', *The Nation*, 9 (1911), 703–5, reprinted in his *Cloud Castle and Other Papers* (London: Duckworth, 1922) as 'Saved time'; see also de la Mare, 'The Vats', in *The Riddle and Other Stories* (London: Selwyn & Blount, 1923), pp. 295–303.
[44] Eng lett 376, fol. 110; cited in *Edward Thomas's Poets*, ed. Judy Kendall (Manchester: Carcanet, 2007), pp. xx–xxi.
[45] Eng lett 376, fol. 221. The spaces in this quotation attempt to represent Thomas's peculiar handwritten orthography. See Appendix 4.
[46] The original line is 'The Mob of Gentlemen who wrote with Ease', in Alexander Pope, *The First Epistle of the Second Book of Horace, Imitated* (London: Cooper, 1737), p. 7.
[47] *Bottomley*, p. 196 (14 December 1909).
[48] *LFY*, p. 111 (16 January 1915).
[49] 'Stone Chat' in *Freedom: Poems* (London: Smith, Elder, 1914), p. 30, cited in *Edward Thomas's Poets*, p. 69; Thomas describes it in a 26 November 1914 letter to Hudson as 'one of the best of all pure bird poems, the bird on a wet stone pure and simple up on a heath', *Edward Thomas's Poets*, p. 68.
[50] Ibid., p. 187 (postmarked 13 February 1916).
[51] *CP*, p. 16.
[52] *Letters to Helen*, p. 1 (21 June 1897).
[53] Edward Thomas, *Keats* (London: T. C. & E. C. Jack, The People's Books, 1916), p. 51.
[54] *PW*, p. 60.
[55] Harry Coombes, *Edward Thomas: a Critical Study* (London: Chatto & Windus, 1956; repr. 1973), p. 92.
[56] See W. H. Hudson, *Green Mansions: a Romance of the Tropical Forest* (London: Duckworth, 1904; repr. 1911), pp. 112–13.
[57] *Bottomley*, p. 158 (26 February 1908); *DC*, 1 March 1904, 3.
[58] *Light*, p. 19.
[59] Ibid., pp. 21, 19.

Notes to Chapter 2

[1] Cited in Roy Palmer, *The Folklore of Gloucestershire* (Launceston: Westcountry Books, 1994), p. 228.

[2] *Norse*, p. 3.

[3] *SC*, pp. 241–2.

[4] *DC*, 21 October 1905; reprinted in *Georgians*, pp. 67–72.

[5] *DC*, 30 January 1912, 24 January 1907, 23 April 1908; reprinted in *Georgians*, pp. 94, 77, 80; cited in *Welsh Writing*, pp. 49, 48.

[6] *ANCP*, p. 47. Further references to this volume will be included in parentheses in the text.

[7] *LFY*, p. 81.

[8] See *OED* entry for 'translate', *OED*, XI (1961), 266.

[9] Linda Dowling, *Language and Decadence in the Victorian Fin de Siècle* (Princeton: Princeton University Press, 1986), pp. 214, 83.

[10] Edward Thomas, *Poetry and Drama*, 1.3 (September, 1913), 370–1.

[11] *DC*, 21 October 1905; reprinted in *Georgians*, p. 68.

[12] *English Review*, August 1914; *New Weekly*, 8 August 1914; both reprinted in Edward Thomas, *A Language Not to be Betrayed: Selected Prose of Edward Thomas*, ed. Edna Longley (Manchester: Carcanet Press, 1981), p. 130.

[13] W. B. Yeats (ed.), *The Oxford Book of Modern Verse 1892–1935* (Oxford: Clarendon Press, 1936), pp. ix, xi, xiii, xxvi.

[14] Review of Frost's *North of Boston*, *New Weekly*, 2.21 (1914), 249 (8 August 1914).

[15] 'Futurism', *Poetry and Drama*, 1.3 (September 1913), 262.

[16] Ibid., 360.

[17] Ibid., 370.

[18] Ibid., 366.

[19] Hodgson's *Eve and other Poems*, in ibid., 370–1 (370).

[20] 'Songs and singers', *Bookman*, February 1912, 266; reprinted in *Georgians*, pp. 94–9 (p. 95); Eng lett, fol. 197 (postmarked 24 June 1913), cited in *Edward Thomas's Poets*, ed. Judy Kendall (Manchester: Carcanet, 2007), p. xxiv.

[21] *Daily News*, 22 July 1914; *New Weekly*, August 1914.

[22] Yeats, *Oxford Book of Modern Verse*, p. xvi.

[23] Edward Thomas, *Elected Friends: Robert Frost & Edward Thomas to One Another*, ed. Matthew Spencer (New York: Handsel Books, 2003), p. 10 (19 May 1914).

[24] Paul Verlaine, 'Art Poétique', in *Jadis et Naguère* (Paris: Léon Vanier, Libraire-Éditeur, 1891), p. 20. My translation.

[25] *SC*, p. 6; Thomas's use of 'superfluous men' is discussed by Stan Smith, *Edward Thomas* (London: Faber and Faber, 1986), pp. 47–8, for more detail, see pp. 11–58; also Piers Gray, *Marginal Men: Edward Thomas, Ivor Gurney, J. R. Ackerley* (Basingstoke: Macmillan, 1991), pp. 8–36.

[26] 'Kasyán from the Fair-Metchá', in 'Memoirs of a Sportsman', *The Novels and Stories of Ivan Turgenieff*, trans. Isabel F. Hapgood, with introduction by Henry

James, 15 vols (New York: Charles Scribner's Sons, 1903), I, pp. 188–220 (p. 205).

27 Review of *The Novels and Stories of Ivan Turgenieff*, trans. Isabel Hapgood, *DC*, 13 December 1905, 3.

28 Circle poem (held in Studio Alec Finlay); line version published in *white peak| dark peak* catalogue (Newcastle: Morning Star Publications and Derbyshire Arts Development Group, 2010).

29 Recorded by Julian Thomas in preface to *The Childhood of Edward Thomas: a Fragment of Autobiography* (London: Faber and Faber, 1938), p. 8.

30 *Portrait*, p. 15.

31 *Norse*, p. 3.

32 *Celtic*, pp. 127–8.

33 *Norse*, pp. 5–6.

34 *Poetry and Drama*, 2.6 (June 1914), p. 188; ibid., 2.8 (December 1914), p. 387.

35 *Bottomley*, pp. 113, 128 (7 July 1906, 9 December 1906).

36 *The Pocket Book of Poems and Songs for the Open Air*, ed. Edward Thomas (London: Grant Richards, 1907), p. viii.

37 *Celtic*, p. 128.

38 Ibid., pp. 128, 3.

39 *Bottomley*, p. 127 (9 December 1906). Original emphasis.

40 Smith, *Edward Thomas*, p. 30.

41 Jonathan Bate, *The Song of the Earth* (London: Picador, 2000), p. 280.

42 See *Portrait*, p. 238; also Thomas to John Freeman, British Library, MS RP 1791, folio 20 (14 August 1914), cited in *Edward Thomas's Poets*, p. xxiv; *LFY*, p. 6; Eng lett, folio 198 (postmarked 29 June 1913), cited in *Edward Thomas's Poets*, p. xxiv.

43 Deborah Thacker, 'Robert Frost and Edward Thomas: poets' stories', in Celia Keenan and Mary Shine Thompson (eds), *Studies in Children's Literature, 1500–2000* (Dublin: Four Courts Press, 2004), pp. 86–93. (pp. 88, 89).

44 *Portrait*, pp. 308–9.

45 Edward Thomas, *Poems and Last Poems*, ed. Edna Longley (London: Collins, 1973), p. 231.

46 *LFY*, p. 172 (postmarked 28 November 1915).

47 *Georgians*, p. 80, cited by Kendall, in *Welsh Writing*, p. 48.

48 *Poems and Last Poems*, p. 244.

49 *Letters to Helen*, ed. R. G. Thomas (Manchester: Carcanet, 2000), p. 1 (21 June 1897).

50 *Poems and Last Poems*, pp. 251–2.

51 Matsuo Bashō, *On Love and Barley: Haiku of Bashō*, trans. Lucien Stryk (Harmondsworth: Penguin, 1985), p. 25. The seventeenth-century itinerant monk-like poet, Bashō, is regarded as the master of haiku.

52 *PW*, p. 62.

53 Myfanwy Thomas, *One of these Fine Days: Memoirs* (Manchester: Carcanet, 1982), p. 124.

54 For inaccuracies in the mythologizing process of Welsh history, see Prys Morgan, 'From a death to a view: the hunt for the Welsh past in a romantic period', in Eric

Hobsbawm and Terence Ranger (eds), *The Invention of Tradition* (Cambridge: Cambridge University Press, 1983), pp. 43–99. Subsequent scholars challenge some claims in this book. The mythologizing process continues.

55 Edward Thomas, *Beautiful Wales* (London: Black, 1905), p. 82; See Bottomley's comment in *Bottomley*, p. 125, n. 3.

56 *Bottomley*, pp. 126–7 (11 November 1906).

57 Ibid., p. 67 (1 November 1904); ibid., p. 75 (18 January 1905); *Beautiful Wales*, pp. 47–8; *Bottomley*, p. 79 (27 February 1905).

58 *SC*, p. 7.

59 Gosse, BL, Ashley A4474, Letter from Edmund Gosse to T. J. Wise, criticizing Edward Thomas's A.C. Swinburne A Critical Study, folio 84/5f (30 November 1912); Alfred Edward Housman also complains, writing 'Pray, who gave Mr E. Thomas leave to print two of my inspired lays in his and your *Pocket Book of Poems and Songs*? I didn't': Housman to Grant Richards, cited in *The Letters of A. E. Housman*, ed. Henry Maas (London: Hart-Davis, 1971), p. 91 (29 June 1907). See Thomas's 2 September 1912 letter to de la Mare, Eng lett 376, folio 16.

60 'Birds in March', *ETF*, 53 (January 2005), 11–3 (13), published in the journal *Young Days*, of the Sunday School Association, February 1895.

61 *Bottomley*, p. 261 (18 February 1916).

62 Thomas's introduction to Isaac Taylor, *Words and Places in Illustration of History, Ethnology and Geography* (London: Dent, 1911), cited in *A Language Not to be Betrayed: Selected Prose of Edward Thomas*, ed. Edna Longley (Manchester: Carcanet Press, 1981), pp. 213–14.

63 *SC*, p. 148.

64 William Shakespeare, *The Winter's Tale*, IV.4, pp. 261–2.

65 F. R. Leavis, *New Bearings in English Poetry* (2nd edn; London: Chatto & Windus, 1950), p. 70.

66 *Times Literary Supplement*, 11 October 1917, 489.

67 *Between*, p. 243. Also *Between*, pp. 134, 136, 181, 215; also Julia Briggs, *Virginia Woolf: an Inner Life* (London: Allen Lane, 2005), pp. 376–8. *Between* discusses relations between the environment, the human voice and creative writing. In Thomas's *George Borrow: the Man and His Books* (London: Chapman & Hall, 1912), chapter 23, entitled 'Between the Acts', follows 'The Bible in Spain' and precedes 'Lavengro' and 'The Romany Rye'. See also George Borrow, *The Zincali: an Account of the Gypsies of Spain* (London: Dent, 1914), p. vii, and 'The Gypsy'.

68 Virginia Woolf, *Moments of Being* (rev. edn; London: Hogarth Press, 1985), pp. 61–137 (p. 67).

69 Virginia Woolf, '"Anon" and "The reader": Virginia Woolf's last essays', in Brenda R. Silver (ed.), *Twentieth Century Literature: Virginia Woolf Issue*, 25 (1979), 382.

70 Virginia Woolf, *A Room of One's Own* (London: Hogarth Press, 1929), p. 98.

71 *ANCP*, p. 70. An earlier version of the second stanza which includes the word 'unnamed'. The *CP* edition prefers a later version. See *CP*, p. 135. Longley, referring to Thomas's recorded dissatisfaction with the poem in a letter dated 28 April 1915 to Farjeon (*LFY*, p. 123), says 'the possibility that Thomas re-thought his "mending" of the poem [. . .] cannot be discounted' (*ANCP*, p. 205).

[72] Woolf, 'Anon', 384.
[73] 'Reading', p. 277.
[74] W. H. Hudson, *Green Mansions: a Romance of the Tropical Forest* (London: Duckworth, 1904; repr. 1911), p. 97; see Bate, *Song of the Earth*, pp. 55–62.
[75] *DC*, 1 March 1904, 3.
[76] Hudson, *Green Mansions*, p. 297.
[77] William Wordsworth, *The Poetical Works of Wordsworth*, ed. T. Hutchinson (London: Oxford University Press, 1904; repr. 1939), p. 199.
[78] Ibid., p. 899.
[79] Ibid., p. 737 ('The prelude', XII, line 208).
[80] *Between*, p. 165.
[81] Woolf, 'Anon', 384.
[82] *Between*, p. 166.
[83] Wordsworth, *The Poetical Works of Wordsworth*, p. 199.
[84] Thomas Browne, *Religio Medici* (London, 1643), cited in Theodore Andrea Cook, *The Curves of Life* (London: Constable, 1914), p. 380.
[85] Review of *Rio Grande's Last Race* by Australian poet A. B. 'Banjo' Paterson, *DC*, 8 February 1904, 3.
[86] *SC*, p. 150.
[87] Hans Ulrich Seeber, 'The retrospective attitude in Edward Thomas and Andrew Motion', in *REAL Yearbook of Research in English and American Literature*, 21 (2005), 155.
[88] *Bottomley*, p. 146 (22 September 1907).
[89] Edward Thomas, *Richard Jefferies, his Life and Work* (London: Hutchinson, 1909), p. 4.
[90] Ibid., pp. 10, 11.
[91] *SC*, p. 150.
[92] 'Reading', p. 276.
[93] Edward Thomas, *The Country* (London: Batsford, 1913; repr. Cheltenham: Cyder Press, 1999), pp. 20–1.
[94] *SC*, p. 147.
[95] Ibid., p. 150.
[96] Ibid.
[97] *Between*, p. 8.
[98] *Times Literary Supplement*, 11 October 1917, 489.
[99] *SC*, p. 147.
[100] Briggs, *Virginia Woolf*, p. 378.
[101] *Sheaf*, pp. 100, 101.
[102] Richard Mabey, *Flora Britannica* (London: Sinclair-Stevenson, 1996), p. 201, see also p. 212; also Oliver Rackham, *The History of the Countryside* (London: Dent, 1986), pp. 199, 184–5.
[103] Review of Frost's *North of Boston*, *New Weekly*, 2.21, 249 (8 August 1914).
[104] *Times Literary Supplement*, 11 October 1917, 489; *SC*, p. 147.
[105] Ibid., p. 150.
[106] Edward Thomas, *The Heart of England* (London: Dent, 1909), p.115.

[107] 'Essay upon epitaphs, I', in *The Prose Works of William Wordsworth*, ed. W. J. B. Owen and J. W. Smyser, 3 vols (Oxford: Clarendon Press, 1974), II, pp. 49–62 (p. 60).

[108] Ibid.

[109] Samuel Taylor Coleridge, *The Notebooks of Samuel Taylor Coleridge*, ed. Kathleen Coburn, 5 vols (London: Routledge and Kegan Paul, 1957), I, p. 1268. Wordsworth quotes this in *Prose Works*, II, p. 118. See 'Essay upon epitaphs, I', in *Prose Works*, II, pp. 49–62 (p. 59); 'Essay on epitaphs, III', in ibid., 80–96 (p. 93).

[110] Alain de Botton, *The Art of Travel* (London: Hamish Hamilton, 2002; repr. Penguin, 2003), p. 154; see Wordsworth, *Poetical Works*, p. 737 ('The prelude', XI, line 208); Edward Thomas, *A Literary Pilgrim in England* (London: Methuen, 1917; Oxford: Oxford University Press, 1980), pp. 263, 265.

[111] Edward Thomas, *Keats* (London: T. C. & E. C. Jack, The People's Books, 1916), p. 37. See also Thomas's section on Keats in *A Literary Pilgrim in England*, pp. 35–43.

[112] *SC*, p. 150.

Notes to Chapter 3

[1] Yone Noguchi, 'The spirit of Japanese poetry', *Selected English Writings of Yone Noguchi: an East-West Literary Assimilation*, ed. Yoshinobu Hakutani (London: Associated University Presses, 1992), 2 vols, II, pp. 55–98 (p. 58). First published as *The Spirit of Japanese Poetry* (London: J. Murray, 1914), p. 16.

[2] Reviews of *North of Boston*, *New Weekly*, 2.21 (8 August 1914), 249, and 'A book of the day: a new poet', *Daily News*, 22 July 1914, 7.

[3] Review of D. H. Lawrence's *Love Poems*, *Bookman*, 44 (April 1913), 47.

[4] Review of *Des Imagistes*, 'Exotic verse', *New Weekly*, 1.8 (9 May 1914), 249.

[5] Kenkō, *The Miscellany of a Japanese Priest*, trans. William N. Porter (London: Humphrey Milford, 1914; repr. Tokyo: Tuttle, 1983), p. 105 (section 137). Also known as *Tsurezuregusa* or *Essays in Idleness*.

[6] W. G. Aston, *A History of Japanese Literature* (London: Heinemann, 1899), p. 24.

[7] Noguchi, 'The Japanese Hokku poetry', *English Writings*, II, p. 68. Published in *The Spirit of Japanese Poetry* (London: J. Murray, 1914), pp 33–53, p. 34.

[8] Lafcadio Hearn, *Kokoru: Hints and Echoes of Japanese Inner Life* (Boston: Houghton, Mifflin, 1896), p. vii; Noguchi, *English Writings*, II, p. 9.

[9] *DC*, 18 January 1907, 3; Edward Thomas, *Lafcadio Hearn* (London: Constable, 1912), p. 90; Basil Hall Chamberlain, *Things Japanese* (4th edn; London: John Murray, 1902), p. 65, cited in *Lafcadio Hearn*, p. 80.

[10] Noguchi, *English Writings*, pp. 11, 19, 9; see also Yone Noguchi, *Yone Noguchi: Collected English Letters*, ed. Ikuko Atsumi (Tokyo: Yone Noguchi Society, 1975), p. 3.

[11] Noguchi, *English Letters*, pp. 210, 204 (2 September 1911, 4 September 1906).

[12] Edward Thomas, *The Icknield Way* (London: Constable, 1913), p. vi.

[13] *The Icknield Way*, p. vii

[14] Edward Thomas, *Keats* (London: T. C. & E. C. Jack, The People's Books, 1916), p. 74.
[15] Ibid., p. vi.
[16] 'Incantation', in *The Collected Poems of Walter de la Mare* (London: Faber and Faber, 1979), p. 256. From *Memory and Other Poems* (London: Constable, 1938), p. 24. Emphasis in original.
[17] Judith Butcher, *Copy-editing: the Cambridge Handbook* (3rd edn; Cambridge: Cambridge University Press, 1992), p. 153; see also John Ellison Kahn, *The Right Word at the Right Time* (London: Reader's Digest Association, 1985), pp. 207–8.
[18] A. S. Byatt, *Possession: a Romance* (London: Vintage, 1991), p. 422.
[19] *CP*, p. 396.
[20] Ibid.
[21] *ANCP*, p. 87. Further references to this volume will be included in parentheses in the text.
[22] *CP*, p. 396.
[23] Ibid.
[24] Edward Thomas, *Elected Friends: Robert Frost & Edward Thomas to One Another*, ed. Matthew Spencer (New York: Handsel Books, 2003), p. 39 (15 December 1914).
[25] Peter McDonald, 'Rhyme and determination in Hopkins and Edward Thomas', *Essays in Criticism*, 43 (1993), 228–45 (243–4).
[26] Wolfgang Iser, *The Act of Reading* (London: Routledge and Kegan Paul, 1978), p. 34.
[27] *Elected Friends*, p. 54 (15 May [1915]).
[28] *Selected Poems of Edward Thomas*, ed. R. S. Thomas (11th edn; London: Faber and Faber, 1964; repr. 1998), p. ix.
[29] *Light*, p. 45.
[30] *SC*, p. 148.
[31] Eng lett 376, fol. 115.
[32] *SC*, p. 4.
[33] *DC* review, 30 January 1912, cited in *Edward Thomas's Poets*, pp. 116, 115.
[34] *Edward Thomas's Poets*, ed. Judy Kendall (Manchester: Carcanet, 2007), p. 182.
[35] *LFY*, p. 124 (12 March 1915).
[36] Iser, *The Act of Reading*, p. 34.
[37] Edward Thomas, *Collected Poems*, ed. Walter de la Mare (London: Selwyn & Blount, 1920), p. x.
[38] *CP*, p. 396; *ANCP*, p. 88.
[39] *ETF*, 53 (January 2005), 11–13 (13).
[40] *Letters of J. Keats*, ed. M. B. Forman (London: Oxford University Press, 1935), letter 32, p. 72 (21 December 1817); *Keats*, p. 75, citing a letter of Keats to Reynolds; *Letters of J. Keats*, p. 104 (19 February 1818). Thomas replaces 'insect' with 'mind'.
[41] Cited in Andrew Motion, *The Poetry of Edward Thomas* (London: Hogarth Press, 1991), p. 90.
[42] Lady Holland, *A Memoir of the Rev. Sydney Smith* (4th edn; London: Longman, Brown, Green and Longmans, 1855), I, p. 363. Sydney Smith is describing the historian T. B. Macaulay.

[43] *DC*, 31 May 1910, 8. By mid-1910 several collections of Noguchi's English poems had been published.

[44] *Lafcadio Hearn*, p. 78.

[45] Noguchi, *English Writings*, II, p. 68. Published in *The Spirit of Japanese Poetry* (London:J. Murray, 1914), p. 34.

[46] Review of *The Spirit of Romance*, *Morning Post*, 1 August 1910; cited in Edward Thomas, *A Language Not to be Betrayed: Selected Prose of Edward Thomas*, ed. Edna Longley (Manchester: Carcanet Press, 1981), p. 122.

[47] Noguchi, *English Letters*, p. 211 (2 September 1911).

[48] *Bottomley*, p. 75 (18 January 1905).

[49] *Celtic*, pp. 127–8.

[50] Unsigned review of Bottomley's poetry, *Chambers of Imagery*, 'Verses and translations', *DC*, 5 August 1907, 2.

[51] *FIP*, pp. 97–8.

[52] William Wordsworth, *Lyrical Ballads*, ed. R. L. Brett and A. R. Jones (London: Methuen, 1963), preface of 1802, p. 251.

[53] *DC*, 23 August 1910, 6; *DC*, 31 May 1910, 8.

[54] Thomas to John Freeman, 14 August 1914, cited in Stan Smith, *Edward Thomas* (London: Faber and Faber, 1986), p. 12.

[55] Review of *Personae of Ezra Pound*, *DC*, 7 June 1909; cited in *A Language Not to be Betrayed*, pp. 116–17.

[56] Review of Frost's *North of Boston*, *Daily News*, 22 July 1914; cited in *A Language Not to be Betrayed*, p. 127; 'The death of the hired man', adapted as an English Noh play and performed by The No East West Company at Oe Noh Gagudo theatre, Kyoto, 16 January 2005; McAteer's motivation for using ellipses in the title was confirmed by him in conversation with Kendall in Kyoto in December 2010.

[57] *Elected Friends*, p. 52 (3 May 1915).

[58] William Wordsworth, *The Poetical Works of Wordsworth*, ed. T. Hutchinson (London: Oxford University Press, 1904; reprint 1939), p. 737 ('The prelude', XI, line 208).

[59] *CP*, p. 436.

[60] *SC*, p. 5.

[61] Ibid., p. 148.

[62] *Bottomley*, p. 165 (19 July 1908). Thomas's emphases.

[63] Jacques Derrida, *Writing and Difference*, trans. Alan Bass (London: Routledge and Kegan Paul, 1978), pp. xvi–xvii.

[64] Cited in Elisabeth Robins Pennell and Joseph Pennell, *The Life of James McNeill Whistler*, 2 vols (London: Heinemann, 1908), II, p. 178. 'Claude' is the seventeenth-century landscape painter, Claude Lorrain.

[65] *DC*, 31 May 1910, 8.

[66] Basil Hall Chamberlain (ed.), *Classical Poetry of the Japanese* (London: Trübner, 1880), p. 6. This passage is also cited by W. G. Aston, *A History of Japanese Literature* (London: Heinemann, 1899), p. 202.

[67] *Light*, p. 176.

[68] Harry Coombes, *Edward Thomas: a Critical Study* (London: Chatto & Windus, 1956; repr. 1973), p. 220.

69 *SC*, p. 6.

70 Lawrence Kramer, *Music and Poetry: the Nineteenth Century and After* (Berkeley: University of California Press, 1984), p. 98.

71 Noguchi on Bashō, in *English Writings*, II, p. 56. Published in *The Spirit of Japanese Poetry* in London in 1914, p. 11.

72 Christopher Ricks, *T. S. Eliot and Prejudice* (London: Faber and Faber, 1988), p. 146.

73 Edward Thomas, *Maurice Maeterlinck* (London: Methuen, 1911), p. 27.

74 Stuart Sillars, *Structure and Dissolution in English Writing, 1910–1920* (Basingstoke: Macmillan, 1999), p. 179.

75 *Bottomley*, p. 41 (10 November 1902).

76 *Elected Friends*, pp. 131–2, 138 (21 May 1916, 10 June 1916).

77 *Bottomley*, p. 53 (17 March 1904).

78 Edward Thomas, *Beautiful Wales* (London: Black, 1905), p. 42.

79 'L'Impressionisme', in *Mélanges Posthumes* (Paris: Société du Mercure de France, 1903; repr. Geneva: Slatkine, 1979), pp. 133–45 (p. 141). 'Object and subject are then irretrievably in motion, inapprehensible and unapprehending': trans. William Jay Smith, cited in Linda Nochlin, *Impressionism and Post-impressionism 1874–1904* (Englewood Cliffs, NJ: Prentice-Hall, 1966), p. 15.

80 *LFY*, p. 237 (27 December 1916).

81 Ibid., pp. 152–3 (postmarked 21 July 1915).

82 Edward Thomas, *Letters to Helen*, ed. R. G. Thomas (Manchester: Carcanet, 2000), p. 94 (5 April 1916). Part of the letter was written on 6 April 1916.

83 *LFY*, p. 219 (postmarked 12 November 1916).

84 See 'Note on the text', p. xiii. Also *CP*, p. xxx; Pikoulis, 'On editing Edward Thomas', *PN Review*, 103, 21.5 (1995), 52–6 (52); Kendall, 'A breath of air', *PN Review*, 164, 31.6 (2005), 62.

85 Jacques Derrida, 'The double session', in *Dissemination*, trans. Barbara Johnson (London: The Athlone Press, 1981), pp. 177–8. Published in *Tel Quel*, 41 and 42 (Paris: Éditions du Seuil, 1970).

86 Ibid., p. 181.

87 Edward Thomas, *Poems and Last Poems*, ed. Edna Longley (London: Collins, 1973), p. 294.

88 Ibid., p. 179.

89 W. N. Herbert, and Matthew Hollis (eds), *Strong Words: Modern Poets on Modern Poetry* (Newcastle: Bloodaxe, 2000), p. 283.

90 Jacques Derrida, 'Signature event context', in *Margins of Philosophy*, trans. Alan Bass (Brighton: The Harvester Press, 1982), p. 320 (first published as *Marges d la Philosophie* (Paris: Les Editions de Minuit, 1972)). Original emphasis.

91 *Beautiful Wales*, p. 166.

92 The duck-rabbit figure, published in *Fact and Fable in Psychology* (Boston: Houghton, Mifflin, 1900), later utilized in 1953 by Ludwig Wittgenstein, *Philosophical Investigations*, trans. G. E. M. Anscombe (Oxford: Basil Blackwell, 1963), pp. 193–6, 197 (part II, section 11). This figure was originally introduced by the Gestalt psychologist Joseph Jastrow in 1900. Popular worldwide on trading

and puzzle cards, the figure was adapted by psychologists Robert W. Leeper and E. G. Boring in 1930, now often referred to as the 'Boring figure'. A similar figure of a young-old woman first appeared on an anonymous German postcard in 1888 and was adapted by British cartoonist W. E. Hill in 1915. For the relation between 'figure and ground', see E. G. Boring, 'A new ambiguous figure', *American Journal of Psychology*, 42 (1930), 444–5.

Notes to Chapter 4

1 Dylan Thomas in W. N. Herbert and Matthew Hollis (eds), *Strong Words: Modern Poets on Modern Poetry* (Newcastle: Bloodaxe, 2000), p. 116. Emphasis in original.

2 See 'gap', *Oxford English Dictionary*, 12 vols (Oxford: Oxford University Press, 1961), IV, p. 48.

3 Edwin Morgan in Chris B. McCully, *The Poet's Voice and Craft* (Manchester: Carcanet, 1994), pp. 54–67 (p. 56).

4 *ANCP*, p. 137. Further references to this volume will be included in parentheses in the text.

5 *LFY*, p. 221 (postmarked 15 November 1916).

6 'Lecture on nothing', cited in McCully, *The Poet's Voice and Craft*, p. 61.

7 See Thomas's use of James's work in Edward Thomas, *The Country* (London: Batsford, 1913; repr. Cheltenham: Cyder Press, 1999), pp. 25–7.

8 William James, *The Principles of Psychology* (London: Macmillan, 1890; Chicago: University of Chicago, 1952), p. 163.

9 Ibid., pp. 165, 163

10 Ibid., p. 165.

11 See G. E. Myers, *William James: His Life and Thought* (New Haven: Yale University Press, 1986), p. 82, 505–6, n. 2; also, unpublished notes to James's *Principles of Psychology*, cited in Myers, *William James*, p. 505, n. 2. Myers writes: 'This note bears no date but has been placed, perhaps by Perry, in folder # 4465, alongside notes for "The Sentiment of Rationality". Since that article originally appeared in 1879, this note may indicate that this key doctrine in Jamesian psychology was formulated before *Principles*. James consistently held that perception and distinct sensation "bloom" out of a "buzzing confusion" or conglomeration of vague sensations.'

12 Lawrence Kramer, *Music and Poetry: the Nineteenth Century and After* (Berkeley: University of California Press, 1984), p. 91.

13 Edward Thomas, *A Language Not to be Betrayed: Selected Prose of Edward Thomas*, ed. Edna Longley (Manchester: Carcanet Press, 1981), p. 271.

14 *CP*, p. 318.

15 *LFY*, pp. 218–19.

16 *Times Literary Supplement*, 11 October 1917, 489.

17 *SC*, p. 147.

18 *CP*, p. 396.

19 *Bottomley*, p. 225 (November 1912), also p. 10; *Bookman*, 44 (April 1913), 47. Thomas favourably reviewed D. H. Lawrence's *Love Poems* in *DC*, February 1913.

[20] Sigmund Freud, 'Creative writers and day-dreaming', in *Art and Literature*, trans. James Strachey, 15 vols (Harmondsworth: Penguin, 1990–3), XIV (1990), pp. 131–41 (pp. 139, 136). This essay was first published in German in 1908. Freud refers to the fact 'that invented dreams can be interpreted in the same way as real ones and that the unconscious mechanisms familiar to us in the "dream-work" are thus also operative in the processes of imaginative writing', in 'An autobiographical study', in *Historical and Expository Works on Psychoanalysis*, trans. James Strachey, 15 vols, XV (Harmondsworth: Penguin, 1993), pp. 183–259 (p. 250). Published in German in 1925.

[21] Sigmund Freud, *The Interpretation of Dreams*, trans. Abraham Arden Brill (1997; London: Allen & Unwin, 1913), pp. 356, 400.

[22] Guy Cuthbertson and Lucy Newlyn, *Branch-lines: Edward Thomas and Contemporary Poetry* (London: Enitharmon, 2007), p. 73.

[23] See Appendix 4.

[24] Eng lett 376, fol. 8; spacing in original.

[25] *CP*, p. 316.

[26] Bodleian, MS Don d 28, p. 44; I am indebted to Piers Pennington for these insights into ligatures.

[27] *CP*, p. xxxi.

[28] Ibid., n. 32.

[29] P. J. Croft, *Autograph Poetry in the English Language*, 2 vols (London: Cassell, 1973), II, p. 161.

[30] Charles Olson, *Selected Writings of Charles Olson*, ed. Robert Creeley (New York: New Directions, 1951; repr. 1966), pp. 22–3.

[31] *CP*, p. xxxi.

[32] Gillian Allnutt, *Sojourner* (Newcastle: Bloodaxe, 2004), p. 54.

[33] Edward Thomas, *In Pursuit of Spring* (London: Thomas Nelson, 1914), p. 220.

[34] *Interpretation of Dreams*, trans. Brill, p. 338. Strachey translates this as 'it fills up the gaps in the dream-structure with shreds and patches': Sigmund Freud, *The Interpretation of Dreams*, trans. James Strachey, 15 vols (Harmondsworth: Penguin, 1990–3), IV (1991), p. 630.

[35] 'An unpublished author', *Atlantic Monthly*, 90 (1902), 834–8 (835).

[36] Edward Thomas, *Walter Pater* (London: Martin Secker, 1913), p. 218.

[37] *Richard Jefferies, his Life and Work* (London: Hutchinson, 1909), pp. 41, 52–3.

[38] *Bottomley*, pp. 81–2 (16 March 1905).

[39] NLW, MS 22917C, folio 159 (letter dated 31 March 1917, with later section written on 1 April). R. G. Thomas marks this list with vertical lines, reading 'leather' for 'buttoned', 'there in a clay' for 'here in a dry', and 'dozed and smoked' for 'dozed or smoked' in Edward Thomas, *Letters to Helen*, ed. R. G. Thomas (Manchester: Carcanet, 2000), pp. 91–2.

[40] British Library, MS 44990. See First World War Poetry Digital Archive, *http://www.oucs.ox.ac.uk/ww1lit* (accessed 13 June 2011).

[41] *The Mikado*, in *Original Comic Operas* (London: Chatto & Windus, 1899), p. 4 (act I).

[42] *Bottomley*, p. 133 (7 March 1907). The editor, R. G. Thomas, replicates significant spaces in Edward Thomas's handwritten orthography. The letter refers to an

introduction Thomas had to write to *The Book of the Open Air*, 2 vols (London: Hodder & Stoughton, 1907), 1, v.

[43] *ETF*, 52 (August 2004), 6 (12 January 1907).

[44] See Appendix 5.

[45] *Bottomley*, p. 140 (14 May 1907); see R. G. Thomas's note in ibid., n. 2.

[46] Ibid., p. 120 (4 September 1906). See *Portrait*, pp. 160, 200. Also, Gordon Bottomley, 'A note on Edward Thomas', *Welsh Review*, 4.3 (September 1945), 166–77 (171). Also, Lucy Newlyn's introduction to Thomas, *Oxford* (Oxford: Signal Books, 2005), pp. xlvi–xlvii.

[47] *Interpretation of Dreams*, trans. Brill, p. 400.

[48] *Bottomley*, p. 118 (27 August 1906).

[49] *SC*, p. 202.

[50] Yone Noguchi, 'The spirit of Japanese poetry', *Selected English Writings of Yone Noguchi: an East-West Literary Assimilation*, ed. Yoshinobu Hakutani (London: Associated University Presses, 1992), 2 vols, II, p. 130. See Clive Wilmer, 'Edward Thomas: Englishness and modernity', *PN Review*, 138, 24.4 (2001), 59–64.

[51] Steven D. Carter, 'A Note on the translations', *Just Living: Poems and Prose by the Japanese Monk Tonna* (New York: Columbia University Press, 2002), p. 25.

[52] *Oxford English Dictionary*, IV, 48; Noguchi, *English Writings*, II, p. 69.

Notes to Chapter 5

[1] Austen to Fanny Knight (23 March 1817), in Jane Austen, *Jane Austen's Letters to her Sister Cassandra and Others*, ed. Robert William Chapman, (2nd edn; London: Oxford University Press, 1952; 2nd repr. 1964), pp. 141–2.

[2] Matsuo Bashō, *On Love and Barley: Haiku of Bashō*, trans. Lucien Stryk (Harmondsworth: Penguin, 1985), p. 73. Translator's emphasis.

[3] *Berridge*, p. 78 (1 June 1915).

[4] William Wordsworth, *Lyrical Ballads*, ed. R. L. Brett and A. R. Jones (London: Methuen, 1963), preface of 1802, p. 251; see *FIP*, pp. 97–8.

[5] *The Stones of Venice*, in *The Works of John Ruskin: Library Edition*, ed. E. T. Cook and Alexander Wedderburn, 38 vols (London: George Allen, 1903–12), X, part 2 (1904), p. 202. Emphasis in original.

[6] *SC*, p. 5.

[7] *Bottomley*, p. 194 (12 October 1909).

[8] Kenkō, *The Miscellany of a Japanese Priest*, trans. William N. Porter (London: Humphrey Milford, 1914; repr. Tokyo: Tuttle, 1983), p. 67 (section 82).

[9] *Garnett*, p. 29 (undated, between 21 April 1915 and 19 January 1917), also in Edward Thomas, *Edward Thomas's Poets*, ed. Judy Kendall (Manchester: Carcanet, 2007), p. 36.

[10] *ANCP*, p. 58. Further references to this volume will be included in parentheses in the text.

[11] Edward Thomas, *Beautiful Wales* (London: Black, 1905), p. 42.

[12] Edward Thomas, *The Happy-go-lucky Morgans* (London: Duckworth, 1913), p. 7.

[13] Edward Thomas, *The Icknield Way* (London: Constable, 1913), p. vii.
[14] *SC*, p. vii.
[15] Edward Thomas, *The Heart of England* (London: Dent, 1909), p. 118.
[16] Edward Thomas, *Richard Jefferies, His Life and Work* (London: Hutchinson, 1909), p. 3.
[17] *Words and Places*, cited in Edward Thomas, *A Language Not to be Betrayed: Selected Prose of Edward Thomas*, ed. Edna Longley (Manchester: Carcanet Press, 1981), p. 214.
[18] *SC*, p. 147.
[19] *Celtic*, pp. 126–7.
[20] Virginia Woolf, *A Room of One's Own* (London: Hogarth Press, 1929), p. 98.
[21] *The Icknield Way*, pp. vi–vii.
[22] Basil Hall Chamberlain, *Things Japanese* (4th edn; London: John Murray, 1902), p. 374.
[23] Kenkō, *Miscellany of a Japanese Priest*, p. 67 (section 82).
[24] *Independent*, 13 August 2005, 10.
[25] Thomas to Harry Hooton while at university, cited in *Portrait*, p. 54.
[26] To Hooton, in Edward Thomas, *Letters to Helen*, ed. R. G. Thomas (Manchester: Carcanet, 2000), pp. 124–5 (13 November 1897).
[27] *PW*, p. 31; also *Portrait*, pp. 131, 173, 239.
[28] Oscar Wilde, 'The critic as artist' and 'The decay of lying', *Intentions* (Leipzig: Heinemann and Balestier, 1891; repr. *The Works of Oscar Wilde* (Leicester: Galley Press, 1987), p. 955, originally published in 1891, cited in Edward Thomas, *Walter Pater* (London: Martin Secker, 1913), p. 219.
[29] Ibid., p. 213.
[30] Ibid.
[31] See *Edward Thomas's Poets*, pp. 69–70, 90–1, 99–100.
[32] 'Reading', p. 276.
[33] Herbert Read, 'Picasso at 75', *The Times*, 27 October 1956, 7.
[34] *Bottomley*, p. 120 (4 September 1906).
[35] *The Heart of England*, p. 207.
[36] *LFY*, p. 199 (*c*. June 1916).
[37] *The Heart of England*, p. 208.
[38] To John Freeman, BL, MS RP 1791, folio 20 (14 August 1914), cited in *Edward Thomas's Poets*, p. xxiv.
[39] *Walter Pater*, p. 218.
[40] 'The critic as artist', p. 955.
[41] Ibid., p. 956.
[42] Linda Dowling, *Language and Decadence in the Victorian Fin de Siècle* (Princeton: Princeton University Press, 1986), p. 185. Quotation from Yeats, *Autobiographies* (London: Macmillan, 1926), p. 160.
[43] Dowling, *Language and Decadence*, p. 187.
[44] Yeats, *Autobiographies*, p. 172
[45] Dowling, *Language and Decadence*, p. 186, n. 14.
[46] A review of 'Wit and dalliance', *DC*, 13 April 1908, 3.
[47] *Pater*, p. 218.

[48] Yeats, *Autobiographies*, p. 160; *Bottomley*, p. 53 (17 March 1904).
[49] *FIP*, p. 76.
[50] *Pater*, pp. 215, 218.
[51] *Richard Jefferies*, p. 203; *Bottomley*, p. 159 (26 February 1908).
[52] Frost to John Cournos, *Selected Letters*, p. 128 (8 July 1914).
[53] *Collected Poems*, ed. Walter de la Mare (London: Selwyn & Blount, 1920), p. x.
[54] Levi, in Jonathan Barker (ed.), *The Art of Edward Thomas* (Bridgend: Poetry Wales Press, 1987), pp. 25–35 (p. 35).
[55] *PW*, p. 67.
[56] *Walter Pater*, p. 213.
[57] *Garnett*, p. 12 (undated, between 13 February and 30 March 1909), also in *Edward Thomas's Poets*, p. 174; Thomas's 'The Attempt' subsequently published in *Light*, pp. 160–73.
[58] *The Seven Lamps of Architecture*, in *The Works of John Ruskin: Library Edition*, ed. E. T. Cook and Alexander Wedderburn, 38 vols (London: George Allen, 1903–12), VIII (1903), p. 214. Original emphasis.
[59] *Miscellany of a Japanese Priest*, p. 170 (section 229).
[60] Noguchi, *English Writings*, II, p. 66. First published in *The Spirit of Japanese Poetry* (London: J. Murray, 1914), p. 32. See also Donald Keene, *The Pleasures of Japanese Literature* (New York: Columbia University Press, 1988), p. 21.
[61] *LFY*, p. 198 (9 June 1916).
[62] Ibid., p. 213. Author's emphasis.
[63] *Garnett*, p. 9 (11 February 1909), and p. 25 (13 March 1915), also in *Edward Thomas's Poets*, p. 17.
[64] Richard Jefferies, *Field and Hedgerow* (London: Longmans, Green, 1889), p. 18.
[65] *Berridge*, p. 78 (1 June 1915).
[66] *Bottomley*, p. 140 (14 May 1907).
[67] Jeremy Hooker, *Writers in a Landscape* (Cardiff: University of Wales Press, 1996), p. 43.
[68] Richard Jefferies, *After London: or Wild England* (London: Cassell, 1885; repr. Oxford: Oxford University Press, 1980), p. 241.
[69] *Richard Jefferies*, p. 260.
[70] Ibid.
[71] *FIP*, p. 141; see Samuel Taylor Coleridge, *Biographia Literaria*, 2 vols (Rest Fenner, 1817); repr., ed. John Shawcross, 2 vols (Oxford: Clarendon Press, 1907), II, p. 259.
[72] *Richard Jefferies*, p. 201.
[73] Cited in ibid., p. 158.
[74] *Bottomley*, p. 165 (19 July 1908). Also George Bottomley, 'A note on Edward Thomas', *Welsh Review*, 4.3 (September 1945), 171–2; also, *Portrait*, pp. 200–1.
[75] *Berridge*, p. 36 (2 November 1902).
[76] *Richard Jefferies*, p. 128.
[77] *Miscellany of a Japanese Priest*, pp. 67 (section 82), 15–16 (section 10).
[78] Guy Cuthbertson and Lucy Newlyn, *Branch-lines: Edward Thomas and Contemporary Poetry* (London: Enitharmon, 2007), p. 11.
[79] Ward, in Barker (ed.), *The Art of Edward Thomas*, p. 56.

Notes to Chapter 6

1. W. G. Sebald, 'As the Snow in the Alps', in *After Nature*, trans. Michael Hamburger (London: Hamish Hamilton, 2002), p. 27.
2. To Bottomley, *ETF*, 55 (January 2006), 15–16 (September 1910); cited in Edward Thomas, *Edward Thomas's Poets*, ed. Judy Kendall (Manchester: Carcanet, 2007), p. xvii.
3. *Edward Thomas: the Collected Poems and War Diary, 1917*, ed. Matthew Hollis (London: Faber and Faber, 2004), pp. xv, xvi, xx.
4. Andrew Motion, *The Poetry of Edward Thomas* (London: Hogarth Press, 1991), p. 77.
5. *Desert Island Discs*, 21 January 2005, BBC Radio 4.
6. *ANCP*, p. 127. Further references to this volume will be included in parentheses in the text.
7. Julia Briggs, *Virginia Woolf: an Inner Life* (London: Allen Lane, 2005), p. 378.
8. See *Between*, p. 243; and Briggs, *Virginia Woolf*, pp. 376–8, 383.
9. Virginia Woolf, '"Anon" and "The reader": Virginia Woolf's last essays', in Brenda R. Silver (ed.), *Twentieth Century Literature: Virginia Woolf Issue*, 25 (1979), 382.
10. W. H. Hudson, *Idle Days in Patagonia* (London: Chapman & Hall, 1893), pp. 151, 162, 152.
11. *SC*, p. 34.
12. Woolf, 'Anon', 382.
13. Ibid., 385.
14. Ibid., 382.
15. 'Reading', p. 277.
16. Walter Benjamin, *Illuminations*, trans. Harry Zohn (New York: Harcourt, Brace and World, 1968; repr. Schocken, 1969), pp. 253–64 (p. 253, section xiv).
17. Sigmund Freud, *The Interpretation of Dreams*, trans. Abraham Arden Brill (1997; London: Allen & Unwin, 1913), p. 190. Also p. 170. Emphasis in original.
18. Sigmund Freud, *The Complete Letters of Sigmund Freud to Wilhelm Fliess 1887–1904*, trans. Jeffrey Moussaieff Masson (Cambridge, MA: Harvard University Press, 1985), pp. 207–8 (6 December 1896).
19. Cited in Nicola King, *Memory, Narrative, Identity: Remembering the Self* (Edinburgh: Edinburgh University Press, 2000), p. 11.
20. Ibid.
21. For German definitions, see *Collins German Dictionary* (2nd edn; Glasgow: HarperCollins, 1991), pp. 661, 473.
22. Eng lett 376, Folio 66 (9 October 1909).
23. Edward Thomas, *George Borrow: the Man and His Books* (London: Chapman & Hall, 1912), p. 165.
24. Hans Ulrich Seeber, 'The retrospective attitude in Edward Thomas and Andrew Motion', in *REAL Yearbook of Research in English and American Literature*, 21 (2005), 147–59, p. 156.
25. Pierre Macherey, *A Theory of Literary Production*, trans. Geoffrey Wall (London: Routledge and Kegan Paul, 1978), p. 68.

[26] *Richard Jefferies*, p. 55.
[27] *Bottomley*, p. 202 (22 April 1910).
[28] Virginia Woolf, *The Diary of Virginia Woolf: Volume 5, 1936–41*, ed. Anne Olivier Bell (London: Hogarth Press, 1984; repr. Penguin, 1985), p. 249 (8 December 1939); Briggs, *Virginia Woolf*, p. 369; 'A sketch of the past', in Virginia Woolf, *Moments of Being* (rev. edn; London: Hogarth Press, 1985), pp. 61–137 (p. 79).
[29] *Between*, pp. 244–5, 248.
[30] Ibid., p. 165.
[31] Ibid., pp. 165–6.
[32] Ibid., p. 165; 'Reading', p. 276.
[33] Wolfgang Iser, *The Act of Reading* (London: Routledge and Kegan Paul, 1978), p. 34.
[34] *Bottomley*, p. 253 (21 July 1915); see also Thomas to John Freeman, BL, RP 1791, folio 29 (21 February 1915).
[35] Woolf, 'Anon', 383, 382, 385.
[36] Berridge, p. 78 (1 June 1915); *Lafcadio Hearn*, p. 78.
[37] *CP*, p. 149.
[38] Ibid., p. 148.
[39] Ibid., p. 151.
[40] *Bottomley*, p. 220 (22 March 1912).
[41] Woolf, 'Anon', 395.

Notes to Chapter 7

[1] Shinkichi Takahashi, 'Time', in *Where We Are*, trans. Lucien Stryk (London: Skoob Books, 1997), p. 168.
[2] *Letters of J. Keats*, ed. M. B. Forman (London: Oxford University Press, 1935), p. 104 (19 February 1818).
[3] Guy Cuthbertson and Lucy Newlyn, *Branch-lines: Edward Thomas and Contemporary Poetry* (London: Enitharmon, 2007), p. 67.
[4] Motokiyo Zeami, *Kinuta*, trans. Iris Elgrichi and Judy Kendall, quoted by Kendall, in 'Translation and the challenge of orthography', in Manuela Perteghetta and Eugenia Loffredo (eds), *Translation and Creativity: Perspectives on Creative Writing & Translation Studies* (London: Continuum, 2006), pp. 127–44 (pp. 140, 142).
[5] Gertrude Stein, *Picasso* (London: Batsford, 1938), p. 12.
[6] Ludwig Wittgenstein, *Philosophical Investigations*, trans. G. E. M. Anscombe (Oxford: Basil Blackwell, 1963), pp. 193–6, 197 (part II, section 11). As noted in chapter 3, the duck-rabbit figure can be traced back to the 1900s.
[7] Ibid., p. 45 (part I, section 103).
[8] Virginia Woolf, '"Anon" and "The reader": Virginia Woolf's last essays', in Brenda R. Silver (ed.), *Twentieth Century Literature: Virginia Woolf Issue*, 25 (1979), 395.
[9] 'Reminiscences of Claude Monet from 1889 to 1909', in *The American Magazine of Art*, XVIII, March 1927, 199–225, cited in Linda Nochlin, *Impressionism and*

Post-impressionism 1874–1904 (Englewood Cliffs, NJ: Prentice-Hall, 1966), p. 35.

[10] Paul Cézanne, *Paul Cézanne: Letters*, ed. John Rewald, trans. Marguerite Kay (Oxford: Bruno Cassirer, 1976), p. 316 (23 October 1905).

[11] Virginia Woolf, 'Mr. Bennett and Mrs. Brown', in *Collected Essays*, 4 vols (London: Hogarth Press, 1966), I, p. 320.

[12] *SC*, p. 253.

[13] Eng lett 376, fol. 66.

[14] *Sheaf*, p. 18.

[15] Edward Thomas, *Letters to Helen*, ed. R. G. Thomas (Manchester: Carcanet, 2000), p. 1 (21 June 1897).

[16] Jeremy Hooker, *Writers in a Landscape* (Cardiff: University of Wales Press, 1996), pp. 60–1.

[17] *Bottomley*, p. 220 (22 March 1912).

[18] *SC*, p. 253.

[19] *A Language Not to be Betrayed: Selected Prose of Edward Thomas*, ed. Edna Longley (Manchester: Carcanet Press, 1981), p. i.

[20] *FIP*, p. 141.

[21] Review of F. A. Hedgcock's 'Thomas Hardy, Penseur et Artiste', *Saturday Review*, 17 June 1911, cited in Edward Thomas, *Edward Thomas on Thomas Hardy*, ed. Trevor Johnson (Cheltenham: Cyder Press, 2002), pp. 27, 26.

[22] *Bottomley*, p. 220 (22 March 1912); *Walter Pater*, p. 213. See Hooker, *Writers in a Landscape*, pp. 56–75.

[23] Eng lett 376, fol. 197. Postmarked 24 June 1913, cited by Judy Kendall, in *Walter de la Mare Society Magazine*, 10, January 2007, 24–9 (26).

[24] Edward Thomas, *The Country* (London: Batsford, 1913; repr. Cheltenham: Cyder Press, 1999), p. 28.

[25] W. H. Hudson, *Idle Days in Patagonia* (London: Chapman & Hall, 1893), p. 216; cited by William James, 'On a Certain Blindness in Human Beings', in *Talks to Teachers on Psychology: and to Students on Some of Life's Ideals* (London: Longmans, Green, 1899), pp. 229–64 (p. 262); and in Thomas, *Country*, p. 26. Hudson's emphases.

[26] *Country*, p. 26.

[27] Nicola King, p. 11.

[28] Ibid., p. 27; citing James, 'On a Certain Blindness in Human Beings', p. 263.

[29] Ibid., p. 259. Emphasis in original.

[30] *Sheaf*, pp. 41–2.

[31] Ibid., p. 43.

[32] *SC*, p. 150.

[33] Bodleian, MS Eng lett c 281, item 141/142.

[34] *Portrait*, p. 234; see letters to John Freeman, MS RP 1791, folio 17.

[35] *Bottomley*, p. 129 (26 December 1906).

[36] Ward, in Jonathan Barker (ed.), *The Art of Edward Thomas* (Bridgend: Poetry Wales Press, 1987), p. 55.

[37] *SC*, p. 253.

[38] *Bottomley*, p. 61 (6 August 1904).

[39] *SC*, p. 4.
[40] *DC*, 31 May 1910, 8.
[41] Yone Noguchi, *Rest and Unrest* (London: Duckworth, 1910), p. 52.
[42] Yone Noguchi, 'The spirit of Japanese poetry', *Selected English Writings of Yone Noguchi: an East-West Literary Assimilation*, ed. Yoshinobu Hakutani (London: Associated University Presses, 1992), 2 vols, II, 117.
[43] *Country*, p. 28.
[44] *FIP*, pp. 101–2.
[45] Ibid., p. 101.
[46] *Bottomley*, p. 220 (22 March 1912).
[47] To Freeman, BL, MS RP 1791, 11 December 1913.
[48] Ibid., 11 December 1913.
[49] Edward Thomas, *The Childhood of Edward Thomas: a Fragment of Autobiography* (London: Faber and Faber, 1938), p. 45.
[50] (Eng lett 376, fol. 234); cited in Edward Thomas, *Edward Thomas's Poets*, ed. Judy Kendall (Manchester: Carcanet, 2007), p. xx.
[51] See Appendix 2 for the relevant passage from 'Insomnia'.
[52] *SC*, p. 4.
[53] Elisabeth Schneider, *Coleridge, Opium, and Kubla Khan* (New York: Octagon Books, 1983), p. 22, also, pp. 16–17, 22, 24–7, 81, 84, 87–8.
[54] 'Anima Poetae', *The Unpublished Notebooks of Samuel Taylor Coleridge*, edited E. H. Coleridge (London: Heinemann, 1895) pp. 37, 206; cited in John Livingston Lowes, *The Road to Xanadu* (London: Constable, 1927), pp. 177, 56. Author's emphasis. For Coleridge's exploration of effects of memory on immediate impressions and his indebtedness to Thomas Wedgewood and Christian Wolfe, see Lowes, pp. 507–8, n. 36, and p. 480, n. 53.
[55] Gertrude Stein, *Picasso* (London: Batsford, 1938), p. 18.
[56] Stan Smith, *Edward Thomas* (London: Faber and Faber, 1986); Stuart Sillars, *Structure and Dissolution in English Writing, 1910–1920* (Basingstoke: Macmillan, 1999). Also, Clive Wilmer, 'Edward Thomas: Englishness and modernity', *PN Review*, 138, 24.4 (2001), 59–64; Ward, in Barker, *The Art of Edward Thomas*, pp. 57–8; Julia Briggs, *Virginia Woolf: an Inner Life* (London: Allen Lane, 2005), pp. 376–9.
[57] See Kendall, *ETF*, 58 (August 2007), pp. 17–20.
[58] *Garnett*, p. 12 (undated, placed between letters dated 13 February and 30 March 1909), also in *Edward Thomas's Poets*, p. 174; Leon M. Solomons and Gertrude Stein, 'Normal motor automatism', *Psychological Review*, 3 (1896), 492–512 (496).
[59] See Solomons and Stein, 'Normal motor automatism', 502. Authors' emphases are left intact in this and subsequent quotations from this text.
[60] William James, *The Principles of Psychology* (London: Macmillan, 1890; Chicago: University of Chicago, 1952), p. 273.
[61] Solomons and Stein, 'Normal motor automatism', 510–11, 499.
[62] James, *Principles of Psychology*, p. 296.
[63] Ibid., p. 284.
[64] Solomons and Stein, 'Normal motor automatism', 499.
[65] James, *Principles of Psychology*, p. 264.

66 *Bottomley*, p. 53 (17 March 1904).
67 Richard Jefferies, *The Hills and the Vale*, ed. Edward Thomas (London: Duckworth, 1909), p. xxvi.
68 Willam James, *The Varieties of Religious Experience* (London: Longmans, Green, 1917), p. 209. Emphasis in original.
69 *FIP*, pp. 101–2.
70 James, p. 209.
71 *Bottomley*, p. 251 (30 June 1915).
72 Virginia Woolf, *A Room of One's Own* (London: Hogarth Press, 1929), p. 10.
73 Robert Frost, *Mountain Interval* (New York: Henry Holt, 1916), p. 9.
74 James, *Principles of Psychology*, p. 297.
75 *LFY*, p. 127 (25 March 1915). Written at Steep.
76 *LFY*, p. 246 (31 January 1917).
77 Laurence Sterne, *Tristram Shandy*, 2 vols (London: Macmillan, 1900), I, p. 36 (book I, chapter 22).
78 Freud to Wilhelm Fliess, Sigmund Freud, *The Complete Letters of Sigmund Freud to Wilhelm Fliess 1887–1904*, trans. Jeffrey Moussaieff Masson (Cambridge, MA: Harvard University Press, 1985), p. 281 (14 November 1897).
79 Virginia Woolf, *The Diary of Virginia Woolf: Volume 5, 1936–41*, ed. Anne Olivier Bell (London: Hogarth Press, 1984; repr. Penguin, 1985), p. 248 (2 December 1939); also p. 249 (8 December 1939).
80 Virginia Woolf, 'A sketch of the past', in *Moments of Being* (rev. edn; London: Hogarth Press, 1985), p. 150.
81 Schneider, *Coleridge, Opium, and Kubla Khan*, p. 241.
82 Jack Stillinger, *Coleridge and Textual Instability: the Multiple Versions of the Major Poems* (Oxford: Oxford University Press, 1994), p. 74. Stillinger refers to Perkins's work on this. See David Perkins, 'The imaginative vision of *Kubla Khan*: on Coleridge's introductory note', in Robert J. Barth and John L. Mahoney (eds), *Coleridge, Keats, and the Imagination* (Columbia and London: University of Missouri Press, 1990), pp. 97–108. Stillinger's emphasis.
83 See also Schneider, *Coleridge, Opium, and Kubla Khan*, pp. 16–17, 22–7; also, Stillinger, *Coleridge and Textual Instability*, pp. 74, 79, 107, 111.
84 Stillinger, *Coleridge and Textual Instability*, pp. 111, 107. Stillinger's emphases.
85 Samuel Taylor Coleridge, *Biographia Literaria*, ed. John Shawcross, 2 vols (Oxford: Clarendon Press, 1907), II, p. 259; *FIP*, p. 141.
86 Ibid., p. 255.
87 Woolf, 'Anon', 390.
88 Eng lett 376, fol. 257.
89 *Bottomley*, p. 248 (*c*.21 May 1915).
90 Woolf, 'Anon', p. 390. For more on dynamic interaction between text and reader, see Wolfgang Iser, *The Act of Reading* (London: Routledge and Kegan Paul, 1978), p. 107 and pp. 163–231.
91 *LFY*, p. 172 (postmarked 28 November 1915).
92 *DC*, 31 May 1910, 8.

Notes to Chapter 8

1. *Garnett*, p. 29 (undated, between 21 April 1915 and 19 January 1917), also in Edward Thomas, *Edward Thomas's Poets*, ed. Judy Kendall (Manchester: Carcanet, 2007), p. 36.
2. Ludwig Wittgenstein, *Philosophical Investigations*, trans. G. E. M. Anscombe (Oxford: Basil Blackwell, 1963), p. 50 (part I, section 129).
3. Guy Cuthbertson and Lucy Newlyn, *Branch-lines: Edward Thomas and Contemporary Poetry* (London: Enitharmon, 2007), p. 11.
4. *SC*, p. 3.
5. Edward Thomas, *Richard Jefferies, his Life and Work* (London: Hutchinson, 1909), p. 151.
6. *This England: an Anthology from Her Writers*, ed. Edward Thomas (London: Oxford University Press, 1915), p. iii; also Edward Thomas, *Oxford* (London: Black, 1903; rev. edn 1922), p. xlv–xlvii; and *Horae Solitariae* (London: Duckworth, 1902), pp. 7–8.
7. Edward Thomas, *Elected Friends: Robert Frost & Edward Thomas to One Another*, ed. Matthew Spencer (New York: Handsel Books, 2003), p. 63 (13 June 1915).
8. *Daily News*, 22 July 1914, 7.
9. Review of *Georgian Poetry* (original publication unknown), 15 January 1913, cited in Edward Thomas, *A Language Not to be Betrayed: Selected Prose of Edward Thomas*, ed. Edna Longley (Manchester: Carcanet Press, 1981), p. 114; review of Pound's *Personae*, *DC*, 7 June 1909, 3.
10. *PW*, p. 43.
11. Stan Smith, *Edward Thomas* (London: Faber and Faber, 1986), pp. 110, 211.
12. Sigmund Freud, *The Interpretation of Dreams*, trans. Abraham Arden Brill (1997; London: Allen & Unwin, 1913), p. 369; 'Recommendations to physicians practising psycho-analysis', in *The Case of Schreber, Papers on Technique and Other Works* (London: Vintage, 2001), pp. 111–20 (pp. 111–12). First published in *Zentralblatt für Psychoanalyse*, 2 (9), June 1912, 483–9.
13. *LFY*, p. 51 (16 December 1913).
14. William Shakespeare, *Hamlet* (London: Methuen, 1982), II. 2, p. 374.
15. *LFY*, p. 48 (8 December 1913).
16. See Appendix 2.
17. Edward Thomas, *Walter Pater* (London: Martin Secker, 1913), p. 213; *Bottomley*, p. 138 (22 April 1907); *Saturday Review*, 17 June 1911, cited in Edward Thomas, *Edward Thomas on Thomas Hardy*, ed. Trevor Johnson (Cheltenham: Cyder Press, 2002), p. 27.
18. *ANCP*, p. 84. Further references to this volume will be included in parentheses in the text.
19. Cuthbertson and Newlyn, *Branch-lines*, p. 35.
20. See Appendix 2.
21. Virginia Woolf, '"Anon" and "The reader": Virginia Woolf's last essays', in Brenda R. Silver (ed.), *Twentieth Century Literature: Virginia Woolf Issue*, 25 (1979), 384.
22. *CP*, p. 471.

[23] See Appendix 2; William James, *The Principles of Psychology* (London: Macmillan, 1890; Chicago: University of Chicago, 1952), pp. 74–5.
[24] Ibid., p. 295.
[25] Sander L. Gilman et al. (eds), *Friedrich Nietzsche on Rhetoric and Language* (Oxford: Oxford University Press, 1989), p. 27. Nietzsche's emphasis. Part of Nietzsche's 1872–4 lecture series.
[26] To Frost, *Elected Friends*, p. 63 (13 June 1915).
[27] From Peter Howarth, *British Poetry in the Age of Modernism* (Cambridge: Cambridge University Press, 2005), p. 97.
[28] John Lucas, 'Plain speaking and the language of the heart', *PN Review*, 158, 30.6 (2004), 38.
[29] Leon M. Solomons and Gertrude Stein, 'Normal motor automatism', *Psychological Review*, 3 (1896), 498.
[30] See Appendix 2.
[31] *Sheaf*, p. 221.
[32] Solomons and Stein, 'Normal motor automatism', 494. The subject is presumably Solomons, since they experimented on themselves.
[33] *LFY*, p. 221 (postmarked 15 November 1916). For a detailed account of the drafting process of this poem, see *LFY*, pp. 221–2 (*c*.15–20 November 1916).
[34] Solomons and Stein, 'Normal motor automatism', p. 493; William James, 'On a Certain Blindness in Human Beings', in *Talks to Teachers on Psychology: and to Students on Some of Life's Ideals* (London: Longmans, Green, 1899), p. 263; *Between*, p. 209.
[35] *The Dhammapada*, trans. Narada Thera (3rd edn; Kuala Lumpur, Buddhist Missionary Society, 1978), p. 35 (verse 33). Originally spoken around 2,500 years ago.
[36] Smith, *Edward Thomas*, p. 33.
[37] Samuel Taylor Coleridge, *Biographia Literaria*, ed. John Shawcross, 2 vols (Oxford: Clarendon Press, 1907), II, p. 262.
[38] James, *Principles of Psychology*, p. 295.
[39] Eng lett 376, fol. 181. The date 5 or 12 February 1913 is added in pencil. Thomas gives no explanation of 'Leftaineronish'.
[40] Ibid. The date 5 or 12 February 1913; see extract in *Edward Thomas's Poets*, p. xxiii.
[41] *Interpretation of Dreams*, trans. Brill, p. 369; Sigmund Freud, *The Interpretation of Dreams*, trans. James Strachey, 15 vols (Harmondsworth: Penguin, 1990–3), p. 388. Strachey cites his source as Bayard Taylor's translation. See Johann Wolfgang von Goethe, *Faust, a Tragedy: the First Part*, trans. Bayard Taylor (London: Strahan, 1871), p. 92 (act I, scene 4).
[42] Virginia Woolf, *Orlando: a Biography* (London: Hogarth Press, 1928), p. 73; W. B. Yeats, 'The circus animals desertion', in *Selected Poetry* (London: Macmillan, 1974), p. 202; see *Bottomley*, p. 133 (7 March 1907).
[43] Woolf, *Orlando*, pp. 73–4.
[44] To Freeman, BL, MS RP 1791, folio 20 (14 August 1914), cited in *Edward Thomas's Poets*, p. xxiv.

[45] Shinkichi Takahashi, 'Stitches', in *Where We Are*, trans. Lucien Stryk (London: Skoob Books, 1997), p. 159.
[46] Judy Kendall, *The Drier the Brighter* (Blaenau Ffestiniog: Cinnamon Press, 2007), p. 11.
[47] Zenji Dogen, untitled haiku, *Where We Are*, p. 140. Dogen was a thirteenth-century Japanese Zen teacher and monk.
[48] Ward, in Jonathan Barker (ed.), *The Art of Edward Thomas* (Bridgend: Poetry Wales Press, 1987), pp. 57–8.
[49] *PW*, p. 26.
[50] *Oxford*, p. 214.
[51] Roland Barthes, *Empire of Signs*, trans. Richard Howard (New York: Hill and Wang, 1983), p. 7.
[52] James, 'On a Certain Blindness in Human Beings', p. 264. These words conclude the essay.
[53] *DC*, 27 August 1901, 3.
[54] *Walter Pater*, pp. 206–8, 208.
[55] See Michael Schmidt, *An Introduction to Fifty Modern British Poets* (London: Pan Books, 1979), pp. 75, 77.
[56] Smith, *Edward* Thomas, p. 97.
[57] Ibid., p. 101.
[58] Paul Cézanne, *Paul Cézanne: Letters*, ed. John Rewald, trans. Marguerite Kay (Oxford: Bruno Cassirer, 1976), p. 316 (1905). Author's emphasis.
[59] Joyce Medina, *Cézanne and Modernism: the Poetics of Painting* (New York: State, 1995), p. 105.
[60] Cézanne, *Paul Cézanne*, p. 316 (23 October 1905).
[61] See Kendall, *ETF*, 58 (August 2007), p. 20.
[62] Virginia Woolf, 'Modern fiction', in *Collected Essays*, 4 vols (London: Hogarth Press, 1966), II, 106.
[63] Yeats, 'The second coming', in *Selected Poetry*, p. 99. Written in 1919.
[64] Review of *Exultations of Ezra Pound*, *DC*, 23 November 1909, 3.
[65] Virginia Woolf, *The Diary of Virginia Woolf: Volume 5, 1936–41*, ed. Anne Olivier Bell (London: Hogarth Press, 1984; repr. Penguin, 1985), p. 250 (9 December 1939).
[66] Ezra Pound, 'Vorticism', *Fortnightly Review*, n.s. 96 (1914), 461–71 (471, n. 1).
[67] Richard Jefferies, *Wild Life in a Southern County* (London: Smith, Elder, 1879), p. viii. See Jeremy Hooker, *Writers in a Landscape* (Cardiff: University of Wales Press, 1996), p. 23.
[68] *Richard Jefferies*, p. 13.
[69] Bayley, in Barker, *The Art of Edward Thomas*, p. 43.
[70] Hans Ulrich Seeber, 'The retrospective attitude in Edward Thomas and Andrew Motion', in *REAL Yearbook of Research in English and American Literature*, 21 (2005), p. 152.
[71] Jonathan Bate, *The Song of the Earth* (London: Picador, 2000), p. 281.
[72] *PW*, p. 122.
[73] Smith, *Edward Thomas*, p. 130.
[74] Ibid., p. 127.

[75] Edward Thomas, *The Heart of England* (London: Dent, 1909), p. 4.
[76] Smith, *Edward Thomas*, pp. 111, 100.
[77] Barker, *The Art of Edward Thomas*, p. 44.
[78] Edward Thomas, *The Country* (London, Batsford, 1913; repr. Cheltenham: Cyder Press, 1999), p. 6.
[79] Hooker, *Writers in a Landscape*, p. 79.
[80] *The Heart of England*, p. 4.
[81] *Oxford*, p. 214. This line is missing in the 2005 Signal edition.
[82] *Country*, pp. 6, 1, 10.
[83] *The Heart of England*, p. 4.
[84] *Country*, p. 10.
[85] Smith, *Edward Thomas*, p. 105. Emphasis in original.
[86] *The Heart of England*, p. 4; Thomas to de la Mare, Bodleian, MS Eng lett c 376, folio 181 (date 5 or 12 February 1913 added in pencil).
[87] Smith, p. 110; Ms Eng lett 376 folio 181.
[88] Edward Thomas, *The Childhood of Edward Thomas: a Fragment of Autobiography* (London: Faber and Faber, 1938), p. 41.
[89] *Oxford*, p. 88.
[90] *Elected Friends: Poems for and about Edward Thomas*, ed. Anne Harvey (London: Enitharmon, 1991), p. 10.
[91] R. P. Eckert (ed.), *These Things the Poets Said* (Flansham: Pear Tree Press, 1935); W. H. Auden, *Juvenalia: Poems 1922–1928*, ed. Katherine Bucknell (London: Faber and Faber, 1994), p. 100. Guy Cuthbertson discusses the term 'Thomasy' in Cuthbertson and Newlyn, *Branch-lines*, p. 51.
[92] Donald Davie, *Under Briggflatts* (Manchester: Carcanet, 1989) p. 176.
[93] D. J. Enright, *The Oxford Book of Contemporary Verse* (Oxford: Oxford University Press, 1980), p. xxviii.
[94] W. N. Herbert and Matthew Hollis (eds), *Strong Words: Modern Poets on Modern Poetry* (Newcastle: Bloodaxe, 2000), p. 11.
[95] Judy Kendall, '"Out in the dark": an exploration of and creative response to the process of poetic composition with reference to Edward Thomas and a self-reflexive study', (Ph.D., University of Gloucestershire, 2005).
[96] Unpublished records kept during the author's academic research into her own poetic composition processes, 10 April 2004. ET refers to Thomas. Published as 'unfamiliar' in Judy Kendall, *The Drier the Brighter* (Blaenau Ffestiniog: Cinnamon Press, 2007), p. 266.

Select Bibliography

Unpublished manuscripts and documents

Bodleian Library, Letters to Walter de la Mare, MS Eng lett c 376.

Bodleian Library, Poems, MS Don d 28.

Bodleian Library, Letters to John Freeman, MS RP 1791.

National Library of Wales, Letters: Edward Thomas to Helen, 1901–13, MS 22915C.

National Library of Wales, Letters: Edward Thomas to Helen, 1916–17, MS 22917C.

Websites

Edward Thomas Fellowship, *www.edward-thomas-fellowship.org.uk*.

First World War Poetry Digital Archive, *www.oucs.ox.ac.uk/ww1lit/collections/thomas*.

Books by Edward Thomas

Poems

Collected Poems, ed. Walter de la Mare (London: Selwyn & Blount, 1920).

Poems and Last Poems, ed. Edna Longley (London: Collins, 1973).

The Collected Poems of Edward Thomas, ed. R. G. Thomas (Oxford: Oxford University Press, 1978).

Edward Thomas: the Collected Poems and War Diary, 1917, ed. Matthew Hollis (London: Faber and Faber, 2004).

Edward Thomas: the Annotated Collected Poems, ed. Edna Longley (Newcastle: Bloodaxe Books, 2008).

Prose

The Woodland Life (London: Blackwood, 1897).

Oxford (London: Black, 1903; rev. edn 1922).

Beautiful Wales (London: Black, 1905).
The Heart of England (London: Dent, 1909).
Richard Jefferies, his Life and Work (London: Hutchinson, 1909).
The South Country (London: Dent, 1909).
Feminine Influence on the Poets (London: Martin Secker, 1910).
Celtic Stories (Oxford: Clarendon Press, 1911).
Light and Twilight (London: Duckworth, 1911).
Maurice Maeterlinck (London: Methuen, 1911).
George Borrow: the Man and His Books (London: Chapman & Hall, 1912).
Lafcadio Hearn (London: Constable, 1912).
Norse Tales (Oxford: Clarendon Press, 1912).
The Country (London: Batsford, 1913; repr. Cheltenham: Cyder Press, 1999).
The Happy-go-lucky Morgans (London: Duckworth, 1913).
The Icknield Way (London: Constable, 1913).
Walter Pater (London: Martin Secker, 1913).
Keats (London: T. C. & E. C. Jack, The People's Books, 1916).
A Literary Pilgrim in England (London: Methuen, 1917; Oxford: Oxford University Press, 1980).
Poems (London: Selwyn & Blount: 1917).
The Last Sheaf (London: Jonathan Cape, 1928).
The Childhood of Edward Thomas: a Fragment of Autobiography (London: Faber and Faber, 1938).
A Language Not to be Betrayed: Selected Prose of Edward Thomas, ed. Edna Longley (Manchester: Carcanet Press, 1981).
Edward Thomas on Thomas Hardy, ed. Trevor Johnson (Cheltenham: Cyder Press, 2002).
Edward Thomas on the Georgians, ed. Richard Emeny (Cheltenham: Cyder Press, 2004).

Articles
'An unpublished author', *Atlantic Monthly*, 90 (1902), 834–8.
'Reading out of doors', *Atlantic Monthly*, 92 (1903), 275–7.
'Birds in March', *Edward Thomas Fellowship Newsletter*, 53 (January 2005) 11–13.

Edited works
The Book of the Open Air, 2 vols (London: Hodder & Stoughton, 1907).
The Pocket Book of Songs and Poems for the Open Air (London: Grant Richards, 1907).
Words and Places in Illustration of History, Ethnology and Geography, by Isaac Taylor (London: Dent, 1911).
The Zincali: an Account of the Gypsies of Spain, by George Borrow (London: Dent, 1914).

Letters

Edward Thomas: the Last Four Years, ed. Eleanor Farjeon (Oxford: Oxford University Press, 1958).

Letters from Edward Thomas to Gordon Bottomley, ed. R. G. Thomas (London: Oxford University Press, 1968).

A Selection of Letters to Edward Garnett, ed. Edward Garnett (Edinburgh: Tragara Press, Edinburgh, 1981).

The Letters of Edward Thomas to Jesse Berridge, ed. Anthony Berridge (London: Enitharmon, 1983).

Letters to Helen, ed. R. G. Thomas (Manchester: Carcanet, 2000).

Elected Friends: Robert Frost & Edward Thomas to One Another, ed. Matthew Spencer (New York: Handsel Books, 2003).

'Letters to Garnett and Hudson', *Edward Thomas Fellowship Newsletter*, 52 (August 2004) 6–17.

Edward Thomas's Poets, ed. Judy Kendall (Manchester: Carcanet, 2007).

Secondary Material

Books

Barker, Jonathan (ed.), *The Art of Edward Thomas* (Bridgend: Poetry Wales Press, 1987).

Barthes, Roland, *Empire of Signs*, trans. Richard Howard (New York: Hill and Wang, 1983).

Bate, Jonathan, *The Song of the Earth* (London: Picador, 2000).

Briggs, Julia, *Virginia Woolf: an Inner Life* (London: Allen Lane, 2005).

Coleridge, Samuel Taylor, *Biographia Literaria*, ed. John Shawcross, 2 vols (Oxford: Clarendon Press, 1907).

Croft, P. J., *Autograph Poetry in the English Language*, 2 vols (London: Cassell, 1973).

Cuthbertson, Guy and Lucy Newlyn, *Branch-Lines: Edward Thomas and Contemporary Poetry* (London: Enitharmon, 2007).

Derrida, Jacques *Dissemination*, trans. Barbara Johnson (London: The Athlone Press, 1981).

Dowling, Linda, *Language and Decadence in the Victorian Fin de Siècle* (Princeton: Princeton University Press, 1986).

Emeny, Richard (ed.), *Edward Thomas 1878–1917: Towards a Complete Checklist of his Publications* (Blackburn: White Sheep Press, 2004).

Freud, Sigmund, 'Creative writers and day-dreaming', in *Art and Literature*, trans. James Strachey, 15 vols (Harmondsworth: Penguin, 1990–3), XIV (1990), pp. 130–41.

Freud, Sigmund, *The Interpretation of Dreams*, trans. James Strachey, 15 vols (Harmondsworth: Penguin, 1990–3), IV (1991).

Freud, Sigmund, *The Interpretation of Dreams*, trans. Abraham Arden Brill (1997; London: Allen & Unwin, 1913).

Gilman, Sander L., et al. (eds), *Friedrich Nietzsche on Rhetoric and Language* (Oxford: Oxford University Press, 1989).

Herbert, W. N. and Matthew Hollis (eds), *Strong Words: Modern Poets on Modern Poetry* (Newcastle: Bloodaxe, 2000).

Hooker, Jeremy, *Writers in a Landscape* (Cardiff: University of Wales Press, 1996).

Hudson, W. H., *Idle Days in Patagonia* (London: Chapman & Hall, 1893).

Hudson, W. H., *Green Mansions: a Romance of the Tropical Forest* (London: Duckworth, 1904; repr. 1911).

Iser, Wolfgang, *The Act of Reading* (London: Routledge and Kegan Paul, 1978).

James, William, *The Principles of Psychology* (London: Macmillan, 1890; Chicago: University of Chicago, 1952).

James, William, 'On a Certain Blindness in Human Beings', in *Talks to Teachers on Psychology: and to Students on Some of Life's Ideals* (London: Longmans, Green, 1899), pp. 229–64.

Jefferies, Richard, *After London: or Wild England* (London: Cassell, 1885; repr. Oxford: Oxford University Press, 1980).

Keene, Donald, *Japanese Literature* (London: John Murray, 1953).

Keene, Donald, *The Pleasures of Japanese Literature* (New York: Columbia University Press, 1988).

Kendall, Judy, 'Translation and the challenge of orthography', in Manuela Perteghetta and Eugenia Loffredo (eds), *Translation and Creativity: Perspectives on Creative Writing & Translation Studies* (London: Continuum, 2006), pp. 127–144.

Kendall, Judy, *The Drier the Brighter* (Blaenau Ffestiniog: Cinnamon Press, 2007).

Kenkō, *The Miscellany of a Japanese Priest*, trans. William N. Porter (London: Humphrey Milford, 1914; repr. Tokyo: Tuttle, 1983).

King, Nicola, *Memory, Narrative, Identity: Remembering the Self* (Edinburgh: Edinburgh University Press, 2000).

Kirkham, Michael, *The Imagination of Edward Thomas* (Cambridge: Cambridge University Press, 1986)

Kramer, Lawrence, *Music and Poetry: the Nineteenth Century and After* (Berkeley: University of California Press, 1984).

Longley, Edna, *Poetry in the Wars* (Newcastle: Bloodaxe, 1986).

Mabey, Richard, *Whistling in the Dark: in Pursuit of the Nightingale* (London: Sinclair-Stevenson, 1993).

McCully, Chris B. (ed.), *The Poet's Voice and Craft* (Manchester: Carcanet, 1994).

Motion, Andrew, *The Poetry of Edward Thomas* (London: Hogarth Press, 1991).

Noguchi, Yone, *Yone Noguchi: Collected English Letters*, ed. Ikuko Atsumi (Tokyo: Yone Noguchi Society, 1975).

Noguchi, Yone, *Selected English Writing of Yone Noguchi An East-West Literary Assimilation*, ed. Yoshinobu Hakutani, 2 vols (London: Associated University Presses, 1992).

Olson, Charles, *Selected Writings of Charles Olson*, ed. Robert Creeley (New York: New Directions, 1951; repr. 1966).

Ruskin, John, *The Seven Lamps of Architecture*, in *The Works of John Ruskin: Library Edition*, ed. E. T. Cook and Alexander Wedderburn, 38 vols (London: George Allen, 1903–12), VIII (1903).

Ruskin, John, *The Stones of Venice*, in *The Works of John Ruskin: Library Edition*, ed. E. T. Cook and Alexander Wedderburn, 38 vols (London: George Allen, 1903–12), X, part 2 (1904).

Schneider, Elisabeth, *Coleridge, Opium, and Kubla Khan* (New York: Octagon Books, 1983).

Sillars, Stuart, *Structure and Dissolution in English Writing, 1910–1920* (Basingstoke: Macmillan, 1999).

Smith, Stan, *Edward Thomas* (London: Faber and Faber, 1986).

Stillinger, Jack, *Coleridge and Textual Instability: the Multiple Versions of the Major Poems* (Oxford: Oxford University Press, 1994).

Thacker, Deborah, 'New voices, new threats', in Deborah Cogan Thacker and Jean Webb (eds), *Introducing Children's Literature* (London: Routledge and Kegan Paul, 2002), pp. 101–13.

Thacker, Deborah, 'Robert Frost and Edward Thomas: poets' stories', in Celia Keenan and Mary Shine Thompson (eds), *Studies in Children's Literature, 1500–2000* (Dublin: Four Courts Press, 2004), pp. 86–93.

Thomas, R. G., *Edward Thomas: a Portrait* (Oxford: Clarendon Press, 1985).

Wilde, Oscar, 'The critic as artist', *Intentions*, in *Works of Oscar Wilde* (Leicester: Galley Press, 1987), pp. 909–31.

Wittgenstein, Ludwig, *Philosophical Investigations*, trans. G. E. M. Anscombe (Oxford: Basil Blackwell, 1963).

Woolf, Virginia, *A Room of One's Own* (London: Hogarth Press, 1929).

Woolf, Virgina, *Between the Acts* (London: Hogarth Press, 1941).

Woolf, Virginia, *The Diary of Virginia Woolf: Volume 5, 1936–41*, ed. Anne Olivier Bell (London: Hogarth Press, 1984; repr. Penguin, 1985).

Woolf, Virginia, *Moments of Being* (rev. edn; London: Hogarth Press, 1985).

Wordsworth, William, *The Poetical Works of Wordsworth*, ed. T. Hutchinson (1939; London: Oxford University Press, 1904).

Wordsworth, William, *The Prose Works of William Wordsworth*, ed. W. J. B. Owen and J. W. Smyser, 3 vols (Oxford: Clarendon Press, 1974).

Yeats, William Butler, *Autobiographies* (London: Macmillan, 1926).

Journals and Newspapers

Bottomley, Gordon, 'A note on Edward Thomas', *Welsh Review*, 4.3 (September 1945), 166–76.

Kendall, Judy, 'A breath of air', *PN Review*, 164, 31.6 (2005), 62.

Kendall, Judy, 'A tale of two poets: Walter de la Mare and Edward Thomas. The Bodleian correspondence', *Walter de la Mare Society Magazine*, 10 (January 2007), 24–9.

Kendall, Judy, 'Edward Thomas and the Impressionists', *Edward Thomas Fellowship Newsletter*, 58 (August 2007), 17–20.

Kendall, Judy, '"A Poet At Last"; William H. Davies and Edward Thomas', in Katie Gramich (ed.), *Almanac: Yearbook of Welsh Writing in English* (Cardigan: Parthian, 2008), pp. 32–54.

Kendall, Judy, 'A genuine contender', *New Welsh Review*, 83 (spring 2009), 25–32.

Kendall, Judy, 'Thomas, absence and Japanese aesthetics', *Edward Thomas Fellowship Newsletter*, 64 (August 2010), 26–30.

Lucas, John, 'Plain speaking and the language of the heart', *PN Review*, 158, 30.6 (2004), 34–8.

McDonald, Peter, 'Rhyme and determination in Hopkins and Edward Thomas', *Essays in Criticism*, 43 (1993), 228–45.

Pikoulis, John, 'On editing Edward Thomas', *PN Review*, 103, 21.5 (1995), 52–6.

Sansom, Ian, 'Where the wood ends', *The Guardian*, 6 November 2004, 25.

Seeber, Hans Ulrich, 'The retrospective attitude in Edward Thomas and Andrew Motion', in *REAL Yearbook of Research in English and American Literature*, 21 (2005), 147–59.

Solomons, Leon M. and Gertrude Stein, 'Normal motor automatism', *Psychological Review*, 3 (1896), 492–512.

Wilmer, Clive, 'Edward Thomas: Englishness and modernity', *PN Review*, 138, 24.4 (2001), 59–64.

Woolf, Virginia, 'Flumina Amem Silvasque', *Times Literary Supplement*, 11 October 1917, 489.

Woolf, Virginia, '"Anon" and "The reader": Virginia Woolf's last essays', in Brenda R. Silver (ed.), *Twentieth Century Literature: Virginia Woolf Issue*, 25 (1979), 382–98.

Index